After the Factory

Comparative Urban Studies

Series Editor
Kenneth R. Hall, Ball State University

Associate Editors
James J. Connolly, Ball State University
Stephen Morillo, Wabash College

The Comparative Urban Studies Series encourages innovative studies of urbanism, contemporary and historical, from a multidisciplinary (e.g., architecture, art, anthropology, culture, economics, history, literature, sociology, technological), comparative, and/or global perspective. The series invites submissions by scholars from the fields of American studies, history, sociology, women's studies, ethnic studies, urban planning, material culture, literature, demography, museum studies, historic preservation, architecture, journalism, anthropology, and political science. New studies will consider how particular pre-modern and modern settings shape(d) urban experience and how modern and pre-modern, Western and non-Western cities respond(ed) to broad social and economic changes.

Titles in the Series

Secondary Cities in the Indian Ocean Realm, 1400–1800 edited by Kenneth Hall
The Evolution of the Ancient City: Urban Theory and the Archaeology of the Fertile Crescent by Alexander R. Thomas
After the Factory: Reinventing America's Industrial Small Cities edited by James J. Connolly
The Growth of Non-Western Cities edited by Kenneth R. Hall

After the Factory

Reinventing America's Industrial Small Cities

Edited by James J. Connolly

LEXINGTON BOOKS
Lanham • Boulder • New York • Toronto • Plymouth, UK

Published by Lexington Books
A wholly owned subsidiary of The Rowman & Littlefield Publishing Group, Inc.
4501 Forbes Boulevard, Suite 200, Lanham, Maryland 20706
www.rowman.com

10 Thornbury Road, Plymouth PL6 7PP, United Kingdom

British Library Cataloguing in Publication Information Available

Library of Congress Cataloging-in-Publication Data

The hardback edition of this book was previously cataloged by the Library of Congress
as follows:

After the factory : reinventing America's industrial small cities / edited by James J.
Connolly.
      p. cm. — (Comparative urban studies)
   Includes bibliographical references and index.
   1. Urban renewal—United States. 2. Cities and towns—United States—Growth.
3. City planning.—United States. I. Connolly, James J., 1962–
   HT175.A625 2010
   307.3'4160973—dc22   2010024291

ISBN: 978-0-7391-4823-5 (cloth : alk. paper)
ISBN: 978-0-7391-4824-2 (pbk. : alk. paper)
ISBN: 978-0-7391-4825-9 (electronic)

~

Contents

Figures and Tables

Figures

Tables

~

Acknowledgments

I am pleased to thank the many people and organizations that helped make this volume possible. The work behind it began with the staging of the 2009 Small Cities Conference, sponsored by the Center for Middletown Studies at Ball State University. Other units at Ball State that helped included University Libraries, the E.B. and Bertha Ball Center, the History Department, the Office of the Provost, the Sponsored Programs Office, and the College of Sciences and Humanities. Ken Hall co-organized the conference. Bob Morris provided support and financial assistance. Marissa Emerson, Beth Simmons, Chris Atkinson, and Katie Campanello helped with the publicity and organization. Thanks as well to all of the participants in the conference, and particularly those who commented: Jay Spaulding, Joel Schrock, Steve Morillo, John Whitmore, Leonard Blussé, Ken Swope, Janet Bednarek, Michael Dodson, Bruce Geelhoed, Jacalyn Welling, Eric Sandweiss, and Richard Longworth.

A number of other people helped with the production of this volume. John Straw, Carolyn Runyon, and the Ball State University Archives staff helped with illustrations and permissions. Bruce Geelhoed and Alison Kelly read portions of the manuscript. Chris Atkinson and Bridget Hahn helped with proofreading and formatting. Ken Hall enthusiastically supported the project and its inclusion in the Comparative Urbanism series. Michael Sisskin and the staff at Lexington Books and Rowman & Littlefield shepherded it through its final phases. I am especially grateful to each of the contributors to this volume for their cheerful tolerance of my editorial demands and the unwieldy process of putting a book with nine authors together. An earlier version of chapter 1 appeared in *Nebraska History* and an earlier version of chapter 9 appeared in the *Boston Review*. Thanks to both publications.

And, as in all things, thanks to Beth, Sarah, and Maggie.

CHAPTER ONE

~

Can They Do It?

The Capacity of Small Rust-Belt Cities to Reinvent Themselves in a Global Economy

JAMES J. CONNOLLY

The term "rust belt" evokes not just a region but a social setting. Geographically, it refers to the band of states running from the Northeast into the Midwest that industrialized extensively during the nineteenth century but experienced a dramatic decline in manufacturing at the end of the twentieth century. The environment it summons to mind is more precise: crumbling city streets, empty factories, abandoned homes, blighted neighborhoods, and desolate downtowns.

These scenes are all urban in character. The policy challenges associated with deindustrialization center on cities as well. They include a diminishing tax base, decaying infrastructure, overburdened social services, increased crime, a poorly educated work force, underfunded schools, and a pronounced civic decline. In its essence, the rust belt is both a regional and an urban phenomenon.

The first cities that come to mind when discussing the rust belt are larger communities such as Detroit, Cleveland, or Pittsburgh. But a number of smaller places—Youngstown, Ohio; Gary, Indiana; Flint, Michigan—make the list as well. The problems of deindustrialization afflict cities of all sizes, but, in terms of how communities experience those changes and respond to them, size matters. Larger cities, with more resources, more diversified economies, and more political clout, have in some instances coped with the economic transformation of the late twentieth century reasonably well. Chicago has emerged as a global city of the first rank, Pittsburgh has made substantial progress as a center of activity in the new knowledge-driven, service economy. Columbus, Ohio and Indianapolis have prospered as state capitals. A few smaller settings have prospered to some extent—Allentown, Pennsylvania, for instance—but most have struggled to adjust. Nonmetropolitan manufacturing cities have more often tended to be dominated by one industry, or even one company. When those firms depart, the community they leave behind has little to turn to economically. Even when a smaller city has some diversity within the manufacturing sector, it has few other options when core businesses disappear. Invented as seats of industry, they struggle to redefine themselves to fit a postindustrial context.

Reinventing the rust belt's small cities is a tall order. A few might still function as nodes of industrial production. But landing a large, foreign-owned auto manufacturing plant or a green energy plant hardly solves every problem: the new jobs likely will not be unionized and thus will not pay nearly as much as the positions lost. The competition among localities for high-tech and knowledge-economy firms is intense. Decaying towns with poor schools and few amenities are hardly in a good position to attract the "creative-class" workers they need to make such a transition. Getting to the point where small cities can lure such companies or keep a home-grown business will require extensive retooling, not just economically but in terms of their built environment, cultural character, political economy, and demographic mix. Such changes often run counter to the historical currents that defined these places as factory towns.

Adding to the challenges small cities face is their limited capacity to act. Compared to metropolitan communities, they have fewer resources—fewer educated workers, fewer amenities, and a smaller tax base, which means less money for the financial incentives that draw businesses. In instances where large companies remain a presence in rust-belt towns, it is generally in the form of an assembly plant or branch office. Key decisions are made elsewhere, by people with little or no connection to the community. The departure of corporate headquarters for more attractive places has not only robbed these communities of economic clout, it has undercut their civic leadership as well. The problem is further compounded by political structures that hamstring urban leaders. Most American cities are legally weak, lacking the authority to annex or exploit surrounding areas, or even to set their own tax rates. As a result, even those communities inclined to reinvent themselves—and many are not—do not have the tools to do so.

This volume examines the fate of industrial small cities from a variety of angles. It includes a selection of essays first presented at a conference that brought together historians, economists, anthropologists, planners, and journalists to consider the sources and character of economic growth and decline in nonmetropolitan urban settings across the globe. Reflecting the multidisciplinary meeting from which they arose, the pieces assembled here delve into the history and present condition of small cities in the American rust belt, discuss the strategies that some of these places have adopted in response to the loss of manufacturing jobs, and propose new tacks for these communities as they struggle to move forward in the twenty-first century. Together, they constitute a distinctive look at an important dimension of economic globalization.

A consideration of how small industrial cities in the American rust belt cope with deindustrialization joins a growing body of work that concentrates on nonmetropolitan urban settings. Often described as a neglected topic, small cities have received increasing amounts of analytical attention in recent years.[1] Scholars have begun to treat such places not simply as the metropolis writ small, but rather as distinctive urban forms. They recognize that both the past experiences of smaller cities and the present challenges they face in a global, neoliberal economic order differ substantially from those of their larger counterparts. The essays collected here combines history and policy analysis to make concrete the often abstract, generalized, or theoretical issues raised in this literature. In doing so, they shed light not only on the opportunities available to rust-belt cities but also their capacity to capitalize on them. *After the Factory* includes historical case studies that explore the deeply rooted economic, cultural, and social patterns that have shaped these communities and continue to define them, accounts of successful redevelopment efforts, a retrospective assessment of income growth across many smaller cities in the Great Lakes region, and consideration of unexplored avenues for reinvention. Other books have outlined approaches for new development or cultural renewal; this one considers both possibilities for the future and the ways in which the contours of the past limit change.

The terms "deindustrialization" and "rust belt" joined the American lexicon during the 1980s. By then the movement of manufacturing operations out of the Northeast and Midwest was well underway. As Barry Bluestone and Bennett Harrison made clear in *The Deindustrialization of America: Plant Closings, Community Abandonment, and the Dismantling of Basic Industry*, these changes, along with the fiscal, economic, and social problems they produced, were symptoms of a structural shift rather than a cyclical downturn. They also raised the question of whether capital flight was inimical to the sustenance of communities, an issue Michael Moore revisited in sharply provocative form with his film *Roger and Me*, later in that decade. That topic has remained at the forefront of discussions among scholars and policymakers into the twenty-first century. [2]

While experts quarrel over the precise causes and consequences of this economic transformation, their broad outlines are clear enough. American manufacturing output did not decline as a whole during the second half of the twentieth century, but technological innovation created efficiencies that increased production while reducing the amount of labor required to sustain or even to increase output levels. Improvements in communication and transportation, combined with increased costs for labor and land, encouraged firms to relocate plants to the southern and western United States, a process that began as early as the 1950s. They did so in part because the absence or weakness of unions in those settings allowed them to reduce labor costs (this became increasingly important as outlays for health and retirement benefits increased). Lighter regulatory burdens and tax levels also made those places more attractive. Much of what remained of union-labor manufacturing in the Midwest and Northeast was further undercut by globalization. As the productive capacity and market size of countries around the world expanded, and as the United States became less protective of its domestic industries, competitive pressures forced companies to shut down expensive, aging plants in what became the rust belt even while opening new facilities overseas. [3]

The flip side of this transformation was the rise of a new service and knowledge-driven economy. Part Walmart and part Google, it relied increasingly on the importation of consumer goods and the exportation of ideas and computer-based technologies. The production of clothing, furniture, toys, and a host of other goods resided increasingly in Asia and other overseas settings. Only the distribution and retail functions of these industries remained in the United States. The high-tech sectors of the economy, characterized by firms such as Google and Microsoft, but including a host of lesser-known, more specialized companies, thrived in places with an abundant supply of highly educated workers such as Palo Alto, California; Austin, Texas; and the communities that make up the research triangle region in North Carolina.

Rust-belt cities, built for and shaped by capital intensive manufacturing, were ill-positioned to capitalize on these changes. Laid-off auto and steel workers lacked the educational foundation necessary to become software engineers, graphic designers, financial analysts, or biomedical researchers, which made it difficult to lure firms that required educated workers. Reductions in local tax revenues precipitated by plant closings and population flight have exacerbated the problem by making it difficult to maintain infrastructure, fund schools, and develop desirable amenities. When high-tech or other knowledge-based businesses began scouting locations, they usually decided that such places would not allow them to draw the young, highly skilled workers they needed. Cities in the Northeast and Midwest that had some features that made them attractive to such firms—a university, a state capital, recreational amenities such as beaches or large parks—have done relatively well amid these changes, but these were never the industrial towns that defined the rust belt to begin with.

Smaller cities face special challenges in this context. The decline of one industry or even the departure of one large plant can send them into a tailspin much more readily than in larger, more diversified places. The decline of the steel industry in the Midwest inflicted extraordinary damage to Gary, Indiana, a city built expressly for steel production, and Youngstown, Ohio, which grew in tandem with that industry. It remains unclear whether these cities can ever rebuild themselves in the wake of this loss of their original purpose. By contrast, Pittsburgh, once the capital of steel making, has been able to regain a degree of economic vitality by redefining itself as a center of finance education and biotechnology partly because its size and diversity provided the resources to do so. The capacity of small cities to remake themselves in light of these economic changes—"random shocks" in the parlance of economists—is considerably more limited.

Despite such difficulties, there are no shortage of plans and programs for the revival of smaller industrial cities. Over the past decade a series of think tank reports and scholarly studies have outlined strategies for the renewal of decaying industrial cities. A growing number of them focus on smaller and mid-sized communities. In broad strokes at least, these analyses have much in common. They recommend that cities first engage in a planning process. Communities, experts agree, need to determine what assets they have—institutions, geographic advantages, unique amenities, clusters of businesses in a particular industry, and so forth—and build upon them. Most analysts also stress the importance of rebuilding infrastructure, rehabilitating and repurposing abandoned properties (both residential and industrial) in order to restore the local tax base, revitalizing existing neighborhoods, improving the quality of life by developing cultural amenities and educational opportunities, and helping local workers retool for a new economy. A few note as well the importance of rehabilitating a community's image, both in the eyes of local residents and among outsider observers.[4]

These proposals reflect a newfound optimism about the future of rustbelt towns. "Given their assets, the moment is ripe for the revival of older industrial urban economies," a Brookings Institution analysis declared in 2007.[5] One reason for such optimism is the scale of life in such settings. The slower pace, ease of living, and sense of community possible in more compact settings offers a distinctive asset that smaller cities can use to attract those unable or unwilling to confront the costs and complications of metropolitan life. Devotees of the new urbanism who seek places built on a scale that encourages a stronger sense of community may find smaller cities attractive. Infused with hope, these prescriptions envision communities restored to fiscal health and with an improved quality of life that will lure educated refugees from big cities and the firms that employ them. The sharp recession of 2008–2009 perhaps curtailed such ambitions temporarily, but these analysts see the potential, at least, for a rosier future if these places act wisely.

There is some evidence that these policy prescriptions have filtered into popular discussion. Virtually every policy paper targeting industrial small cities is peppered with examples of cities taking innovative steps to improve themselves. Another indication is the work of citizens and civic leaders in Muncie, Indiana, one of the cities featured in this volume. During 2009–2010, community members participated in the creation of the "Muncie Action Plan." This city-wide effort to form a vision of Muncie's future—a step that in and of itself that corresponds to the prevailing advice of experts—reached much the same conclusions that policy analysts and scholars offer. The list of priorities produced by local participants could easily have been cribbed from a think tank white paper: neighborhood revitalization; greater community pride; restored infrastructure; smarter land use; education and skill development; more parks, cultural, and entertainment options; improvement of the community's appearance; and increased civic cooperation.[6]

While some analysts have questioned whether small cities can do anything at all, at least in terms of policy, to reverse their slide, there is at least some evidence that their actions matter. In a systematic study of 267 small cities, George A. Erickceck and Hannah McKinney compared "winners" and "losers" (in other words, those cities that either exceeded or failed to reach predicted expectations for income growth). Factors such as industrial mix, firm size, location, quality of life factors, and the presence of educated workers explained the lion's share of a city's economic success or failure, they found. But there was enough variability among cities that shared similar profiles in these areas to suggest that public policy choices made a difference. Erickceck and McKinney do not consider exactly what those policies should be, but their analysis indicates that it was possible, even likely, that decisions made by local governments had an impact. In Massachusetts, researchers surveyed business leaders and real estate specialists about the prospects for locating new businesses in the state's older industrial cities. They found a surprising degree of optimism among local economic development officials, who had discovered a number of ways to lure new firms, often to brownfield sites in the center of town. Sounding a hopeful note, they formulated a list of steps local officials could take to improve a community's chance of doing so more consistently.[7]

Assuming local policies matter, the key question facing smaller rust-belt cities is not what to do but whether they can do what is necessary. The obstacles to economic development in these places, while not insurmountable, are nevertheless high. Compared with metropolitan communities, they are dependent places, subject to economic and political currents over which they have little control. The flight of capital has taken with it not only jobs, but access to the corridors of power. Industrial cities included homegrown elites who not only filled seats on local civic boards but had connections to economic and political leaders from around the country and even the world. The economic structures that produced such people are gone and with them went the links to corporate and governmental authority. This difficulty is compounded by the comparatively weak position of cities with the American polity. Creations of state governments, U.S. cities are bound by a set of rules and regulations that limit their capacity to act independently in matters such as setting tax levels or exerting influence over the surrounding region. Smaller cities even struggle to define their own identities, which are often determined as much by labels stamped upon them by national media as they are by the experiences of local residents.

The most obvious obstacles to restoring growth and prosperity are economic. Simply put, at least some smaller cities lack the basic resources necessary to generate economic growth on their own. The local labor market in these places cannot accommodate hundreds, if not thousands, of newly unemployed, low-skill workers. The absence of large sums of capital within the community means that any substantial new undertakings require external investment. Since so many places are competing for a limited pool of private money, cities have often had to provide tax breaks and incentives in what amounts to a race to the bottom. Luring a plant to a community through tax breaks and other financial incentives yields a few jobs but often little in the way of business and property taxes, key drivers of the municipal revenues necessary to maintaining and improving a community in ways that promote its long-term economic health.

But other, less obvious factors constrain the small cities of the American rust belt. Perhaps the most salient is the American tendency to conceive of cities as independent entities, an idea with roots in the model of cities as free of feudal authority in medieval Europe. That sense of autonomy, magnified in the highly decentralized system of government in the United States, has encouraged the idea that cities are separate corporate units (as indeed they are in a legal sense) and has created a climate of competition among cities for economic advantage. The most famous example of such contestation was the clash between Chicago and St. Louis for predominance in the American middle west during the nineteenth century, but it has occurred at all levels of the urban hierarchy as localities have battled to attract railroad lines, factories, universities, and other institutions. This tradition of viewing cities as individual competitors in an open market, responsible for their own improvement and development, has encouraged the assumption that cities themselves are to blame for their own failures.[8]

The sense that American cities are independent actors is especially ironic given the legal and political restrictions placed upon them. Comparisons with cities from other countries underscore the distinctive limits to municipal power in the United States. Chinese cities, for example are creatures of the national government, which steers foreign investment to them, provides necessary financial resources, and gives them control over the surrounding regions. In Europe, cities with roots as independent walled communities during the medieval period retain at least a residual influence over their immediate hinterlands, as well as greater support from and influence upon regional and national governments. American cities, particularly smaller ones, have very little ability to shape the national policies that affect them (such as the location of a military installation). While urban leaders may have somewhat more influence over state-level decisions, such as the location of a highway or a community college, those choices remain largely out of their hands. And as products of state legislation, in the form of charters, American cities of all sizes are also hemmed in by legal restrictions that prevent them from annexing surrounding areas or otherwise extracting the tax revenues from the people and businesses that have decamped to their outskirts. State laws can also limit their capacity to levy property taxes or raise money in other ways. Meanwhile, state and federal policies in education, housing, environmental improvement, and numerous other areas further constrict municipal action.[9]

The prescriptions for urban policymaking contained in the recent think tank plans inadvertently underscore the dependency of American municipalities. Many of their proposals require either permission or formal action by state governments. In *To Be Strong Again*, the rehabilitation program for rust-belt cities produced by PolicyLink, the plans for infrastructure improvements and repairs require state or federal funding, as do the calls for new forms of rail transit and the revamping of state-sponsored local development authorities. Tellingly, when the Brookings Institution took up the issue of revitalizing older industrial cities, it focused not on municipal-level action but on state government. It calls for investment in infrastructure, safety, job training, and housing, all areas where state governments are the crucial actors, not cities. None of this means small cities cannot or should not act, but it underscores the degree to which they are reliant on state legislatures (often dominated by less-than-sympathetic suburban, rural, or metropolitan interests) to move ahead.[10]

Deindustrialization and its side effects have frayed other political ties to the detriment of rust-belt small cities. Business elites heading manufacturing firms had the clout necessary to lure state and federal investment to their communities (as LaDale Winling's essay in this volume on the Ball family's role in the development of Muncie, Indiana shows). Their departure has severed key connections between small industrial cities and corridors of state and federal power. Industrial unions once constituted the core constituency of the Democratic Party in factory towns across the Northeast and Midwest and a powerful force in local politics. Plant closings and cutbacks, most common among heavily unionized steel and automaking manufacturers, have reduced the numbers and clout of organized labor in these communities considerably, severing yet another tie to decision making at the local, state, and even national level. More broadly, the demographic shift fueled by the reordering of the American economy has moved the nation's electoral clout decisively to the south and west. While population growth has slowed in the states that make up the rust belt, it has increased sharply in states such as Texas, Nevada, and California. Congressional seats and electoral votes have followed accordingly, leaving the older industrial states and the municipalities within them in a weaker position when it comes to influencing federal policy.[11]

Internal social dynamics can work against small cities as they seek to reinvent themselves for a new economy. In an intriguing book, Sean Safford makes the case that these structures can have a considerable impact on whether or not it can adjust to new economic realities. He examines the fortunes of two cities, Allentown, Pennsylvania and Youngstown, Ohio. Both were steel cities that fell on hard times as deindustrialization set in. From there, their respective stories diverged. Allentown managed to remake itself for a new economy while Youngstown languished, plagued by poverty and civic decay. Allentown had a more open, flexible social structure that made it open to change.[12]

More specifically, Safford argues that Allentown was more nimble than Youngstown in the face of this crisis because it had long before developed a dense, interconnected web of institutional networks. By virtue of its demographic history and social geography, Allentown had a robust civic life that incorporated not only business leaders but also representatives of the city's ethnic groups. Interaction within the public realm fostered a tradition of cooperation and mutual trust that served it well when economic changes forced the community to realign itself to fit a global economy. Youngstown's civic life developed differently, with business leaders dominating philanthropic and social organizations to the exclusion of representatives from other groups. The failure to establish the habit of civic collaboration with other elements of the community bred division and made cooperation and innovation much more difficult when economic changes demanded it. Safford's analysis is richer and more complex than a brief summary can convey. But his key idea—that many, if not most, rust-belt cities have inflexible civic cultures in which class and racial tensions prevent the coordinated effort necessary for economic transformation—reminds us of another, internal obstacle small cities encounter as they aim to remake themselves.[13]

Safford's exploration of the roots of local civic configurations points toward the most fundamental challenge small cities face as they retool for a new economy. These communities arose as industrial places and any transformation that takes place will involve not just a redefinition of their economic roles or a reconstruction of their built environment, but a cultural reinvention as well. The prescriptions laid out in the various think tank proposals and academic analyses all point to particular policies, but rarely acknowledge the deeper change that must take place for these cities to even begin to implement the agenda they lay out. Small-city residents have to imagine themselves as members of a different kind of community. Even those places fortunate enough to retain a significant manufacturing base will still need to attract a culturally diverse set of educated, cosmopolitan workers and their families. That is a tall task that entails not just opening a few coffee shops and boutique stores but reorienting deeply rooted local mores regarding everything from race and education to gender roles, sexuality, parenthood, and marriage. Such changes cannot happen overnight.[14]

Some observers have noted the importance of a community's identity in connection with its ability to respond to economic hardship. John Russo and Sherry Lee Linkon examine how Youngstown became the nation's "poster child" for deindustrialization, as well as a symbol for political corruption and civic decline. Those images not only shaped how outsiders represented the city, but also influenced the ways that local residents imagined their own community. In particular it fostered among them a sense that Youngstown's difficulties were the product of the community's moral and civic failures, rather than the result of specific business decisions and larger economic trends. That perspective in turn imbued in them a sense of hopelessness, a belief that their town was fundamentally flawed and could not return to prosperity.[15] In much the same way, S. Paul O'Hara has traced the way that Gary, Indiana has become the classic case of a rust-belt city, albeit one in which racial tensions have complicated the story. It now seeks to redefine itself as a lakeside gambling destination, a task made all the more difficult by the widespread perception of the city as an urban dystopia held by locals as well as outsiders.[16]

Every smaller rust-belt city faces this same challenge—to remake itself into something new. Some aim to become tourist destinations. Those fortunate enough to be in the orbit of a larger city can evolve into suburbs. Others seek to lure high-tech or other knowledge-driven businesses. While the recipe for all of these transformations includes lower taxes and a modest cost of living, attributes many rust-belt towns already possess, it also includes becoming a physically attractive place that offer the kinds of educational, recreation, and leisure opportunities that young, well-educated workers seek. Conceived chiefly as the home of factories and their workers, these communities rarely possess such amenities. Convincing a blue-collar town to invest in parks, preserve historic buildings, revive its downtown as an upscale shopping district, foster cultural diversity, or fund new school construction is difficult in the best of times. When resources are scarce, when filling potholes and clearing snow overtax municipal resources, such steps seem like luxuries. It is even more difficult to get locals on board when they appear to cater to upper- and middle-class outsiders rather than to the immediate needs of the thousands of struggling blue-collar workers who grew up there. Such choices only make sense if residents have bought in to a new vision of their community, one that looks dramatically different from the place that they, their parents, and their grandparents knew as home.

The essays collected in this volume each speak to the questions of whether and how small industrial cities can reinvent themselves in the face of such obstacles. The first section presents a series of concrete case studies that either explore deeply rooted cultural, economic, and social patterns that have shaped responses to economic change or offer accounts of successful redevelopment efforts. The second part considers strategies for redevelopment in more general ways. While hardly exhaustive in scope, the contributions to this volume do touch on a range of issues that have attracted the attention of urbanists in recent decades, including suburbanization, the role of business leaders and large institutions, the fate of downtown, sustainability, and the evolution of class relations. One thread that ties them together is their import for understanding the fate of rust-belt small cities in the postindustrial era. Each speaks in some fashion to the challenges and opportunities cities face as they try to reinvent themselves.

In the book's first chapter, S. Paul O'Hara reminds us of the power of narratives to shape our understanding of deindustrialized cities and to constrain their ability to act. It traces popular representations of two manufacturing cities sited within the orbit of metropolitan communities, Gary, Indiana and Norwood, Ohio. His account of the changing depictions of both cities complicates the Detroit-versus-Pittsburgh duality that frames so much current discussion of the rust belt (with Detroit as the exemplar of urban decay and Pittsburgh of a new-economy renaissance). During the early twentieth century commentators used these "satellite cities" as examples of the beneficent possibilities of industrialism. Gary was a planned model community and Norwood a seemingly organic industrial town. Observers cast both as victims of deindustrialization and the social problems it bred during the second half of the twentieth century, when a decline in the U.S. steel industry undercut Gary and the departure of a GM plant robbed Norwood of its leading employer. Today, Gary remains a steel producer, albeit with much lower employment levels and extensive poverty, while Norwood has yet to make the transition to a middle-class suburban enclave of Cincinnati that observers anticipated when the GM plant closed. As O'Hara demonstrates, the prevailing narrative of postindustrial life in the rust belt has no role for these in-between places, a particularly acute problem when such frameworks shape the expert advice and policy plans that shape the fortunes of small cities.

Allen Dieterich-Ward finds the usual accounts of deindustrialization problematic as well. He explains how Steubenville, Ohio has transformed from decrepit industrial city to bedroom community for Pittsburgh. As recently as the 1990s the city suffered from many of the ills that plague other factory towns in the rust belt, including a declining population and tax base, an empty downtown, and heavy pollution. Highway construction connecting it to the Pittsburgh metropolitan area, including its airport, has allowed Steubenville to begin redefining itself as low-cost, high-amenity option for commuters. To be sure, Pittsburgh's revival has made this strategy possible, as has the willingness of governments in two states to build highways and bridges. But accompanying state action has been energetic efforts by local leaders and citizens to redefine the character of their city and to reimagine themselves as part of a metropolitan community. Geography, augmented by state-level action, made reinvention possible, but so too did an internal cultural shift.

Janet Bednarek presents another account of a city that was able to remake itself. She focuses on the remaking of downtown Omaha, Nebraska, a city once famous for meatpacking and other industries. With state support, and considerable public-private collaboration, downtown was reconfigured, both literally and in a metaphorical sense, as part of an effort to revive the city's economic fortunes. The core effort was the reorientation of the downtown toward the Missouri River, turning what had once been the center of the city's commerce and industry into a destination for recreation and entertainment. As Bednarek explains, it became the city's "image center." The meaning of this transformation, not only for the downtown but for the city as a whole, was captured in the tension over what to call the new downtown riverfront park. The rejection of the initial plan to call it "Union Labor Plaza," in honor of the city's workers, and the ultimate choice of "Lewis and Clark Landing," reflected the rethinking of Omaha's identity. No longer a city with a strong industrial base, it was now home to financial services companies and other knowledge-intensive activities. Its appealing downtown bolstered that image, though it no longer served as the principal site of local economic life.

One reason Omaha has been able to reengineer its own image so effectively is because its size gives it advantages over most other Midwestern industrial communities. Though far from a global metropolis, a population of more than 400,000 gives it influence that smaller places usually lack. For less substantial cities and towns, the loss of an important firm dramatically lessens their political clout. LaDale Winling underscores this point in his analysis of the role of the Ball family in shaping the institutional and spatial character of Muncie, Indiana. He details how the wealthy Ball family used not only their economic resources, derived from their famous glass jar company, but also their political connections to state and federal government to create a public college in their hometown of Muncie, Indiana, in 1918, and to expand it dramatically in ensuing decades. In much the same way, they established a regional hospital in Muncie. They also used their wealth to jump-start construction of an exclusive residential district that sharpened the geographic character of the city's well-established class divide. As Winling rightly notes, these developments were testimony to the "gravity of capital." But they also represented the exploitation of political influence. The university and hospital, both of which bear the Ball family name, now serve as the cornerstones of the city's economic development plans, while the subdivision they launched remains an enclave for the well-to-do, including numerous professors and doctors. The source of these changes is gone—neither the Ball family nor the Ball Corporation reside in Muncie today. But the imprint of the Balls' actions not only remains clear but now provides the blueprint for the blue-collar town's struggle to transform itself into a center for medical services and higher education.

Such a transition is fraught with tension, as Alison Goebel shows in her ethnographic portrait of Mansfield, Ohio. A small manufacturing city located midway between Cleveland and Columbus, Mansfield finds itself in the midst of changes similar to those Muncie is experiencing. Industrial production—now chiefly in small, nonunionized plants—remains the largest slice of the local economy by a slight margin, but health care is now the fastest growing sector and a firm running two hospitals is the county's largest employer. Locals without college degrees are more and more likely to work as medical technicians or ambulance drivers rather than on an assembly line. Meanwhile the new professional jobs tend to go to outsiders, including many from other countries. That pattern has produced new tensions that overlay longstanding class and racial frictions. The new mix has thus far generated considerable unease, as old-timers clash with newcomers—many with only limited sense of attachment to the community—on a variety of fronts. This split, reproduced in many rust-belt towns making the shift from manufacturing to medical care, higher education, and other knowledge- and service-economy activity, makes it difficult for Mansfield to act in the coordinated, forward-thinking fashion that policy analysts prescribe.[17]

The two essays by economists that are included here reinforce the argument that a focus on amenities and other quality of life issues is an essential element in the reinvention of small industrial cities. The first, Michael Hicks' statistical analysis of the correlates of urban growth in Great Lakes region small cities, underscores the difficulties small cities face in making the transition to a new economic order. Hicks found that human capital plays a strong role in regional economic performance, local amenities are important, though less so than human capital, and social capital measures are also correlated with economic growth. These findings, which conform to the results of other studies, only hint at growth strategies and policies. There is "no silver bullet," Hicks points out. Regions can do little about random shocks to their economy due to demand fluctuations for their dominant industries. But his analysis nevertheless indicates that human capital (broadly defined as workers with at least minimal educational attainments), local amenities, and social capital are more likely to lead to higher levels of per capita income and population. Public policies that seek to enhance these qualities seem most appropriate to small cities in the Midwest.

Thomas Lehman's examination of income patterns in rural counties points in the same direction. Their best chance of improvement comes, perhaps counterintuitively, from becoming more urban. Counties with relatively higher population density, closer proximity to metropolitan areas, outside-county employment opportunities for their residents, a more educated workforce, and greater labor force attachment exhibit consistently higher levels of median household income. Additionally, and to a lesser degree, counties with relatively more immigrants and a relatively higher proportion of same-sex partner households tend to have higher median household incomes. These findings tentatively support the theory that rural economies that can capture urban characteristics such as higher population density, greater population diversity, increased human capital, and workforce connections to metropolitan areas exhibit the best chance for economic development. Lehman advises county leaders (and these counties include smaller cities and towns) to "seek to attract and retain younger, more educated workers." Doing so may involve reducing taxes and regulations but it also involves improving the quality of life and educational opportunities.[18]

The book closes with a provocative proposal that goes beyond the plans stressed by most urbanists. Catherine Tumber, in an essay first published in the *Boston Review*, argues that the customary neglect of smaller cities in urban studies have prompted analysts to overlook key advantages. By virtue of their intermediate scale and their access to nearby open land (as well as empty lots within their borders), they can become epicenters of more sustainable energy and agricultural practices. Such innovations can pave the way for greater prosperity in these places and Tumber's ideas deserve careful and serious consideration. There are reasons to question whether small rust-belt cities can reorient themselves in the way that Tumber lays out, at least for the near term. Many of the steps she proposes require at least the assent, and more often the initiative, of local leaders and citizens. A prerequisite of such action is a willingness to innovate. Some small rust-belt cities, usually aided by inherent advantages of location, scale, or pre-existing institutions, have begun to make such leaps. But other places remain mired in longstanding identities and new cultural conflicts that make the changes in values and priorities inherent in Tumber's agenda difficult to achieve.

Can small industrial cities change in the ways that the more optimistic urbanists propose? The evidence collected in this volume suggest the answer is, provisionally, yes. Some communities, recognizing the advantages they have in hand and acting upon them, have broken with the past. But the obstacles—economic, political, and cultural—to a successful transition remain substantial. Part of the problem is structural—small American cities are legally, politically, and financially weak and thus cannot act aggressively. Perhaps the greater impediment is the ability of communities long accustomed to a certain place in the world to accept that that role and the social, cultural, and civic order it produced can no longer be sustained. It does not mean that all factories will disappear. But manufacturing will no longer be the engine of prosperity that it was for the better part of a century. Only when and if residents of small cities recognize that fact, and acknowledge that they will be different kinds places, are they likely to thrive again.

Notes

1. Key works include David Bell and Mark Jayne, eds. *Small Cities: Urban Experience Beyond the Metropolis* (New York: Routledge, 2006), which addresses issues of economic growth around the world but includes only a handful of chapters on U.S. cities. W.F. Garrett-Petts, ed., *The Small Cities Book: On The Cultural Future of Small Cities* (Vancouver: New Star Books, 2005) examines cultural experiences and identity formation in small cities, chiefly through an analysis of Kamloops, British Columbia. It has relatively little to say about the economic, cultural, and civic challenges facing industrial small cities in the United States. Essays on the history of small cities in the modern world can be found in James J. Connolly, *Decentering Urban History: Peripheral Cities in the Modern World*, special issue of the *Journal of Urban History* 35, no. 1 (November, 2008), but it includes just one piece on an American city. PolicyLink recently released Radhika Fox and Miriel Axel-Lute, *To Be Strong Again: Renewing the Promise in Smaller Industrial Cities* (Oakland, CA: PolicyLink, 2008), a 64-page publication outlining development strategies for smaller industrial cities in the United States. Other key policy reports include Jennifer S. Vey, *Restoring Prosperity: The State Role in Revitalizing America's Older Industrial Cities* (Washington, D.C.: The Brookings Institution, 2007); Lorlene Hoyt and Andre LeRoux, eds., *Voices from Forgotten Cities: Innovative Revitalization Coalitions in America's Older Small Cities* (Oakland, CA: PolicyLink, 2007). Timothy Mahoney, "The Small City in American History," *Indiana Magazine of History* 99, no. 4 (December 2003): 311–30 provides a valuable introduction to the history of small cities in the United States.

2. Barry Bluestone and Bennett Harrison, *The Deindustrialization of America: Plant Closings, Community Abandonment, and the Dismantling of Basic Industry* (New York: Basic Books, 1982).

3. Thomas J. Sugrue, *The Origins of the Urban Crisis: Race and Inequality in Postwar Detroit*, First Princeton Classic Edition (Princeton, N.J.: Princeton University Press, 2005), 125–152. See also Steven High, *Industrial Sunset: The Making of North America's Rust Belt, 1969–1984* (Toronto: University of Toronto Press); Jon C. Teaford, *Cities of the Heartland: The Rise and Fall of the Industrial Midwest* (Bloomington: Indiana University Press, 1993); Richard C. Longworth, *Caught in the Middle: America's Heartland in the Age of Globalism* (New York: Bloomsbury, 2008).

4. Fox and Axel-Lute, *To Be Strong Again*; Vey, *Restoring Prosperity*; Hoyt and LeRoux, *Voices from Forgotten Cities*.

5. Vey, *Restoring Prosperity*, 4.

6. See the Muncie Action Plan, "Community Choices Public Workshop." www .cityofmuncie.com/upload/assets/map/communiy%20choices%20presentation%20 slides.pdf (accessed April 23, 2010).

7. George A. Erickcek and Hannah McKinney, "Small Cities Blues": Looking for Growth Factors in Small and Medium-Sized Cities," Upjohn Institute Staff Working Paper No. 04-100, June 2004, www.upjohninst.org/publications/wp/04-100.pdf (accessed May 20, 2010); David Soule, et al., *The Rebirth of Older Industrial Cities: Exciting Opportunities for Private Sector Investment* (Boston: Center for Urban and Regional Policy, Northeastern University, 2004).

8. On medieval urban forms and their connections to American city development, see Eric H. Monkonnen, *America Becomes Urban: The Development of U.S. Cities and Towns, 1780–1980* (Berkeley: University of California Press, 1988), 31–68.

9. James J. Connolly, "Decentering Urban History," *Journal of Urban History* 35, no. 1 (November, 2008): 12.

10. Fox and Axel-Lute, *To Be Strong Again*; Vey, *Restoring Prosperity*.

11. Election Data Services, "2009 Reapportionment Analysis," December 23, 2009 www.electiondataservices.com/images/File/NR_Appor09wTables.pdf (April 23, 2010).

12. Sean Safford, *Why the Garden Club Couldn't Save Youngstown: The Transformation of the Rust Belt* (Cambridge: Harvard University Press, 2009).

13. Safford, *Why the Garden Club Couldn't Save Youngstown.*

14. For an intriguing discussion of the interplay between economic change and cultural norms in the contemporary United States, see Naomi Cahn and June Carbone, *Red Families v. Blue Families: Legal Polarization and the Creation of Culture* (New York: Oxford University Press, 2010). The cultural fault line Cahn and Carbone describe often runs right through rust-belt towns as they attempt to adjust to the new economic order.

15. John Russo and Sherry Lee Linkon, "Collateral Damage: Deindustrialization and the Uses of Youngstown," in *Beyond the Ruins: The Meanings of Deindustrialization*, ed. Jefferson Cowie and Joseph Heathcott (Ithaca, N.Y.: Cornell University Press, 2003), 201–18.

16. S. Paul O'Hara, "Envisioning the Steel City: The Legend and Legacy of Gary, Indiana" in *Beyond the Ruins*, ed. Cowie and Heathcott, 219 36.

17. It is worth noting just how far this state of affairs leaves Mansfield from embracing the cultural diversity that Richard Florida argues is the essential precursor to prosperity in the new knowledge economy. See Richard Florida, *The Rise of the Creative Class and How It's Transforming Work, Leisure, Community, and Everyday Life* (New York: Basic Books, 2002).

18. The analyses offered by Lehman and Hicks support, at least in its broad strokes, the argument advanced by Richard Florida in *The Rise of the Creative Class.*

CHAPTER TWO

~

Model Cities, Mill Towns, and Industrial Peripheries

Small Industrial Cities in Twentieth-Century America

S. Paul O'Hara

In the March 2009 issue of the *Atlantic*, urban sociologist Richard Florida offered his predictions on what the economic crash of late 2008 and early 2009 would mean to the American economy and the shape of American cities. The front cover offered in bold letters Florida's predictions of "how the crash will reshape America." In the zero-sum game of twenty-first-century urbanism, the "suburbs lose, the Sunbelt fades, [and] Chicago wins." In his article Florida lays out his rationale for such predictions. Global crises, he argues, cause geographic transformations. Just as the long depression of the nineteenth century consolidated industrial production and migration in Midwestern cities such as Chicago, Cleveland, and Pittsburgh, so too had the economic crises of the 1970s and 1980s shifted growth to sunbelt cities and suburbs. The current crisis, says Florida, signals a similar shift in American urbanism. However, he points out, these economic crises do not create the shifts in economic and spatial patterns but rather accelerate shifts already under way; thus some cities will win while others lose. Those cities that are part of mega-regions are particularly well positioned to continue to grow. New York, the center of the financial world currently in crisis, is also a center of what Florida calls "talent-clustering" (highly educated and diverse in occupation) and has a high rate of "urban metabolism" (i.e., new ideas and creative endeavors quickly come to fruition) and thereby will be fine. The key to understanding the crisis, Florida tell us, is to comprehend that "the economy is shifting away from manufacturing and toward idea-driven industries—and that too favors America's talent-rich, fast-metabolizing places."[1]

To trace this shift from "manufacturing regions whose heydays are long past" to sunbelt cities built upon real estate "Ponzi schemes" to talent-rich and thriving mega regions, Florida offers several key examples. New York will thrive, he argues, because its economy and culture encompasses more than finance. Las Vegas and Phoenix will fade as their speculative real estate bubbles burst. To make sense of the declining industrial rust belt, Florida turns to the same example so many commentators use. "Perhaps no major city in the United States today looks more beleaguered than Detroit," Florida concludes. "Perhaps Detroit has reached a tipping point," he speculates, "and will become a ghost town." Possible but unlikely, he continues, because too many residents are tied to the home mortgages and will not or cannot leave. Still others have nowhere else to go. Detroit will continue, Florida concludes, but it will never be the city that it once was. For Florida, what was necessary was a kind of political triage with industrial cities. Some, such as Pittsburgh, could be saved; others such as Detroit would decline. "Finally we need to be clear that ultimately we can't stop the decline of some places, and that we would be foolish to try," he summarizes. The best and last hope for industrial cities is a policy which "in limited ways . . . can help faltering cities to manage their decline better."[2]

Placing Detroit at the center of industrial collapse and urban decline was a common narrative in the fall of 2008. Florida was far from alone in using the Motor City as a key example of industrial cities. Often within this narrative, the decline of Detroit is juxtaposed against the redevelopment and rejuvenation of Pittsburgh, which Florida praises as a place which has "shown that a city can stay vibrant as it shrinks by redeveloping its core to attract young professionals and creative types." Within these narratives, Detroit became an adaptable metaphor for industrial decline. For some Detroit was a tragic story of lost prosperity, the so-called Arsenal of Democracy abandoned and broken. For others Detroit stood as a cautionary tale of stagnant growth and overdependence on a single and increasingly outdated industry. Within these narratives the concept of Detroit becomes a metaphor because there is often a blurred line about what people mean when they say "Detroit." Only some of the time did descriptions and eulogies of Detroit actually refer to the city. During the public debate over federal money to save the auto industry, "Detroit" was a metonym for the big three auto companies. For those who lament the decline of industrial unionism and the liberal state, "Detroit" comes to mean the lost potential of Walter Reuther and the United Autoworkers (UAW). Yet in many ways it was in Flint, on the outer edges of the city of Detroit, where the UAW was born. Part of the urban decline described in a December 2009 piece in the *Economist* is in Highland Park, a mill town separate from the city of Detroit that once held its own historic Ford factory.[3] Much of the history of industrial production and industrial urbanism in the United States during the twentieth-century is not the story of major industrial cities but rather the rise and fall of small industrial centers built on the edges of other cities. For Detroit there is Flint, for Pittsburgh there is Braddock, for Chicago there is Gary. Even in cities that Richard Florida declares will win in the postindustrial economy, there is still severe loss in the deindustrialized periphery.

Yet these cities are often forgotten in the public debate. Rather it focuses upon cities such as Detroit because that city serves as a powerful metaphor within which we can debate the history of neoliberal economics, race relations and riots, industrial unionism and the collapse of the liberal consensus, or any of the other narratives of the Reagan epoch. It is fitting to remember that although our public memory dates the fall of Detroit in 1967, the motor city served as the convention host to Ronald Reagan's 1980 campaign. In other words, for the last twenty to thirty years, Detroit has served as a convenient way for us to discuss ourselves. Places such as Braddock, Gary, or Flint (despite Michael Moore's desperate attempts) do not work as well and thus fall from the public debate.

This was not always the case however. Throughout much of the twentieth century, these industrial outskirts were deemed to be of terrific importance and great attention was paid to their constructions, their functions, and their dysfunctions. "We are familiar with Chicago and Detroit, Cleveland and St. Louis," wrote the *Survey* in 1912, "but do we know overmuch about Argo and Gary, Corey, Norwood, Granite City and the other industrial satellites which are springing up under the eaves of the great urban centers?" The writers and editors of the *Survey*, led by Graham Romeyn Taylor, were convinced that not only were industries moving out onto the urban periphery, but that this "industrial exodus . . . is in its individual parts a consciously directed movement" and thus worthy of close scrutiny and attention. This phenomenon:

> presents repeated opportunities for shaping the civic and social conditions under which large groups of people are to live for decades to come. It raises in new and searching ways questions as to the obligations which go with economic control; as to the future of local self-government in relation to the same; and as to the organization and large-scale development of our industrial districts.

These new industrial cities may have been on the periphery of the urban landscape but they were far from peripheral to the American economy or the American imagination. Rather they demanded close attention in their construction as well as close supervision in the development. For all of their potential for growth, these cities also held such great potential for upheaval and conflict. They were paradoxically planned and unplanned, American and foreign, important and peripheral. They were brand new and held the potential for anything. "Like the foundlings which were dropped in the turn-cradles of the old time orphanages, these young communities which industry is leaving at the door-steps of our cities are no longer things apart and by themselves," concluded Taylor in the *Survey*. "For better or worse, they come to share in the common lot."[4]

This article revisits the history of these industrial outskirts in order to rethink their place within the patterns of industrial and urban growth in the twentieth century. In particular it traces the meaning and history of two of Taylor's satellite cities: Gary, Indiana, and Norwood, Ohio. These were small secondary cities tied to the fates of larger economies and cities. They were also cities built by single industries and designed for a single purpose. Thus they present a distinct pattern of urban growth, development, and decline. On the one hand, both of these cities share a great deal of history because both were key parts of the industrial narratives of twentieth-century America. Their history stretches from the industrial expansions of the late nineteenth and early twentieth century to deindustrialization and plant closures. Yet, on the other hand, the histories of these cities vary greatly because they developed in very different ways, focused upon different industries, and (perhaps most importantly) served different roles within the American imagination. Gary was always the model city that served as a metaphor for both the best and worst of industrialism, while Norwood was the urban periphery of Cincinnati that observers assumed grew "organically" and thus did not carry the same kind of symbolic importance. Yet narrative and meaning still very much mattered for Norwood as the city became a key site of twentieth-century labor relations.

Gary was a city planned and built by the United States Steel Corporation. Constructed on what was essentially open sand dunes on Lake Michigan just across the Indiana border from Chicago, Gary was designed to be a concentrated supercenter of steel production. The first and most prominent structure of Gary was its massive steel works along the lake shore; the rest of the city of Gary developed literally in the shadow of these works. Begun in 1906 and producing steel by 1909, Gary was an instant city made from scratch by a massive and seemingly omnipotent corporation. It was quickly populated by steel workers, especially immigrants from Eastern Europe and migrants from the American south. Norwood began very differently as an industrial outgrowth of Cincinnati. Several factories had begun to move out to the suburb by the late 1880s, but Norwood's industrial future would become intimately tied to the General Motors (GM) body plant that opened in 1923. This plant not only gave Norwood its industrial identity but it also provided the city with the tax base and political independence to remain apart from the city of Cincinnati which grew around it. Not only did Norwood's production of automobiles differ greatly from Gary's production of steel, but migration patterns differed in the cities as well. The GM plant was filled largely by southern migrants from Appalachia; very few of whom chose to live in the city. Both cities would peak in population in the middle of the twentieth century; Gary with over 178,000 people and Norwood with about 35,000.

The two cities developed in different ways and at different times and were very different cities, yet Taylor chose to combine his analysis of the two cities under the larger social phenomenon of "satellite cities." Both cities had working communities centered on a single industry and the plants in both cities left a considerable impact (both physical and psychological) on their cities, however these industries also varied greatly in the kinds of work, the kinds of workers, and the kinds of pollutants associated with the production. Both cities would also play very different roles in the narratives of twentieth-century race relations. For all of Taylor's comparisons, these two cities represented very different forms of small city industrialism. At the same time, however, both cities demonstrate the importance of small city industrialism in the twentieth century.

What the comparative histories of these two cities give us is an opportunity to trace the role of these cities as metaphor. There is a pattern of meaning attached to the industrial outskirts. Some, like Gary, served as model cities of perfect planning. Others such as Norwood became industrial peripheries shaped by its relationship to the larger metropolis. By mid century, however, both cities were reimagined as cauldrons and crucibles of the key social forces of race, work, class, and ethnicity. While Florida and others may use Detroit as the key site to understand postindustrial urbanism, for observers in the twentieth century it was not in the major industrial cities but rather the industrial outskirts where the meaning of twentieth-century American industrial urbanism was to be written. From 1880s to 1970s these cities were peripheral in geography but central to the American imagination of urban industrialism.

The Death and Life of Small Industrial Cities

In her famous treatise on urban growth and vibrancy, Jane Jacobs argues that the death and life of great American cities can be explained by the presence or absence of vibrant public spaces. Diverse economies, diverse people, and diverse professions all intermingle in the dense public spaces of great metropolises, giving these cities great vibrancy. Yet there are important differences between major metropolises and peripheral industrial cities. In many ways the modern metropolis comes to serve as a microcosm of the liberal state and the modern nation.[5] At the same time, the struggle for power and identity in so-called "second cities" was quite different. While such cities thrived on the rise of bourgeois liberalism and industrialized urbanization, much of their autonomy and importance were eclipsed by the central metropolis.[6]

The industrial cities that emerged in the twentieth century were neither capital cities embodying the nation nor second cities fretting over their growth or future. Nor were they the expolis of multiple spaces and far ranging meanings that cities such as Los Angeles have come to symbolize.[7] Rather they were planned spaces that promised order and continued production. This meant a specific kind of industrial geography that resulted from a shifting relationship to industrialism. Through their efforts to expand and find new markets and resources, capitalists wanted to redefine not only capital but also time and space. As David Harvey points out, the only way capital can expand was to create permanent physical structures that are tied into the landscape. Thus the moment capital created a structure, such as a factory, a sidewalk, a road, or port, expansion tried to make that structure obsolete.[8] Since these industrial spaces were new there were not the long-standing traditions, separations, or cultures that would create *habitus* as described by Pierre Bourdieu. Rather they were brand new spaces with new structures and populated by new arrivals. These industrial cities may not have been organic in their growth or diverse in economy and culture, but they were certainly cities. They may not have developed in a long process of urbanization but they were certainly urban. It was this very reality that made these cities such important metaphors for the American imagination. What these cities meant, and thus what American industrialism in the twentieth century meant, was largely up for grabs.

The histories of peripheral industrial cities not only challenge many of our assumptions about deindustrialization and postindustrial economies, but they also add new dimensions to our understanding of the origins and histories of urban growth, especially the growth of smaller cities. Far from the organic environments of big city urbanization with its diverse interplay of large social forces, industrial cities were fabrications designed and built for a single purpose. In a summary of trends within urban history, James Connolly has argued that one way to revitalize the study of cities is to recognize the dual importance of space and place. The study of space, informed as it is by the theories of Henri Lefebvre, Michel Foucault, and David Harvey, suggests that urban environments are more than stages onto which actors move. Rather, the very structure of the city is an exercise in social construction and power. Cities are constructed environments, both in terms of physical structures as well as the meaning and use of its spaces. At the same time, studies of place recognize that each city has its own unique geography, social environments, and transformative moments that make each city its own site.[9] Such an understanding of place would serve industrial satellite cities well. Most of these former mill towns get organized together under an umbrella of structural deindustrialization. Recent histories of deindustrialization, however, show that the chronology, causes, and aftermaths of capital flight and deindustrialization vary dramatically by location.[10] Gary and Norwood are quite different from other mill towns such as Youngstown and Flint, just as they differ from other peripheral cities such as East Saint Louis or Camden, New Jersey. Yet at the national level they all play an important role (although these roles differ) as metaphor in national debates about the meaning of industrialism in the twentieth century.

Such debates mattered because, at the same time these cities were emerging, Americans came to frame their descriptions and comprehensions of culture and society in industrial terms. Across the class spectrum of nineteenth-century America, people tended to look backward to evoke a pre-industrial past. The struggle over culture and meaning in the twentieth century took a very different direction. All of the efforts to establish order and social control assumed the realities of industrialization. Instead of evoking an ideal past, these movements tended to imagine an industrialized future. Even those who wished to reject the industrial vision were forced to critique the system from within the parameters of industrialism. As James Barrett points out, worker radicalism still used revolutionary language at the turn of the century, yet the revolutionary movements European immigrants evoked were not the republican ideals of the American Revolution but the proletarian traditions of 1848.[11] Likewise, middle-class efforts in the Progressive Era did not seek to overturn industrialism but rather reform it through pragmatic efforts to make industrial society better.[12]

Political understandings of industrialism and order changed dramatically as workers were integrated into the New Deal state in the 1930s. The rhetoric of economic nationalism stressed the importance of industrial labor and industrial production to the stability and power of the nation, but it also recognized the place or workers and their industrial unions within the nation. By mid century, however, the key definitions of progress, success, and citizenship had changed again. As Lizabeth Cohen has pointed out, citizenship in the twentieth century was increasingly defined by consumerism. Thus one's status and importance was decided less by what one did at work than what one owned at home. Instead of the steel mill, the key site for Americanism was the suburban home.[13] By the last decades of the century, the quest for order and fears of instability had less to do with industrialism than the social divisions of race. However, as Thomas Sugrue and Robert Self have shown, structural changes in industrial production, highway construction, state investment and disinvestment, and capital mobility created the environment from which the "urban crisis" of the 1960s emerged. Far from a "natural" and inevitable death of American cities due to racial animosities, actions by industrialists and politicians created this new urban environment. However, by the 1980s, American cities, especially rusted industrial centers, seemed to many to be not only disordered but also perhaps uncontrollable and unredeemable.[14]

The paradox of industrial spaces is that they were specifically designed to not have the kind of diversity and vibrancy that Jane Jacobs points to as essential to urban growth. Rather industrial cities were constructed environments designed to serve the needs of industrial production and capitalism, just as New England mill towns had before and cities such as Los Angeles would later. The industrialists of this epoch, however, chose to place their industrial production on the periphery of larger metropolitan areas. Yet such peripheral spaces were not margins in the sense that they were disregarded. Indeed the planning and development of industrial spaces at the turn of the century suggests that industrialism, while placed upon the periphery of the metropolis, had moved to the center of the American consciousness. Only at the end of the twentieth century as they deindustrialized did these spaces become marginalized. Instead, during the twentieth century people assumed that these cities mattered and what happened in these cities reflected a great deal about their own understanding of class, race, industry, and urbanism.

At the same time, however, different ideas of what purpose these cities served led to different understandings of the industrial outskirts. For some these spaces were model cities, for others they were mill towns. By mid century, these cities had become, within the public imagination either industrial peripheries of larger socioeconomic forces or crucibles of humanity representing the best and worst of twentieth century possibilities. What the public thought about the industrial outskirts said a lot about how they felt about

American industrialism. The histories of Gary and Norwood, and the way people understood the place of Gary and Norwood, each come to represent both their own specific origins and the era in which they emerged.

The Origins of Industrial Outskirts

The Model City: Or, the Origins of Gary, Indiana

Designed and built by U.S. Steel, Gary, Indiana, was supposed to be a centralized site for steel production. The corporation started with a blank slate (or at least what they chose to believe was a blank slate) and designed the mill and its city with care and precision. As such, Gary came to represent the culmination of urban planning and industrial consolidation in the nineteenth century. Yet at the same time, the evolution of urban planning and the corporation's refusal to engage in utopian discourse also marks an important shift away from industrial utopian thinking.

The earliest form of industrial age utopianism was a rejection of both the metropolis and the market as well as a critique of modern social relations. In the United States such communalist utopias often centered upon religion and religious community. Thus, for instance, there was the experimental community of Oneida which not only rejected the role of market individualism but also private property and Victorian marriage as well. Likewise the Pietists of Harmony, Indiana, removed themselves from the larger society in order to create a perfect community. When he took over the failing Harmony community and transformed it into New Harmony, Robert Owen embraced a slightly different idea of utopianism. Instead of rejecting industrialism and machines, the utopia of New Harmony tried to fix the inequalities of the market and create a different form of industrialism. The colony of New Harmony would be mechanized and modern, but would offer a different social system around industrial production. What this utopia promised was not a pre-industrial religious community but rather a more fair and equal modern society, yet one still small in scale and communal in purpose.

For many Americans their fears of the social and political ramifications of industrialization came through their understanding of Northern English industrial cities such as Manchester. When people looked at these industrializing cities many saw a dark and dystopic wasteland of belching smoke, abject poverty, and constant danger; a space dominated by what William Blake would call the "dark Satanic mills."[15] For Americans, this kind of industrial system based as it was on poverty, class structures, and machinery seemed in stark contrast to the agrarian republic that the revolution had created. Yet when Samuel Slater founded his first textile mill in Pawtucket, Rhode

Island, the city quickly became known as the American Manchester. For a republican system that valued independence measured in land and patriarchal structures of power, the mills offered work only for those who had been broken elsewhere including widows and small children with no other choice. At the same time, however, the process of tending machines soon created an artisan class of mule spinners who demanded the autonomy and recognition of artisan work.[16]

Because of the seeming paradox between the social realities of industrial mill towns and the political ideals of the early republic, many industrialists turned to the ideal of the planned and/or peripheral community. One option was the removal of industrial interests onto the urban periphery, such as the grand plan to industrialize the city of Paterson, New Jersey. Despite these ideals, however, growth in Paterson did not come as quickly as industrialists might have hoped. Another option was to plan not only an industrial city, but to design a model industrial city. The builders of Lowell, Massachusetts, for instance, sought to combine republican community and industrial production within a pastoral setting. Thus when planning their new industrial center of Lowell, the Boston Associates intentionally tried to infuse the city with republican virtues (including a rotating workforce of young women) and natural surroundings so as not to create industrial classes, poverty, pollution, and moral decay. By the 1840s, however, Lowell manufacturers had already begun to hire Irish laborers, including children, for lower wages.[17]

If the first half of the nineteenth century saw the rise of the model city as a possible solution to the paradoxes of industrial production in a republic, by the second half of the nineteenth century, the ideologies of industrial modernity, which demanded massive scale and technological advancements, challenged the size and implementation if not the underlying assumptions of the industrial model city. Many utopianists such as Etienne Cabet did not envision small, close-knit communities but rather used their utopian planning to model a better future. Cabet's cities were to be large and modern, yet clean and ordered. By the end of the nineteenth century, this brand of broad utopianism would be the basic blueprint for experiments like Pullman, Illinois. Because George Pullman sought to control and reform the lives of his workers through planning and structure, he envisioned his city as a social utopia. Clean water, library books, and green spaces were supposed to eliminate social tensions and class conflicts. Such conflicts, tensions, and upheavals seemed not to be inevitable outcomes of modernization, but rather stemmed from the improper practices of modern society. What separated Pullman from previous utopian plans was its embrace of large-scale modernization and its faith that the answers to modern problems lay in scientific technology and sanitation. Long an advocate for sanitary and moral reforms in Chicago, Oscar DeWolf looked to Pullman as confirmation of his ideals. "The erection of such towns as Pullman . . . has a very valuable and decided sanitary educational influence on the general population," he concluded, ". . . such towns, by improving the social surroundings of the working classes, tend to diminish the unrest, which is one great factor in capital and labor conflicts." By providing uplift instead of support, Pullman provided a model of social and moral reform. "This field is one which especially deserves the attention of philanthropists," DeWolf continued, "since it increases the power of the person aided to help himself, does not take from him self-respect, and therefore has no paupering tendencies, like the greatest number of other philanthropic schemes."[18]

Although Dr. DeWolf believed that the utopian schemes of Pullman maintained the self-respect of its workers, the foundation of Pullman's social utopia was paternalistic control. Workers not only had to embrace the middle-class standards of moral uplift, leisure, and entertainment, but they also had to accept the company's ownership and control of everything. At the same time, while the social planning and reliance on moral uplift assumed that social unrest could be planned away, the economics of capital and labor relations remained an important part of social relations in the city. These paternalistic controls, a series of wage cuts, and the continued high rents in company houses led to a major strike in 1894. For a city that assumed that labor unrest could not occur within its planned environment, the strike shook the foundations of the experiment. The strikers in Pullman were soon joined by the American Railway Union, led by Eugene Debs, which refused to carry Pullman cars. By claiming that the strike was preventing the delivery of the mail, President Grover Cleveland secured a court order to end the conflict. He also sent in federal troops to uphold this order. The result was violence in Pullman between strikers and soldiers that resulted in twelve deaths.[19]

In the aftermath of the Pullman strike it became clear to all that Pullman's paternalism and his attempt at social utopia had failed. Among those hardest hit by Pullman's failure were the social reformers and urban planners who had placed so much hope in the idea of the social utopia. After the strike, Jane Addams, founder of Hull House in Chicago, wrote of Pullman:

The sense of duty held by the president of the Pullman Company doubtless represents the ideal in the minds of the best of the present employers as to their obligations toward their employees, but he projected this ideal more magnificently than the others. He alone gave his men a model town, such perfect surroundings. The magnitude of his indulgence and failure corresponded and we are forced to challenge the ideal itself: the same ideal which, more or less clearly defined, is floating in the minds of all philanthropic employers.

For Addams, Pullman represented a modern King Lear. Just as Lear tried to give all to his daughters yet was ultimately rejected, so did Pullman try to indulge his workers without fully understanding what they desired. In the *Survey*, Graham Taylor also lamented the end of the Pullman experiment:

> For those who early hailed the town as providing that alchemy by which the labor problem was to be transmuted into Utopian paternalism, the mention of the name [Pullman] brings memories . . . [of a] dream which vanished. . . . For "practical" men it signifies the futility of social betterment schemes and marks the battleground where law and order triumphed over anarchy. . . . But for the host of warm-hearted, sane believers in the better day that is coming, it stands for a great human tragedy.[20]

The failure of Pullman made many question the viability of the model town and the possibility of social utopianism.

The discourse surrounding the construction of Gary, Indiana, coming only fifteen years after the end of Pullman, developed out of these uncertainties. All of the traditional assumptions in Pullman were also applied to Gary. Yet the utopian discourse of Gary was slightly different. Pullman represented an attempt at social utopia because it sought to better its residents and eliminate industrial strife and conflict. Through betterment, the working class of Pullman would cease to be the dangerous element that they were in Chicago. In addition, the scientific planning of production and the general cleanliness of the city would make the structures of industry less imposing upon the urban landscape. Indeed the factories that produced the Pullman sleeping cars were only part of the master plan for the city. To accomplish social betterment the factories would have to work in conjunction with libraries, schools, shared housing, and other elements of worker life. In essence, the city of Pullman sought to solve the problems and anxieties of modernization. The creators of Gary made no such attempt in their construction. Instead they assumed that the problems of industrialization and urbanization were inherent within modernization. The cause of anxiety within the modern city was not the presence of industry and the working class. Rather, it was the uncontrolled interaction between and the lack of definition of urban spaces. Thus the creators of Gary sought to clearly define, confine, and restrain the spaces of their city. Gary was to be more the model city than the industrial utopia.

For its part, U.S. Steel made it clear that its role in choosing to build Gary was economic geography and steel production. The foot of Lake Michigan, it claimed, was advantageous for its access to iron ore, coal, and trunk lines for shipping. Limitless space along the lake also insured that the corporation could plan its mill to be as large, efficient, and modern as possible. The company was completely uninterested, it claimed, in creating a model city or an industrial utopia. The city of Gary, again according to this official narrative, was an afterthought to the careful planning of the mills. Much of the coverage of the opening of the Gary Works followed this line of reasoning. Journals such as *Scientific American*, the *System*, and the *Independent* lauded the scientific accomplishments of U.S. Steel in constructing its mill.[21]

Other observers, however, could not help but read onto the new industrial space hopes for social order and memories of past experiments. "Fresh in the minds of us all," concluded *Harper's Weekly*, "is the failure of the Pullman Company to maintain its authority over the village affairs." It also suggested that "the new enterprise will avoid the excess of paternalism which put something of a blight on Pullman, and the hit-or-miss planlessness which has filled South Chicago with discord and cross purposes."[22] U.S. Steel insisted that it built Gary solely for economic reasons. "The officials of the steel company say frankly," reported *Survey*, "that the building of the town was incidental, that their main concern was to construct a steel plant." Newspaper reports echoed similar justifications. "The selection of Gary as the site of the colossal plant to be constructed," voiced the *Indianapolis News*," is because of its general understanding that the industry can be assembled there as cheaply as at any place in the United States."[23] Still others, however, saw in the new city limitless potential and possibility. *Harper's Weekly* declared Gary a "land of opportunity" and the "city that rose from a sandy waste." It expressed amazement that "three years ago the wild duck used to flock in the lazy reached of backwater all about the sluggish bends" where now the city of Gary stood. Likewise the *Survey* concluded that "Gary is probably the single greatest single calculated achievement of America's master industry." Embracing the notion of strategic planning, the *Independent* proclaimed that Gary represented the "most interesting economic development of all time." "Surely in Gary we see the so-called trust at its best," it concluded. "The old order is passing away. Man, the conqueror, and man, the liberator, takes on new dignity and glory as man, the creator."[24]

For many contemporary urban theorists and social reformers, the building of the city represented both the promise of limitless possibilities and the lost opportunity to engage rather than confine urban problems. The notion of beginning a city anew attracted a great deal of attention. "In Gary, the town," commented the *Survey*:

there was absolutely unhampered opportunity to arrange the streets, provide the fundamental necessities of community life, determine the character of

its houses, and predestine the lines of growth, all in the best and most en-
lightened way.

"Each dwelling has been provided with a small garden," noted the Chicago
Tribune, "it is clean and has adequate space for the family which it is designed
to accommodate." Harper's Weekly stated that "Gary is nothing more than
the product of effort along practical lines to secure right living conditions
around a steel-manufacturing plant."[25] Perhaps Eugene Buffington, president
of Indiana Steel Company, best understood the industrial utopian nature of
Gary and the role U.S. Steel sought to play in social questions. "In approach-
ing consideration of the model village," he wrote in Harper's Weekly in 1909,
"our thought naturally gravitates toward problems associated with the complex social relations found in present-day urban life." "Who can doubt," he
continued, "that the future of our nation will be worked out, for weal or for
woe, in the rapidly increasingly centres of concentrated population?" However, the future of the nation and the responsibilities for controlling complex
social relations did not fall to U.S. Steel. Rather the company claimed it
built the city solely for steel production and not for social experiments. "The
material welfare of Gary is an accomplished fact," Buffington concludes, "its
social welfare is held within the desires and aspirations of its future citizens."
U.S. Steel, it seemed, was not responsible for the development, success, or
future of the city of Gary.[26]

Mill Towns: Or, the Origins of Norwood, Ohio
Despite this celebration of the possibilities of urban planning, however,
the shape of Gary disappointed many others. "While it may fall short in its
community features," lamented Graham Taylor in 1912, "there are those
who see in it an extraordinary degree of industrial strategy." To Taylor's
eyes, Gary, because it was planned as a site for industrial production and
not for model urbanism, was less the model city than U.S. Steel's mill
town. Yet the construction from scratch of the city presented several
missed opportunities. Among the complaints Taylor leveled at the planners of Gary were the use of a rectangular street pattern instead of a more
modern design utilizing diagonal streets, the monopoly by the corporation
of the lakeshore thus preventing the development of Chicago style parks,
and the boom of saloons within the city. In essence Taylor wanted to apply
the newest notions of urban planning popularized by Georges Haussmann
in Paris and proposed for Chicago by Daniel Burnham. Yet Taylor was most
concerned about the deterioration of sanitation, health, and housing. "The
failure of the company to work out the housing needs of its low-paid im-

migrant labor," he concluded, "was emphasized by its apparent indifference as to where the 'hunkies' found a new abode."[27]

If Taylor led the voices of disappointment for the missed opportunities for social and progressive planning, he also tried to place the growth of Gary into the larger context of urban and industrial development. While many of his articles focused upon U.S. Steel's failure to take full advantage of Gary's new construction, he also penned a series of articles that examined the phenomenon of other industrial peripheries. Serialized first in the *Survey* and then collected into a book, Taylor's articles examined the development of what he called "satellite cities." These places were industrial centers that grew upon the periphery of larger urban centers and retained economic and cultural connections to the larger city. Taylor included in this list not only Gary but also East St. Louis, Illinois; Corey, Alabama; Argo, Illinois; and Norwood, Ohio.[28] What made these cities important to the mind of the urban planner and sociologist, Taylor argued, was their rapid growth and their social potential. These were not only new cities but cities that contained many of the key forces of twentieth century industrialism. "Towns made to order entirely, or with some little village as a core," wrote Taylor:

> snatch bundles of papers from the morning trains, smudge new postmarks over sheet after sheet of red postage stamps, edge their way into the telephone toll books and the freight tariffs, scrawl their names on the tags of new-coming immigrants at Ellis Island and become part and parcel of up-and-doing municipal America before most of their slower going sister cities have even heard of their existence.

Such social laboratories should appeal, Taylor argues, to social scientists. "In our general municipal development," he states, "we pay more and more heed to the counsel of the city planner, housing expert and sanitarian." The role of manufacturer who "has to tear out, rebuild and build higher" in these newly conceived satellite cities should receive close attention in order to understand the place of these cities in the larger "struggle to reshape our rigid, old-established conditions to fit newer and more workable molds."[29]

Although these were built environments for industrial production, "the suburban industrial community is, however, something more than a framework of streets," Taylor warns. "It is a compact of life and labor—a community of living beings." Great social forces were at play in these cities. This is where new technologies in production were implemented and new efforts at sanitation and housing could be tried. These cities were on the destination tags of "new-coming immigrants at Ellis Island" and thus stood at the center

of Americanization efforts at assimilation. Such industrial cities were also fo-
cal points of labor conflict, unionization, and efforts at social control. There
are multiple reasons, Taylor points out, beyond the extra space and cheap
land that drove industrialists to the urban outskirts. "Some company officials
act on the belief that by removing working men from a large city that it is
possible to get them away from the influences which foment discontent and
labor disturbances," Taylor reports. "The satellite city is looked to as a sort of
isolation hospital for the cure of chronic 'trouble.'" Yet in many of these cities, and especially in Gary, "one feels that friction and antagonisms between
townspeople and the industrial control are always just under the surface if
not cropping out."

Of all the cities that Taylor traced in his survey of satellite cities, he admits
that the industrial environs of Cincinnati present a unique case. "This community study deals not so much with the separate suburban community as
with that constant offshooting of factories to the city's edge," introduced the
editor of the magazine, "which in bulk and social consequences transcends
the more spectacular company towns." If Pullman and Gary represented too
much industrial control then the environs of Cincinnati represented too
little control and central planning. "The average American factory moves
to the edge of the city when the old quarters become too small for the expanding business of the concern . . . ," wrote Taylor in his study of Norwood
and Oakley, Ohio, "this trend is not spectacular, but in volume and human
consequences it is worth perhaps more attention than the separate and more
conspicuous 'model towns.'" The social processes that created Norwood, he
argues, may not be as noticeable as those that drove Gary, yet they are as, if
not more, important. "The removal of industries to the outskirts is ordinar-
ily gradual and piecemeal, and often escapes public notice," he concludes,
"until the chance for rational guidance from the standpoint of community
efficiency has all but gone."[30]

Taylor offered a solution to this oversight through a close study of Cincinnati's northeastern suburbs. While Cincinnati's Procter and Gamble, with
its massive "Ivorydale" plant, received the most public attention, Taylor
argued that the most important developments were occurring along the
Baltimore and Ohio line. It was along this line that the two distinct industrial communities of Norwood and Oakley were growing. Founded in 1888,
Norwood was the older and more established of the two and also, to the eyes
of its boosters, held the greatest potential. "It was little more than a decade
ago that a town chronicler hailed Norwood as 'Gem of the Highlands, the
brightest jewel in Cincinnati's sylvan crown,'" Taylor reported. "At a recent

legislative hearing in Columbus," he added, "she had become, in the words of her spokesman, 'the Chicago of Hamilton County.'" Despite the slightly mocking tone Taylor takes toward these boosters, he agrees that Norwood had seen great industrial growth; in 1909, he reported, the city was home to forty-nine different manufacturers, including the Bullock Electric Works of the Allis-Chalmers Company (which was one of the city's first industrial residents establishing the plant in 1898) and the United States Playing Card Company. Despite this industrial growth, however, incoming factories "encountered local indifference and even antagonism" about worker housing. The great flaw in Norwood for Taylor was that so few workers lived in the city and so few houses were built for workers. Instead workers piled into streetcars and passenger cars of the B&O to make the trip from their homes in Cincinnati to work in Norwood. If part of the plan of satellite cities was the removal of workers from the bad environments of cities into the planned and sanitary conditions of factory towns, then the reluctance of workers to move into Norwood undermined this experiment. Oakley, which was newer and better planned with its "factory colony" (or cooperative efforts by factory grouping), held greater potential for organized and efficient growth but it too lacked housing for workers. Some experiments in worker housing, such as the Schmidlapp Bureau for Women and Girls (created by JG Schmidlapp) offered cooperative living and shared housing in Oakley. Yet overall the conditions of Oakley and Norwood were underplanned and did not bode well for the future of industrial conditions and American urbanism. "We may inquire, therefore, what efforts have been made to adapt this suburban area to the needs of the people brought together by its industries," concluded Taylor. "If modern science and technical ability secured the highest degree of efficiency in plant arrangement and construction," he questioned, "were similar skill and ingenuity applied to the community life, to town planning, housing, health, and recreation?"[31]

While these remained important questions for the success of American social order, and clearly spaces such as Norwood would play an important role in the answers, these satellite cities were no longer the utopian spaces of perfection that shaped Pullman and Gary. By the time Taylor penned his articles in 1912, such utopian plans seemed no longer possible or desirable. In 1922, Lewis Mumford would eulogize these earlier efforts at utopia. Grand utopian schemes had failed precisely because they were so grand, making them disconnected, he would argue, from any social reality. Utopian thinkers had failed to catch Thomas More's playful pun in creating "utopia." It was a place caught in between outopia (nothingness) and eutopia (a good place): thus a utopia could never really exist. Efforts at reform had been "spotty and inconsecutive and incomplete." "It was not, let us remember, by any legislative device that the cities of the industrial age were monotonously patterned in the image of Coketown," Mumford would say. "It was rather because everyone within these horrid centers accepted the same values and pursued the same ends." Far from a social ideal, industrial spaces "expressed the brutality and social disharmony of the community." Epitomizing the cultural pessimism of the 1920s as well as the shifting thought on utopias in the twentieth century, Mumford argued that utopias were not possible, instead we should borrow the methods of the utopianist thinker to "project an ideal community" but use it in a "practical way" to carve out smaller eutopias where we could. The age of the industrial utopia, it seemed, was at an end.[32]

At the same time, by the 1920s the development of new industrial spaces largely broke away from both the paternalism of model cities and the orbit of the large metropolis. Henry Ford's River Rouge plant outside of Detroit would follow established patterns of planned and efficient production without the burden of social planning. While Ford's company certainly strove for social order, it did so through the intervention of the "sociological" department, not the structural planning of a model town. By mid century even Ford had abandoned the industrial monolith model, instead creating smaller factory towns spread throughout Michigan. As Howard Segal has argued, Ford's earliest efforts at creating rural factory towns was an effort to instill a kind of pastoral rural sensibility in Ford's workers and create a kind of model industrialism. Much of Ford's efforts were an attempt to undo the kind of centralized urban industrialism that Ford himself had created at River Rouge.[33] The branch assembly plants of Ford's competitors, however, were far more pragmatic in their design. Branch assembly plants were a way to decentralize production (not corporate control which stayed centralized) and produce products more efficiently for a national market. By the 1920s, these plants, scattered as they were in small cities across the country, became the standard of industrial expansion. It was this pattern of industrialism that would ultimately shape the industrial history of Norwood. While the city described by Taylor in 1912 was a disorganized collection of forty-nine different manufacturers, after General Motors established a massive production plant in the city in 1923 the city became a kind of company town. From 1923 until the plant closed in 1987, nearly all of Norwood's economy, culture, politics, and policies revolved around the GM plant. Yet unlike Gary, which was designed by U.S. Steel and named for its chairman, Norwood was but one of many branch assembly plants within the General Motors family. As such it became a mill town beholden to the fortunes of the auto industry.

Industrial Peripheries: Or, How the Outskirts Became Cauldrons of Humanity

If Taylor offered the "satellite city" as a key site for understanding early twentieth-century industrialism, the meanings of both Gary and Norwood had changed by 1945. Yet they still remained important spaces within American discourse on race, work, and politics. For the first few decades of its existence, Gary served as both a model of industrial planning and a cautionary tale of industrial chaos and foreign populations. As early as 1912, Woodrow Wilson campaigned against the kind of industrial consolidation and power that U.S. Steel represented by suggesting that Gary was an unAmerican city.[34] By the late 1930s however, as the New Deal state integrated industrial classes, unions, and ethnic workers into the nation state, the meaning of Gary shifted. However, as Detroit emerged from World War II as the "Arsenal of Democracy" (which came to epitomize all of the promises of Keynesian nationalism, New Deal liberalism, and middle-class home ownership), Gary came to stand as the juxtaposition to this idealism. Instead of Detroit's integrated democracy and suburban growth, Gary was seen by outside observers as a hotbed of vice, gambling, corruption, and racial hostilities. As such, it still very much played a prominent role in the public imagination. So too would Norwood continue to play a prominent role in discussions of postwar American industrialism; yet instead of a juxtaposition to Detroit's paradigm, Norwood was considered a part of the larger story of Detroit's world of labor relations and automobile production. However both of these storylines would change dramatically in 1972.

It is, of course, not without coincidence that the years between 1945 and 1972 also represent the high years of Keynesian economic nationalism which valued industrial production as the center of the American economy. Little wonder then, that industrial cities such as Detroit and Gary would stand at the center of the American debate about this economy. But Gary's image after 1945 was also increasingly about race. Gary, to the outsiders' mind, became a space where the meanings, conflicts, possibilities, and failures of post-war race relations would be played out. When white students of Froebel High School walked out of classes in 1945 to protest the integration of their school, for instance, Frank Sinatra, who had become a sort of ambassador for post-war race relations due to his hit song "The House I Live In," flew to Gary to offer this new vision of toleration.[35] Yet only two years after Sinatra's visit, students from another Gary high school walked out to protest integration. Calling the city a "crucible of steel and humanity," *Time* concluded that there had been no change in Gary. "Two years ago Crooner Frank Sinatra flew from Hollywood to Gary to try to persuade Froebel High students to end a strike over Negro pupils," the magazine concluded, "the bobby-soxers squealed with delight but didn't take any of his line of reasoning."[36]

Between 1945 and 1972, narrative descriptions of the city often focused upon its pollution, crime, and racial conflicts. Often these descriptions juxtaposed the strength suggested by the massive Gary Works and the pollution and environment that the mills created. "Gary is a steel town," concluded James O'Gara in 1949, "when you have said that, you have just about covered the ground." When Harry Waters of *Newsweek* wrote of the steel city in 1970 he described in detail the ecology of the city. "You drive only five minutes out of the Loop on the Chicago Skyway before the huge, gray, flame-flecked cloud mushrooms into view to the southeast," he wrote. "Then the sulphuric fumes hit, overriding the stench from the Chicago stockyards, forcing you to hastily wind up the windows. 'Welcome to Gary, Ind.—City on the Move' proclaims the grimy green sign off Exit 2." Upon leaving what he calls a "drab steel city," Waters states that, as he drives away, "through the rear window, the sky smolders in an eerie false sunset, as if a nuclear holocaust were subsiding." At the same time, the racial politics of the 1960s made the steel city a site of both racial possibilities and hostilities. The election of black mayor Richard D. Hatcher in 1967 both offered an example of black politics and black power and triggered a backlash of white flight and racial conflicts. By the early 1970s, Gary was defined as much by its racial politics as its steel production. Frequent layoffs and slowing production made this split more acute. If in 1909, Gary had been declared an "industrial utopia," white flight and job loss had changed not only the city but the role it played as urban metaphor. By 1972, *Time* magazine declared that, "for all the hosannas sung to it in *The Music Man*, Gary, Ind., is not one of those garden spots that perennially win community-service awards. Indeed, it is in some respects the very model of modern urban decay." [37]

Norwood's place within the narratives of American industrialism was always quite different from either Gary's or Detroit's. Much like Graham Taylor had argued in 1912, Norwood seemed a quieter example of industrial growth and thus drew less attention. While Gary served as an example of model urbanism turned to a crucible of humanity turned to a model of urban decay, few cited Norwood in their discussions of American industrial cities. Which is not to say that the city never held the nation's attention; major media publications did offer analyses of Norwood in order to understand American industrialism in the twentieth century. Yet the discussions of Norwood focused upon labor issues between General Motors and the UAW, especially the Norwood local of the UAW. From its creation in the 1930s to its epic 174-day strike in 1972, Local 674 and the UAW dominated public discussions of Norwood (not coincidently these again were the key years of American Keynesian nationalism where industrial work and industrial politics were the key issues of public debate).[38] If Gary was the counter narrative to the city of Detroit throughout much of the twentieth century, Norwood was a part of the narrative of Detroit. However, instead of Detroit the city, this narrative was about Detroit the auto industry and Detroit the system of capital and labor relations.

Between 1937 and 1972, Norwood appeared within the public consciousness as part of the larger conflict within the auto industry. Throughout the 1930s, the Fisher Body Plant in Norwood was a key site for the United Autoworkers struggle to gain union recognition. Between 1937 and 1945, Norwood's name featured prominently in national stories of labor conflict and coming strikes. After the war and the "Treaty of Detroit" in 1950, stories that mentioned Norwood talked of Walter Reuther's politics or the production numbers for GM. By 1967, however, the narrative shifted to temporary plant closures, retooling, and production halts. In 1972, Local 674 struck in protest over production changes to the General Motors plant, especially the creation of General Motors Assembly Division which combined the previously autonomous assembly division and immediately began pushing for improved productivity. With its Appalachian heritage, its many familial connections to the United Mine Workers, and its intensity in these strikes, the Norwood local quickly earned a reputation as one of the feistiest and most militant locals within the UAW.

Both Gary and Norwood became centers of debate over postwar race relations and unionization, but their place within the industrial paradigm gave the workers and residents of both Gary and Norwood a chance to form their own meanings, communities, narratives, and resistance. *Time* may have written off Gary as the "very model of urban decay" but that same year the city hosted the National Black Political Convention. The city of Norwood may have been one part of a larger universe of automobile production and labor relations, but the presence of the General Motors plant gave the local the opportunity to militantly resist not only GM but at times the UAW international as well. This local culture of work, identity, and pride, however, was built upon industrial production and industrial jobs.

From Industrial Outskirts to Industrial Wastelands

If the satellite cities of American industry, such as Gary and Norwood, were major sites of debate about the meaning of industrial work through much of the twentieth century, the shift from an industrial economy to a neoliberal economy changed that. By the early 1990s, these sites had largely fallen out of the public discussion replaced by neoliberal concerns about free trade and melting borders. At the same time, heavy industries such as U.S. Steel and General Motors (the central industries for Gary and Norwood) became marginalized by the slow rise of neoliberal economics from the late 1960s through the early 1980s. Free trade imports of both steel and automobiles undercut much of American industries' markets and seemed to force, in the minds of executives, rounds of wage cuts, automations, and plant closures. The relationship between U.S. Steel and the United Steel Workers as well as GM and the UAW, steeped as they were in suspicion and animosity, did little to help this situation. Gary's history, and thus its place within the American imagination, changed with deindustrialization and job loss. By the mid 1970s, much of American steel production began shifting away from the aging mills of Gary. The economic crisis of the early 1980s would finish off steel work within the city. Through a series of cutbacks and reinvestments, U.S. Steel decided to close many of its subsidiary mills in the region and it heavily mechanized the major Gary Works. By the middle of the 1980s Gary had become, in both reality and in national narratives, a deindustrialized city. So too did the city of Norwood reenter the public discussion in 1987 when General Motors closed their plant, eliminating 4,000 jobs and taking away 35 percent of the city's tax base. Old mill towns, including not only Gary and Norwood but also Youngstown, Flint, and many others, were suddenly a very American story again.

But unlike Taylor's articles in 1912 that positioned these cities as sites of the future, these news stories were about the past. These were places and cities that the new economy had left behind. The heavy industries that created these cities were not beneficiaries of the new neoliberal economic order that rewarded global finance and foreign debt payments; rather, heavy industries were far more invested in the political and economic system that neoliberalism strove to replace. Despite its conflicts with the United Steel Workers and government regulation, U.S. Steel was not only heavily involved in Keynesian economic nationalism, it was, as Judith Stein has shown, a key corporate citizen within the twentieth-century New Deal compact. By the early 1980s, however, U.S. Steel responded to the steel crisis by closing many plants and automating others. Likewise, General Motors and the rest of the big three U.S. automakers were deeply involved in the Keynesian liberal state. Not only did Walter Reuther and the UAW wield considerable influence, as Kevin Boyle has shown, but leaders of this system such as George Romney and Robert McNamara came to political power out of auto industries. None of this mattered, however, for the workers of Gary and Norwood; the automation of U.S. Steel's mills in Gary and the closure of GM's Norwood plant were felt in terms of immediate job loss, not long term economic and political trends. Indeed, one of the great paradoxes of deindustrialization is that its origins and causes often exist within the *longue durée* of economic and political transformations that are transnational in scope, yet its effects, especially plant closure and unemployment, are most deeply felt at the local level. Capital mobility may be a long process but plant closure is an immediate and shocking transformation.[39]

At the same time, the loss of jobs in Norwood and in Gary, despite being part of the same large economic shifts, were understood very differently because of the different roles the two cities had played through the century. For Gary, the model city which had long served as a projection of all the possibilities and pitfalls of urban industrialism, the loss of steel jobs combined with white flight, racial conflict, and urban decay was presented as tragic loss and betrayal. The 1996 film *Original Gangstas*, set in the steel city, eulogized Gary with a similar narrative. Against shots of abandoned buildings, the film's opening voiceover established the city's tragic transformation.

> You're looking at Gary, Indiana, USA. A city with the highest murder rate in America, maybe the world; a factory town that somehow became a gang town. Back in the [19]50s, the community was supported by the U.S. Steel mill. It was damn hard work but people raised their families well. Then just twenty years later, without warning, U.S. Steel shut down 70 percent of the mill. First the workers thought it was temporary, but it wasn't. Their savings went, unemployment ran out, and slowly the former steelworkers lost the last two things they had left: their pride and their hope. And that has been the inheritance of the children of Gary.

In a fitting piece of symbolism the final battle between the protagonists and antagonists of the film takes place within the rusting shell of abandoned steel mills.

For Norwood, the story of deindustrialization was written quite differently. Established first as a satellite city for Cincinnati's industries and expanded as a branch assembly site for General Motors, Norwood never carried the symbolic meaning of Gary's model city. Instead, commentators dating from Graham Taylor in 1912 attributed a kind of organic development and life to Norwood. By the 1960s and 1970s, discussions of Gary always focused upon race; stories on Norwood focused upon labor relations not race relations (which itself is a commentary upon the assumed whiteness of the city). Thus the loss of General Motors was written less as tragedy than as new opportunity. The city's own official narrative of this transformation relates the odds the city faced. "General Motors was such a dominant part of Norwood's economic base that many experts questioned Norwood's ability to survive such a loss," states Richard Dettmer, the city's Community Development Director, on the city's own Web site. "Even the more optimistic prognosticators discounted Norwood's ability to substantially recover the lost economic, job and tax base," he writes. "The critics had history on their side. In the national casebook of major industrial plant and military base closings, few success stories have emerged."

The *New York Times* visited the city in 1992 to comment upon the possibilities of reinvention and regrowth. New office spaces and its proximity to downtown Cincinnati meant that the loss of General Motors, according to the *Times*, did not necessarily mean inevitable decline for the city. "On Nov. 6, 1986, General Motors delivered a body blow to this city of 24,000," commented the paper. While "residents feared that GM's departure would mean the end to life as Norwood had know it for generations . . . ," the paper gladly reported that "Norwood has discovered that there is life after GM." The city certainly missed the tax revenue; since 1986 the city had cut forty employees and the school district had cut thirty-nine positions and closed an elementary school. Yet within this 1992 article, the loss of GM and GM's tax revenue offered not a tragic loss, but an opportunity. Although faced with rising city costs and the possibility of bankruptcy, city auditor Donnie Jones concluded that "we grew fat with General Motors." The city, it seemed, was making a necessary transition into the new economy. In place of the old plant, which the city demanded General Motors tear down before it left, was a new office complex which promised to not only recover the lost tax revenue but rewrite the history of the city. New white-collar jobs, shopping centers, and rising house values were to drive the new growth of the city. "It's been rough, but it's given us the only opportunity in the next 100 years to change the image of Norwood," the newspaper quoted Mayor Joseph E. Sanker. "I think we're going to be a much better city in the long run." "I'm tickled to death that GM is gone," echoed resident Thomas Hooks. "The city depended upon GM like a crutch."[40]

For a moment in 1992, Norwood seemed to offer a very different future for postindustrial spaces. Indeed the *Times* visited the Ohio city in 1992 because General Motors had just announced plans to close another 21 plants and cut 70,000 jobs around the country. Those cities, the narrative went, could follow the example of Norwood in reinventing themselves. The realities for Norwood, of course, were quite different. For those who lost their jobs, deindustrialization in the city was quite real and twenty years after the closure of the GM plant, redevelopment has been slow in Norwood. Housing values that were supposed to match those of neighboring Hyde Park have yet to materialize (ironically, the housing boom of the past decade has happened largely in Oakley, a neighborhood bordering both Norwood and Hyde Park. Oakley was the other industrial satellite city Graham Taylor described in 1912). A 2009 report showed that the city now has the second-oldest housing stock in the United States and housing construction has been largely nonexistent for the past twenty years. Yet such loss and struggle has never been a part of the city's postindustrial narrative; Norwood was supposed to be an example of a postindustrial city. By the turn of the century, just as Detroit had come to represent the lost opportunities of the deindustrialized city, Pittsburgh would take the place as the key example of the new economy.

There are multiple ironies in the way in which Gary and Norwood fell away as metaphors of industrial urbanism to be replaced by the iconography of Detroit and Pittsburgh. If branch assembly plants and small industrial cities still mattered in 1992, by the turn of the century they had been completely overlooked by this new postindustrial paradigm. Detroit and Pittsburgh were not only cities but also centers of American heavy industries: Detroit, the auto industry with branch assembly in places such as Norwood; and Pittsburgh, the center of U.S. Steel with its largely automated steel production in cities such as Gary. Race also remained an important, if sometimes unspoken, part of deindustrial and postindustrial narratives. Between 1945 and 1972, the public perception of Gary was defined by racial conflicts. After 1972, Gary became, both in terms of actual population and national reputation, a black city. In the most recent census, Gary's population was 84 percent black. Norwood's population was not only smaller (at its peak in 1950 Norwood numbered about 35,000 people; Gary at its peak in 1960 numbered over 178,000), but also 94 percent white. Thus when the *New York Times* declared the city of Gary the "model of urban decay" in 1972, its article focused upon issues of race. But in the paper's 1992 piece on Norwood's postindustrial future, no mention of race is made.

Conclusion: The Narratives of
Postindustrialism in Industrial Cities

For all their differences, however, the storylines of both Gary and Norwood have important dates and themes in common. Both were reshaped by the economic nationalism of the 1930s and 1940s, both were key parts of national debates over work and race in the 1950s and 1960s, both were dramatically redefined first by events in 1972 and then by massive job loss in the 1980s. Both cities then reemerged briefly within the public consciousness in the early 1990s as either cautionary tales or possible paths for postindustrialism. The history of industrial outskirts and their place within the American imagination, then, follows an arc. In the 1880s Pullman represented an effort to create model utopian spaces for both industrial production and social order. By 1906, the creation of Gary represented the culmination of these efforts and, at the same time, the abandonment of these ideals. Some intended Gary to be a utopia, others did not. In 1912 Graham Taylor laid out the social and political significance of the industrial outskirts that would follow these cities through the 1940s. They were sites of social interaction and rapid growth that demanded attention and social planning. They were paradoxical sites because they were planned yet unplanned, organic yet unorganic. They were sites worth watching. After World War II and the triumph of New Deal politics, these cities became quintessentially American, either as the best examples of "arsenals of democracy" or the worst examples of "crucibles of humanity." By 1972 these cities no longer seemed like models of industrial communities but rather urban decay and disintegration. By the 1980s these cities were sites of deindustrialization and, by the 1990s, spaces left behind and thus largely ignored by a postindustrial and neoliberal economy.

For a brief moment in the fall of 2008 and spring of 2009, the story of former industrial cities returned to the national consciousness. The collapse of the financial system gave rise to not only critiques of the economic system and the sunbelt urbanism that it seemed to encourage (such as Florida's critiques mentioned above) but also a return to the cities long abandoned by deindustrialization. Thus in national publications, the storylines were no longer just about postindustrial triumphs such as Pittsburgh's biomedical technology-based economy, but journalists also told the stories of Braddock's job loss and urban blight on Pittsburgh's periphery.[41] The possibility of collapse within the American auto industry also moved branch assembly mill towns back to the forefront of American politics. All of which serves as a reminder that postindustrialism never meant the end of industry but rather a shift of focus and perspective. Capital moved and mills closed, but industrial production still occurred, it just no longer stood at the center of American politics, priorities, or imaginations.

Yet for every discussion of Braddock's history of steel production and its realities of deindustrial poverty, there were many more stories on Detroit. Much of this can be attributed to the need for a good and simple narrative. The storyline of Detroit, as presented by these articles, is very simple. It can be tragic or poignant. It can have specific villains (take your pick of either the big three companies or the UAW) or can be an inevitable and blameless shift. The story of deindustrialization and postindustrialism in satellite cities is far more complex and problematic. There is a certain level of irony to the notion of postindustrialism for Gary because the U.S. Steel Gary Works is still there and it still produces steel (along with the pollution and smoke that comes with it), but it is automated production and the jobs are few and far between. Likewise there is a certain level of irony to talk of the auto industry and economic stability in Norwood. The argument could be made that General Motors was far too significant a company to fail and that the lack of government loans would destabilize the larger economy. Yet this meant little to Norwood, since GM had been gone since 1987. If we, like Florida, want to talk about urban triage and think about which cities will win and which should lose, we would do well to remember how these industrial cities developed, what roles they once played, and what roles they still play in our larger national discourse.

Notes

1. Richard Florida, "How the Crash will Reshape America," *The Atlantic* (March 2009).

2. Florida, "How the Crash will Reshape America," 2009.

3. "The Art of Abandonment," *The Economist*, December 17, 2009.

4. Graham Romeyn Taylor, "Satellite Cities: The Outer Rings of Industry," *Survey* 29, no. 1 (October 5, 1912): 13–24.

5. Jane Jacobs, *The Death and Life of Great American Cities* (New York: Vintage, 1961). The symbolic importance of the capital metropolis is central to Walter Benjamin's analysis of nineteenth-century Paris's urban culture and the role of the *flaneur*. Walter Benjamin, "Paris: Capital of the Nineteenth Century," in ed. Philip Kasinitz *Metropolis: Center and Symbol of our Times* (New York: New York University Press, 1994).

6. Maiken Umbach, "A Tale of Second Cities," *American Historical Review* 110, no.3 (June 2005): 659–92.

7. Mike Davis argues that L.A. is a city of "pure capitalism" that is founded entirely upon real estate values and civic image. Its foundation, development, and continued growth depend upon its urban image, thus the imagined city of L.A. always precedes the lived realities of its streets. This new kind of global city, symbolized by LA, is a sprawling metropolis with many different centers of population and political power. Despite their high population density, these centers are disparate from and unconnected to each other. Mike Davis, *City of Quartz: Excavating the Future in Los Angeles* (New York: Verso, 1990); eds. Allen J. Scott and Edward W. Soja, *The City: Los Angeles and Urban Theory at the End of the Twentieth Century* (Berkeley: University of California Press, 1996); Norman Klein, *The History of Forgetting: Los Angeles and the Erasure of Memory* (New York: Verso, 1997).

8. David Harvey, *Urbanization of Capital* (Oxford: Blackwell, 1985); David Harvey, *Consciousness and the Urban Experience* (Oxford: Blackwell, 1985).

9. James Connolly, "Bringing the City Back In: Space and Place in the Urban History of the Gilded Age and Progressive Era," *Journal of the Gilded Age and Progressive Era* 1, no. 3 (July 2002): 258–78.

10. Jefferson Cowie and Joseph Heathcott, "The Meanings of Deindustrialization," in eds. Jefferson Cowie and Joseph Heathcott, *Beyond the Ruins: The Meanings of Deindustrialization* (Ithaca: Cornell University Press, 2003), 1–18; Steven High and David W. Lewis make a similar argument about the folklore of "smokestack nostalgia" in *Corporate Wasteland: The Landscape and Memory of Deindustrialization* (Ithaca: Cornell University Press, 2007).

11. James Barrett, "Americanization from the Bottom Up," *Journal of American History* 79, no. 3 (December 1992), 1,000.

12. Michael McGerr offers an analysis of the progressive movement as a culmination of middle-class identity and pragmatic, not utopian, reform. Michael McGerr, *A Fierce Discontent: the Rise and Fall of the Progressive Movement in America, 1870–1920* (New York: Free Press, 2003).

13. Lizabeth Cohen, *A Consumers' Republic: The Politics of Mass Consumption in Post-War America* (New York: Vintage, 2003).

14. Thomas Sugrue, *The Origins of the Urban Crisis: Race and Inequality in Postwar Detroit* (Princeton: Princeton University Press, 1996); Robert O. Self, *American Babylon: Race and the Struggle for Postwar Oakland* (Princeton: Princeton University Press, 2005).

15. Despite this dystopic reputation, Victorian industrial cities, Tristram Hunt has shown, were also vibrant sites for discussions on the meaning of industrialism. Not only were they critiqued as Dickensian cesspools, but industrial cities were also the center of hopeful visions of an industrial future. Far from writing off industrial centers and urban environments, the Victorians strove to reform, reclaim, and redeem their cities. Instead of being pessimistic or fatalistic, Victorians, Hunt argues, saw great utopian potential in cities. Tristram Hunt, *Building Jerusalem: The Rise and Fall of the Victorian City* (New York: Metropolitan Books, 2005).

16. On the meaning of work, masculinity, and artisanship in early industrial Pawtucket and Paterson see Paul Johnson, *Sam Patch: The Famous Jumper* (New York: Hill and Wang, 2004).

17. John Kasson argues that the builders of Lowell, Massachusetts, tried to accommodate industrialization with republican theory by creating a pastoral city where young women would work for only a few years. Instead of corrupting male citizens, mill work could create good wives and mothers. John Kasson, *Civilizing the Machine: Technology and Republican Values in America, 1776–1900* (Toronto: Penguin Books, 1976).

18. "Sanitary Drainage and Sewerage," *Industrial Chicago: The Building Interests*, vol. 2 (Chicago: The Goodspeed Publishing Company, 1891), 146–88.

19. On the Pullman strike, see Richard Schneirov, et al., ed., *The Pullman Strike and the Crisis of the 1890s: Essays on Labor and Politics* (Champaign: University of

Illinois Press, 1999), and Richard Schneirov, *Labor and Urban Politics: Class Conflict and the Origins of Modern Liberalism in Chicago, 1864–97* (Champaign: University of Illinois Press, 1998).

20. Jane Addams, "A Modern Lear," *Survey* 29, no. 1 (November 2, 1912): 131–37. Addams wrote her piece in 1894 and first delivered it as an address. Graham Romeyn Taylor, "Satellite Cities: Pullman," *Survey* 29 (November 2, 1912): 117–31.

21. Examples of this fascination with the mill and its technology include "Gary: The Largest and Most Modern Steel Works in Existence," *Scientific American* (December 11, 1909); "Gary—Pittsburg's Future Rival," *American Review of Reviews* 39 (February 1909); Daniel Vincent Casey, "The Sum of a Thousand Short Cuts," *System* 15 (January 1909); John Kimberley Mumford, "This Land of Opportunity: Gary, the City that Rose from a Sandy Waste," *Harper's Weekly* 52 (July 4, 1908); Charles Pierce Burton, "Gary—A Creation," *Independent* 70 (February 16, 1911).

22. Eugene J. Buffington, "Making Cities for Workmen," *Harper's Weekly* 53 (May 8, 1909), 15–17; Henry Fuller, "An Industrial Utopia: Building Gary, Indiana, to Order," *Harper's Weekly* 51 (October 12, 1907), 1482–83, 1485. On Homestead see Paul Krause, *The Battle for Homestead, 1880–1892: Politics, Culture, Steel* (Pittsburgh: University of Pittsburgh Press, 1992).

23. Graham Romeyn Taylor, "Creating the Newest Steel City," *Survey* 22 (April 1909); Buffington, "Making Cities for Workmen"; Fuller, "An Industrial Utopia"; *Indianapolis News*, March 19, 1906.

24. John Kimberley Mumford, "This Land of Opportunity: Gary, the City that Rose from a Sandy Waste," *Harper's Weekly* 52 (July 4, 1908), 22–23, 29; Charles Pierce Burton, "Gary—A Creation," *Independent* 70 (February 16, 1911), 337–45.

25. Eugene Buffington, "Making Cities for Workmen"; Fuller, "An Industrial Utopia."

26. Graham Taylor, "Satellite Cities: Gary," *Survey* 29, no. 22 (March 1, 1913): 781–97.

27. Taylor, "Satellite Cities: Gary."

28. Graham Romeyn Taylor, *Satellite Cities: A Study of Industrial Suburbs* (New York: D. Appleton and Company, 1915)

29. Taylor, "Outer Rings of Industry."

30. Taylor, "Outer Rings of Industry."

31. Graham Romeyn Taylor, "Satellite Cities: Norwood and Oakley," *Survey* 29, no. 10 (December 7, 1912): 287–301.

32. Lewis Mumford, "The Foundations of Eutopia," in ed. Donald Miller, *The Lewis Mumford Reader* Donald Miller (New York: Pantheon Books, 1986), 217–27; originally published as Lewis Mumford, *The Story of Utopias* (New York: Boni and Liveright, 1922).

33. On Ford's industrial communities, see Howard P. Segal, *Recasting the Machine Age: Henry Ford's Village Industries* (Amherst: University of Massachusetts Press, 2005).

34. Woodrow Wilson, "The Fear of Monopoly," *Annals of American History* http://america.eb.com/america/print?articleId=386648 (21May 2008).

35. "As the Twig is Bent," *Time*, Oct. 8, 1945.

36. "No Gain," *Time*, Sept. 15, 1947.

37. James O'Gara, "Big Steel, Little Town: The Recent Steel Settlement has not Settled Everything," *Commonwealth*, November 25, 1949; Harry Waters, "Gary: A Game of Pin the Blame, *Newsweek*, January 26, 1970; "Godfather in Gary," *Time*, November 12, 1972. For other examples of national descriptions of Gary see J.D. Ratcliff, "It's Murder," *Saturday Evening Post*, January 28, 1948; "Steel and Sex," *Quick*, May 1955; "The Abandoned County," *Time*, April 29, 1966; "Vote Power," *Time*, May 12, 1967; "Black Power & Black Pride," *Time*, December 1, 1967; "Real Black Power," *Time*, November 17, 1967; Marshall Frady, "Gary, Indiana: For God's Sake Let's Get Ourselves Together," *Harper's*, August 1969; Godfrey Hodgson and George Crile, "Gary: Epitaph for a Model City," *Washington Post*, March 4, 1973; Joel Weisman, "Every Major City Problem Seems More Acute in Gary," *Washington Post*, December 2, 1974.

38. Numbers on the length of the strike vary depending upon when one begins to count and how one ties the local struggle to the larger UAW conflict with GM. The *New York Times* declared it a 174-day strike in Norwood, Sept. 28, 1972.

39. Judith Stein, *Running Steel, Running America: Race, Economic Policy, and the Decline of Liberalism* (Chapel Hill: University of North Carolina Press, 1998). For a political and economic history of neoliberalism see David Harvey, *A Brief History of Neo-Liberalism* (New York: Oxford University Press, 2007).

40. Adam Bryant, "G.M.'s Gone, but This City's Alive," *New York Times*, January 21, 1992. Steven High documents this tendency to see deindustrialization as both a form of nostalgia but also as an inevitable change that brings new opportunities. Steven High and David W. Lewis, *Corporate Wasteland*.

41. On Braddock, for instance, see David Streitfeld, "Rock Bottom for Decades, but Showing Signs of Life," *New York Times*, January 31, 2009.

CHAPTER THREE

~

From Satellite City to Burb of the 'Burgh

Deindustrialization and Community Identity in Steubenville, Ohio

ALLEN DIETERICH-WARD

In the spring of 1998, early morning commuters along Route 22, a four-lane highway running west from Pittsburgh, woke to find a new billboard touting "Pittsburgh's New Suburb . . . in Ohio." The billboard was part of an advertising campaign spearheaded by Alliance 2000, a pro-growth coalition of local officials and business leaders formed to take advantage of new transportation links extending across the Pennsylvania border through the narrow West Virginia Panhandle to eastern Ohio.[1] "It accomplished what we needed to do," explained Alliance member Gary Dufour. Pennsylvania residents and business leaders "began to think, 'Oh yeah, it isn't that far.'"[2] Indeed, by the time the first billboard went up announcing the newest "Burb of the 'Burgh," metropolitan growth had already reached the community, with a new upscale residential project built by a Pittsburgh developer and a number of tenants in a new industrial park along the highway.[3]

Suburban historians from Sam Bass Warner to Owen Gutfreund have extensively documented the expansion of urban services to the metropolitan periphery in the wake of new transportation links.[4] While the story of Pittsburgh's new suburb may sound like just another narrative of decentralization and sprawl, however, the community seeking to attract new residents and businesses was the small city of Steubenville, a withering, polluted and poverty-stricken jewel of the deindustrialized rust belt.[5] "You could let off a howitzer down on Market Street in Steubenville and not harm a soul," declared one local resident in 1994. "In fact, I'm not even sure there would be enough people there [to notice] a big bang."[6] Nevertheless, by the late 1990s the completion of Route 22 and other highways fostered increased commuting for work and play and the articulation of a "postindustrial" vision of the landscape that provided an opportunity to symbolically recreate the battered hinterland as a vital part of the larger metropolitan region.

The story of the "Burb of the 'Burgh" reflects a larger social and cultural evolution in the relationship between U.S. industrial cities and their metropolitan hinterlands during the latter half of the twentieth century. Recent scholarship has provided persuasive evidence that the narrative trope of deindustrialization (and its geographical auxiliary, the "rust belt") dominating scholarly discourse in the 1980s and 1990s is no longer adequate for describing the multitude of economic and social changes taking place "beyond the ruins."[7] By acknowledging the limits of the postwar declension narrative, Howard Gillette's recent study of Camden, for example, assigns agency to urban residents working to recreate the community after the decline of the region's industrial base.[8] Indeed, as Bruce Schulman and other "Sunbelt" scholars have pointed out, cities from Oakland to Phoenix to Charlotte faced the same issues of spatial inequality as their counterparts above the Mason-Dixon line, suggesting there may be greater disparities within metropolitan communities than between them.[9]

Addressing the deficiencies of an overly simplified postwar declension narrative and expanding the historical record past the late 1970s also requires a new metropolitan framework that can encompass the changing spatial patterns of the late twentieth century.[10] Over the last twenty-five years, two generations of suburban scholars have used the lens of urban social history to expand the field from an emphasis on the white middle and upper class to also include a more diverse landscape of industrial, working-class, and African-American communities.[11] Matthew Lassiter, Robert Self, and other scholars have worked to combine these insights into a synthetic narrative of both city and suburb. In focusing on the metropolis as a whole, these new studies have highlighted the breadth of metropolitan spatial inequality, while connecting previously isolated movements—in Self's case, Black Power politics and suburban tax revolts in Oakland—and revealing unexpected political alliances, such as the cross-race working class alliance supporting broad-based busing in Charlotte illustrated in Lassiter's work.

Despite the considerable strengths of this new urban/suburban focus, the case of Steubenville suggests that the field remains limited in its ability to account for postwar changes taking place "beyond the metropolis."[12] While urban decentralization removed factories and residents from central cities to suburbs, equally powerful centripetal forces drew formerly discrete areas into closer contact with the metropolitan core.[13] Postwar historians have largely ignored the lessons of William Cronon's *Nature's Metropolis*, as well as other recent studies by historical geographers and urban theorists that underscore the interdependence of communities throughout wider regions.[14] Edward K. Muller's work on the Pittsburgh region, for example, convincingly links developments in the city to changes in the mining communities and mill towns of the Pennsylvania countryside.[15] While overshadowed in the postwar literature by suburban decentralization, these longer-term trends of economic centralization and increasing community interdependence suggest the need for a new "metropolitan regional" model that can encompass both aspects of the evolving postwar community.[16]

The story of the "Burb of the 'Burgh" is ideal for pushing the narrative of postwar urban history both "beyond the ruins" and "beyond the metropolis." At the beginning of the twentieth century, Pittsburgh and its metropolitan hinterland in southeastern Ohio, southwestern Pennsylvania, and northern West Virginia was a celebrated example of America's industrial power. This region, the "Steel Valley," was tied together by an extensive web of railroads that connected the densely settled mill towns of the narrow river valleys with mining camps and villages in the surrounding mountainous countryside.[17] In

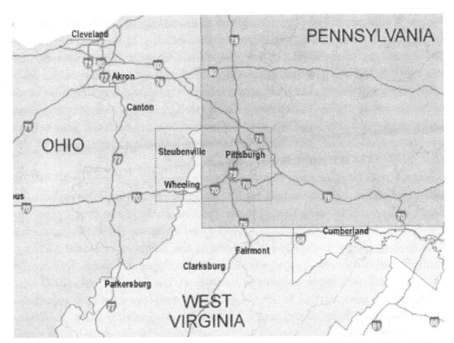

Figure 3.1. The "Steel Valley"—Metropolitan Pittsburgh and the Upper Ohio Valley

addition to these economic bonds, Steel Valley residents shared a culture shaped by the topography and grounded in the unique mix of nationalities that settled throughout the region. Issues both economic and environmental eventually derailed regional prosperity as changes in production lessened locational advantages, while the rugged landscape and pollution problems made much of the area unsuitable for postwar growth industries. As a result of these limitations, by the 1990s abandoned mines and mills stood silent sentinels over a scarred landscape and aging communities wracked by rampant poverty, massive unemployment, and high out-migration, particularly among the young and educated.

Within this overall framework of deterioration a new regional identity began to form that, to an extent, challenged the long-cherished equation of environmentally destructive heavy industry with economic and community prosperity. The decline in Pittsburgh's fortunes prompted the creation of a powerful progrowth partnership that worked to reinvent the city, first as a center of corporate administration and later as a "postindustrial" hub of the high-tech and service sectors. Centered in the region's universities, hospitals, and growing commuter suburbs, this more consumption-oriented vision of community emphasized environmental protection as a "quality of life" issue necessary for attracting and retaining economic talent.[18] This Pittsburgh "Renaissance" and its subsequent manifestations, however, remained largely confined to select neighborhoods and certain wealthy suburbs, while the remainder of the region continued to face chronic unemployment and out-migration. Failing either to develop sufficient highway links to the metropolitan core or revitalize their urban infrastructure, older and smaller communities in the industrialized river valleys declined in population and were increasingly isolated. In effect, they became *more* rural with few resources to overcome the massive economic dislocations following the collapse of the steel industry in the mid-1980s.

Steubenville's efforts are thus best situated as part of a broader transition whereby former mill towns and rural mining communities, both within the Steel Valley and in other metropolitan regions, struggled to find a place for themselves within a new economic and spatial order. By the 1990s, strategies for urban development shifted from serving the interests of existing heavy-industrial and other corporate employers to building highways that would connect declining areas to growth centers in the postwar suburbs. Many communities also worked to attract potential employers to new suburban-style industrial parks along major highways, emphasizing their proximity to Pittsburgh while highlighting quality of life issues associated with small towns. For Steubenville, as in other communities seeking to transcend their roots as industrial satellites, the goal was not merely to build new highway links to the metropolitan core, but to define a new role for itself as a low cost/ high service alternative to the traditional suburbs.

"A Community of Interest"

In 1909, industrialist Ernest T. Weir began construction of a new tin mill thirty-five miles west of Pittsburgh, just across the Ohio River from Steubenville. The site sat at the intersection of river and rail transportation with good connections to both Steubenville and Pittsburgh, and featured a ready supply of cheap land. The relative isolation of the site also allowed Weir, a veteran of Pittsburgh's contentious labor wars, more control over his employees' environment. Cities, Weir believed, "if not breeders, were certainly magnifiers of discontent among workers." "In a small town," he concluded, "workers and management lived near each other; they belonged to the same churches and fraternal organizations; they participated in the same recreations; their children attended the same schools, and . . . workers and managers were friendly . . . relatives or close friends."[19] By 1920 the new community of Weirton already counted 9,500 residents and in 1940 its population of approximately 25,000 made it the largest unincorporated community in the nation.

Despite Weir's sentiment his community was not simply a self-contained island of industrious workers, nor was the creation of Weirton a matter of straightforward urban imperialism. Indeed, Steubenville boosters played an instrumental role in attracting development to the area. Cyrus Ferguson, who made his initial fortune as an oil speculator, sold the land to Ernest Weir and laid out some of the first lots in the new community. Dohrman Sinclair, a dominant figure in Steubenville's history, pushed for the Market Street Bridge across the river in 1905 and later extended the city's streetcar line to Weirton. [20] Indeed, Steubenville and Weirton quickly formed a symbiotic relationship of "sales place" and "workshop," with many Steubenville residents, including company executives such as David Weir and J.C. Williams, commuting across the river to work and Weirton residents crowding the larger city's business district on the weekends.[21]

The industrial expansion of Steubenville was part of the enormous growth in manufacturing and corporate reorganization of industrial production driving the spatial extension of development far beyond the region's older urban centers. This trend gained momentum during the 1870s with the construction of huge integrated steel mills, such as Andrew Carnegie's Edgar Thomson Works completed in 1875 and located twelve miles south of Pittsburgh on the Monongahela River. A variety of factors contributed to the decentralization of industrial development in the Steel Valley. A new breed of industrial executives wanted to integrate various parts of the production cycle while increasing demands for heavy industrial products created a need for a large physical plant. New mills required access to river and rail facilities while the region's rugged landscape prevented simple contiguous growth. As time went on, the construction of an extensive transportation system made up of railroads, streetcars and inter-urban lines facilitated the continued dispersal of manufacturing centers. Finally, as the Weirton example suggests, while economic issues most often underlay the decision to develop a green field site at the turn of the century, management sometimes had social and political reasons as well.[22]

Between 1870 and 1920, capital from Pittsburgh played a dominant role in knitting together and reorganizing the region's physical and social landscape.[23] While Pittsburgh was most successful in managing this transition during the late nineteenth century, other communities in the Upper Ohio Valley also reoriented their economies away from agriculture and small-scale craft industries toward heavy industrial manufacturing and the extraction of natural resources. Wheeling and Steubenville emerged as important centers of heavy industry with their own steel and iron producers, railroad links, and burgeoning workforce. This process of industrialization tended to centralize control in the urban areas, especially Pittsburgh, which by the late nineteenth century had established itself as the region's dominant metropole. This left former downriver rivals looking increasingly to the city for economic and cultural leadership.[24] "Pittsburgh overshadowed Wheeling and took the profit out of the iron and steel business here," wrote a dispirited local businessman to Andrew Carnegie in May 1899. "Should you ever care to interest yourself in [our] city, the appreciation and gratitude of a minority will be correspondingly keen and strong."[25]

The rise of the railroads and dispersal of manufacturing strengthened the connections between areas within the larger metropolitan region that had previously been largely autonomous. As new mills and mines sprang up throughout the rapidly urbanizing river valleys and the rural countryside, manufacturers, political leaders, and engineers developed an extensive railroad system spreading throughout the region. Trunk lines and regional carriers connected the major cities, while inter-urban lines and streetcars enabled speedy movement within communities and out to their growing hinterlands. By the late nineteenth century, a trip from Pittsburgh to Steubenville or Wheeling that had once been counted in days by steamboat or wagon road (if the season permitted the journey at all) could now be accomplished in a matter of hours (or less), no matter what the weather.[26] This transportation system largely transcended municipal and even state boundaries and knit together the region culturally, socially, and economically, if not politically.

Industrial decentralization in the Steel Valley region went hand in hand with the creation of new urban forms.[27] Between 1880 and 1920, developers built dozens of enormous mills and factories that hugged the narrow flatlands up the Monongahela and Allegheny Rivers from Pittsburgh and down the Ohio Valley through Steubenville and Wheeling. In addition to Weirton, corporate managers laid out entirely new mill-oriented communities, such as Homestead (1881), Monessen (1896), and Follansbee (1905). These community-building projects were part of a larger North American phenomenon that belies the easy urban-suburban dichotomy developed by more contemporary scholars.[28] In contrast to the middle-class model, recent studies of pre-World War II suburbia have affirmed the importance of understanding mill towns and mining camps as a part of a heterogeneous landscape encompassing a wide variety of community types.[29] This emerging model of metropolitan complexity is particularly important for understanding the trajectory of the Steel Valley, which by 1920 featured the nation's most decentralized metropolitan region.

Further complicating this picture, Pittsburgh scholar Edward Muller has suggested that what contemporaries and later historians often viewed simply as industrial decentralization also involved the creation or expansion of local production systems.[30] Consequently, older settlements that had previously been oriented toward riverine or agricultural economies experienced a massive influx of new immigrants as existing industries grew or entrepreneurs built entirely new facilities. The relationship between Steubenville and the new community of Weirton provides an excellent example of this trend. While Steubenville developed its own heavy-industrial base, thousands more residents crossed the Ohio River daily to work in the mills of Weirton Steel. Lacking a highly developed downtown core, Weirton consumers regularly traveled to their larger neighbor for shopping. At midnight on a Saturday night, people had no room to walk on the sidewalks [on] 4th and Market Streets," Steubenville resident Nicholas Kaschak recalled. "They spilled over into the street walking. It was absolutely tremendous."[31]

The expansion of massive vertically integrated corporations transformed the Steel Valley region's physical and economic landscape into a form suitable for large-scale production and natural resource extraction. At the same time, mill towns and mining camps joined a preexisting pattern of river cities and market hamlets, resulting in heavily developed corridors that extended throughout the river valleys. Industrial recruitment brought new immigrants, particularly from southern and eastern Europe, that when coupled with the fragmented topography created a mosaic of nationalities and ethnic enclaves that came to define regional culture and politics.[32] An extensive network of railroads, necessary for the centralized coordination of diverse corporate interests, connected Steel Valley communities, fostering industrial growth in some rural areas and allowing residents to commute to the larger cities for work, shopping, and leisure. Finally, smoke, sewage, and surface mining increasingly spoiled the environment as corporations extracted resources and emitted pollutants that reshaped the relationship between Steel Valley residents and the region's natural landscape. By the end of World War II, the Upper Ohio Valley, which had always been "closely identified with" its neighbors in southwestern Pennsylvania, had become "in effect, a continuation of the heavy industrial concentrations upstream toward Pittsburgh."[33]

"Issues in a Region of Contrasts"

On a late November evening in 1973, the crème of Pittsburgh's civic elite streamed into the beautiful surroundings of Oakland's Carnegie Music Hall for the annual meeting of the Allegheny Conference on Community Development, the progrowth coalition that had spearheaded the city's economic "Renaissance" following World War II.[34] As they walked through the grand foyer with its crystal chandeliers and elaborately carved pillars, the university presidents, industrialists, financiers, labor leaders, and politicians gathered there had reason to be proud of their accomplishments in the downtown Golden Triangle, new suburban industrial parks, and the handful of state parks dotting the rural periphery.[35] The neighborhood of Oakland, home to Carnegie-Mellon University and the University of Pittsburgh, was also a good setting for the evening's keynote speech, which touched upon the city's growing reputation as a center for research.[36] That night's speaker, former Appalachian Regional Commission executive director Ralph Widner, congratulated the audience on the many gains of the Pittsburgh Renaissance, but counseled that "because of very poor and inconvenient highway access to the surrounding areas of western Pennsylvania, eastern Ohio, and northern West Virginia, Pittsburgh suffered from a shrunken retail trade area for a metropolis its size" as well as the inability effectively to harness the tourism potential of the rural periphery.[37] "The future of the region," Widner concluded, "rests as much with what can be initiated in the outlying areas as with what can be done downtown."[38]

Despite its reputation as an economic powerhouse, Pittsburgh reached its peak in the 1920s and by the 1950s showed the signs of decline associated

MAJOR BASIC INDUSTRIES
in the UPPER OHIO VALLEY

Plate 3

Figure 3.2. Map from Regional Industrial Development Corporation, A Community of Interest Between the Pittsburgh Metropolitan Area and the Upper Ohio Valley: A Preliminary Analysis, 1959.
Courtesy of the Regional Industrial Development Corporation

with both older industrial cities and rural Appalachia, a combination that made it particularly difficult for the region to accommodate itself to the postwar economy. The makeup of the regional economy and contentious employee-employer relations combined with the geographical obstacles of a hilly, broken terrain to make the area unattractive to the growing industrial sectors of the postwar period. Contentious local politics and a populace conditioned to expect corporate paternalism compounded these issues and made effective responses to industrial decline difficult. As the authors of the landmark *Economic Study of the Pittsburgh Region* explained in 1963, "it is a long step from a coal miner to an electronics technician: from an obsolete steel mill to a modern industrial park; from a giant corporation to a multitude of innovators and ambitious small entrepreneurs."[39]

Despite these obstacles, the coalition between Pittsburgh officials and the corporate leaders of the Allegheny Conference had considerable success in reinventing the region in the 1950s and again in the 1980s, first as a center of corporate administration and later as a postindustrial hub of the high-tech and service sectors.[40] The Pittsburgh "Renaissance" of the late 1940s and 1950s centered on revitalizing the downtown Golden Triangle through a program of environmental improvements, such as smoke and flood control as well as the demolition and replacement of older mixed-use neighborhoods with gleaming skyscrapers and public facilities. A powerful partnership between Republican businessmen associated with the Allegheny Conference, particularly financier Richard King Mellon, and the Democratic administration of Mayor David Lawrence guided the urban renewal program. "The city welcomed tomorrow, because yesterday was hard and unlovely," Lawrence explained. "The town took pleasure in the swing of the headache ball and the crash of the falling brick. Pittsburgh, after all the grim years, was proud and self-confident."[41]

As Widner's remarks suggest, the transformation of the Steel Valley region had as much to do with outlying areas as it did with the celebrated urban redevelopment of the Pittsburgh Renaissance. Postwar highway construction prompted a boom in middle-class commuter suburbs with available land and easy access to the city's revitalized central business district. Monroeville, a small farming community at the junction of the new Penn-Lincoln Parkway and the Pennsylvania Turnpike, boomed from 3,100 residents in 1950 to 33,000 by 1976.[42] Other new suburban communities, including Cranberry Township north of Pittsburgh and the area surrounding Pittsburgh International Airport west of the city posted similar gains in the 1960s and 1970s. The growth in regional infrastructure mirrored attempts by boosters in the Allegheny Conference to symbolically link urban revitalization with an improved quality of life in suburban and even rural areas. "Look around," declared a 1972 advertisement in the *Wall Street Journal*. "You'll find parks that were once strip mines. New colleges, lakes, ski slopes and skating rinks [as well as] the big city amenities of . . . a rebuilt downtown Pittsburgh with its bustling new nightlife."[43]

This suburban boom came partly at the expense of older and more isolated river valley communities, such as Steubenville, that according to one 1961 report were "losing many of their traditional economic functions and, in the process . . . acquiring the mirror-image characteristics of contemporary suburbia."[44] With the decline of river and rail transportation, local officials increasingly saw highways as the key to economic development in many parts of the region. Despite the challenges in building roads over hilly terrain and through densely populated areas, the small city of Kittanning in rural Armstrong County had particular success in this regard. Following the completion of the Allegheny Valley Expressway in the mid-1980s, a 925-acre mixed-use industrial campus called Northpointe formed the centerpiece of a marketing campaign, "Armstrong County, The Best Thing Next to Pittsburgh," emphasizing the community's rural atmosphere combined with easy access to the metropolitan core.[45] "We're in a paradigm of change," declared one local leader. "Look at Northpointe. We're into new age manufacturing [and] jobs for the twenty-four- and twenty-five-year olds."[46]

The urban industrial river communities of Ohio and West Virginia faced even greater challenges in attracting new investment than their counterparts in Pennsylvania. During the 1950s and 1960s, workers in the Upper Ohio Valley's numerous mills generally prospered, with median family income higher than the national average and, after a wave of strikes in the late 1940s, a high percentage of unionized workers with generous health and pension benefits.[47] "If you were fortunate enough to work in a mine or a mill or a glass factory, that was the higher grade of employment," recalled local resident Don Myers of his childhood during the early 1960s. "It was a struggle, but as long as . . . dad never got killed in a mining accident or a mill accident, you survived and you ate and you were clothed and you went to school."[48]

While jobs in the local steel mills and factories remained steady during the 1950s and 1960s, the region's traditional residential and commercial core along the river increasingly suffered from aging and poorly maintained buildings as well as air and water pollution from nearby steel mills.[49] A steep rise in automobile traffic and frequent disruptions from the railroad lines crisscrossing the crowded river valleys also overwhelmed market areas designed for horse-carts. Despite relative prosperity for many residents, between 1950 and 1980 the Upper Ohio Valley lost nearly 6 percent of its population largely

When we brag about our area's growth, we mean white oaks and mountain laurel, too.

Figure 3.2. During the 1970s, a regional marketing campaign sponsored by the Allegheny Conference merged the diverse economic and urban development strategies adopted by business and political leaders during the 1950s and 1960s into a comprehensive vision of a metropolitan "neighborhood" that was marketed in the *Wall Street Journal* and other national newspapers.
Courtesy of the Pittsburgh Regional Alliance

due to declining employment in the coal, steel and glass industries.[50] Out-migration among the young and better educated disproportionately affected older urban centers in Steubenville, Wheeling, and other river valley communities. "The children started to move away and the workforce started to get older," explained Myers. "Older people do not have children the majority of times and they don't produce like a twenty- and thirty-year-old. Deaths started to exceed births. It just took your breath away."[51]

By the late 1960s, a study of the downtown area concluded that Steubenville itself had also grown old, "with little or no attention given to the renewal, rehabilitation, design, and planning [necessary to establish] a new and inviting image of the downtown central business district in an urban community."[52] This is not to suggest that local leaders were blind to their community's deterioration. Indeed, in 1966 John King Mussio, the Catholic Bishop of Steubenville, requested federal funding for a housing project that he believed would slow out-migration and "help in the process of keeping those young people near the downtown area, a move that would help in the process of revitalizing the central business district, now being discussed by [downtown] merchants."[53] The proposal was the latest from the energetic bishop who also helped build a new Catholic high school, the city's first college, numerous churches and schools, and an expanded hospital.[54] Municipal officials also embarked on a number of projects during the 1960s, including improvements to the central business district and the city's roads.[55]

Despite increasing federal funding from the War on Poverty, urban redevelopment in small cities such as Steubenville faced a number of important obstacles.[56] Comprehensive planning, the basis for many federally subsidized programs, had a limited history in many local communities.[57] "When I arrived in Jefferson County, planning was regarded with suspect, with suspicion," recalled one local official. "It was as if it had little 'Pinko' shades to it."[58] No single community commanded the political or economic resources needed for large projects, which left local officials at the mercy of competing politicians. In 1968, for example, colorful Democratic Congressman Wayne L. Hays of Ohio accused the state's Republican governor James Rhodes of stealing credit for local development programs and threatened "that no other Appalachia project would be automatic in [Hays'] district."[59]

Weak urban administrations also made it difficult to marshal the political power to make controversial decisions within a climate of ethnic, religious, and social divisions. "A serious impediment to progress derives from the strange ethno-nationalism that prevails" in the region, reported one state official in 1972. "The various European émigrés' and their offspring have retained strong ties to their region, thus a melting pot that didn't melt, which has perpetrated factionalism that approaches total chaos."[60] Finally, the Upper Ohio Valley's declining population helped remove potential challengers to the existing leadership and lessened the impetus for expanded services and opportunities. "With the industrial move to the Sunbelt . . . the college-educated engineers, chemists, and business people left their hometown for greater opportunities in the South," concluded one study in 1983. "This trend has deprived Steubenville of fresh ideas and the potential leadership these people could provide."[61]

The decline of downtowns corresponded to and stimulated the development of hilltop residential areas throughout the Steel Valley region. Despite the desire of municipal authorities to strengthen downtown business districts, employers also began leaving the crowded and dirty river valleys.[62] Under the auspices of Bishop Mussio and other religious leaders, the Catholic Church became a major employer and developer in Steubenville as well as an important part of the region's religious life. The bishop persuaded administrators of the local Catholic hospital to move from their downtown location to expanded quarters on the periphery and convinced a group of Franciscans to found a college on a bluff overlooking the city.[63] Mussio "didn't speak much, but when he spoke, people listened," recalled a local planning official. "Of course, [the new facilities] had an impact and still do, but they were not done in concert with the locals, the civic officials."[64]

Of course, not everyone was free to relocate to the region's new hilltop neighborhoods, as poverty among the elderly and racist housing practices against African Americans limited many residents to the aging urban core.[65] In 1967, a group of civil rights activists, calling themselves Community Organization Members Build Absolute Teamwork! (COMBAT), dispatched a white couple to inquire about renting a home on Steubenville's west end. "The figure they were quoted was $87," recalled Rose Marie Schick. "But, when the owner's next inquiry came from a COMBAT! planted black couple, it had jumped to more than $200."[66] "Steubenville moved in terms of its population to the western part of the city," explained Nicholas Kaschak. "The downtown is still populated with the poor and unemployed and so forth. It is not a desired place to live."[67]

Despite some successes in redeveloping the community's infrastructure, urban redevelopment had a limited impact on the structure of the overall economy. Increasingly, local boosters turned to highway construction as a potential way to connect the region to the national marketplace. Because railroads and trolleys declined in the face of competition from the automobile, volume on the twisting local highways grew dramatically as residents of the region's relatively small and scattered communities traveled for work, education, and shopping.[68] By 1973 Joseph Kennedy, vice president of the Steubenville Chamber of Commerce, had come to equate highways with economic opportunity itself as he described watching "more affluent and seemingly more important counties enjoy the benefits of modern highways. . . and all the while our citizens are fighting to work in outmoded, substandard two-lane roads." Kennedy went on to cite a poll in which 78 percent of local businesses listed "highways and access into the area as being the number one problem of our area."[69]

Pittsburgh's progrowth coalition between the Allegheny Conference and municipal officials provided a means to marshal the enormous political and economic resources necessary to build highways through the region's rugged, densely populated terrain. The Allegheny Conference presented a vision of the region centered on an urban core functioning as a corporate headquarters, regional shopping area, and center for government and specialized services. Highways formed an integral part of this vision, knitting the region together and providing quick movement from the Golden Triangle to Pittsburgh International Airport west of the city as well as east to the Pennsylvania Turnpike.[70] As in Monroeville, during the 1950s and 1960s rural Moon and Robinson Townships, for example, grew rapidly due to their location near new highway and airport investment. "Out in the coal-stripped hills that form the Western pocket of Allegheny County, giant townships are stirring from a deep slumber," wrote journalist Edwin Beachler in 1951. "They have been awakened by the whoosh of jets at Greater Pittsburgh Airport and rumble of bull-dozers on the Penn-Lincoln Parkway West."[71]

Southwestern Pennsylvania's relative success in highway construction contrasted with a glaring lack of development in the West Virginia and Ohio portions of the Steel Valley, particularly around Steubenville.[72] Larger regions with growing populations offered expanding tax bases to support new services and highway development, but a declining and increasingly elderly population doomed local communities to shrinking revenues and little state incentive to develop outlying areas. While the Upper Ohio Valley had more than 350,000 residents in 1950, a population scattered over two states meant the dispersal of funding through separate legislatures.[73] Political calculations also played a major role in the distribution of highway funds. The Ohio portion of the region generally voted for Democrats during a period of Republican state control.[74] Conversely, Wheeling and Weirton residents consistently returned Republican Arch Moore to Congress, while "it was the Democratic Party that ran West Virginia." Consequently, explained an aide to Moore, who was elected state governor in 1969, "the northern panhandle historically did not get its share of any resources that had to be funneled through state government."[75]

The absence of strong support among the region's heavy industrial employers also hindered highway planning and construction in the Upper Ohio Valley. "Weirton Steel was employing about 13,000 people at that time," recalled Weirton City Manager Robert Wirgau. "They were the powerhouse in this town, you know. I found that out quickly. You don't do anything unless Weirton Steel says its o.k. They taught me what this town was about, it was about steel."[76] Many local business and civic leaders did take a strong stance advocating highway construction, but the issue was less important for a heavy industrial sector served by the river and the railroads. Some companies were interested in selected projects, but because most mills shared the flat lands adjacent to the river with the major highways, they often opposed road construction that might disrupt production. Indeed, a major bridge project between Steubenville and Weirton was delayed for nearly thirty years as residents and corporations wrangled over its precise location in the crowded river valley.[77] "I mean there were all of the big cities that had to be taken care of, first, with federal dollars, and these communities were progressive in going after it," Wirgau explained. In the Upper Ohio Valley, the mines and mills were "taken care of by the river and the railroad and the highway really

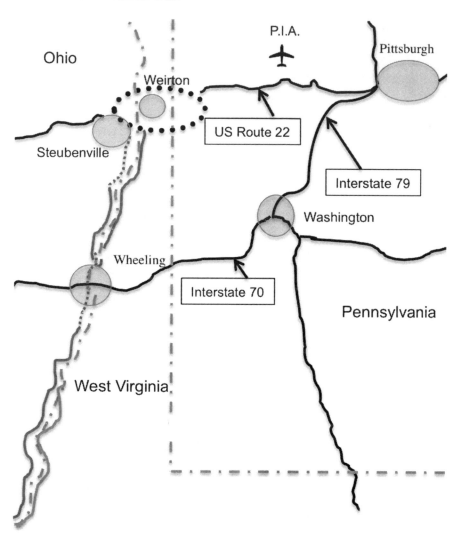

Figure 3.4. **Major highway connections between metropolitan Pittsburgh and the Upper Ohio Valley, ca. 1970. The missing link that would upgrade U.S. Route 22 between the Pennsylvania state line and Steubenville was not completed until the early 1990s.**

wasn't that big a deal. So therefore the powers that be [decided] it wasn't important enough to organize and go after it."[78]

Increasing federal intervention by the mid-1960s offered new opportunities for highway planning and construction. The Federal-Aid Highway Act of 1962 required a "continuing, comprehensive and cooperative" process for regional highway planning and the 1966 Demonstration Cities and Metropolitan Development Act expanded these requirements to a wide variety of federal environmental and development programs.[79] In response, local and state officials in the Steubenville-Weirton area formed the Brooke-Hancock-Jefferson (BHJ) Metropolitan Planning Commission, while to the south the Belmont-Ohio-Marshall (Belomar) Metropolitan Planning Commission encompassed the Wheeling area.[80] At Belomar's first meeting in March 1969, chairman Charles Steele declared that, "for the first time in the two-hundred year history of the area, various government bodies had agreed to cooperate in the establishment of an organization that can be of real assistance to the entire area."[81]

By the early 1970s, existing political rivalries already threatened the fledgling organizations, which had little local political support. "Self-interest is probably the key phrase to describe" the Upper Ohio Valley, concluded one 1970 report. "The federal government, with its offer of funds for updating the area, is the only measure which will bring the area together." [82] Commission members from smaller communities were "always suspicious of what Steubenville would do or not do," recalled BHJ representative Nicholas Kaschak.[83] The voluntary structure of the two commissions also left construction projects up to the local units, limiting the ability of staff to implement their designs. In 1971, BHJ completed a plan for Weirton that emphasized civic and commercial improvements downtown.[84] Concerned about the cost of carrying out the renewal program, administrators in Weirton drastically reduced financial support for the commission. At the same time, leaders in Steubenville and Jefferson County also cut payments because they were upset at a decision to locate the BHJ office in Weirton. While the participating governments later reached funding agreements, this type of fiscal restraint kept BHJ's staff to a minimum and limited its effectiveness.[85] "Since we really didn't have a history of an integrated area, we still thought in terms of Brooke Countians and Hancock Countians and Jefferson Countians, [each] pushing their own kind of agenda whenever they could," Kaschak concluded. "And it wasn't really much in the way of progress as far as the general area was concerned."[86]

Rivalry at the state and federal levels mirrored competition among local leaders. Ohio Congressman Wayne L. Hays used his connections in Washington and Columbus to control federal spending in his district, channeling it to local political supporters.[87] Hays continually struggled with Ohio Governor James Rhodes over control of government spending in eastern Ohio, and, according to numerous local officials, violently opposed cooperation between communities in his district and those across the river in West Virginia.[88] A staunch partisan, he had a particular animosity for the West Virginia Republican congressman, later state governor, Arch Moore. In one episode from the early 1970s, Hays was attending a meeting at a local country club when a county official announced funding approval for a highway study linking a local community to I-70. Upon hearing the news, the congressman stood up, struck the table with his fist and with the entire room staring, declared, "God damn they will. That organization [Belomar] is controlled by West Virginia and Governor Moore."[89]

The possibilities and problems exposed by attempts at regional highway planning were part of a series of larger conflicts over control of Steel Valley markets and institutions. The self-image of most local residents remained firmly defined by those economic and social institutions developed during the region's heyday in the early twentieth century. While paying lip service to the need for new roads, the region's mills and mines remained well served by river and rail links. As a result, many business leaders saw little need to invest in construction projects that might disrupt operations at their plants in the narrow river valleys.[90] A tradition of weak civic administration left Steubenville officials incapable of overcoming contentious local politics hindering economic and urban development programs. "The greatest inhibitor of economic development is unanimously reported to emanate from poor transportation linkages," concluded a 1972 survey of local business leaders. But "the alternatives set forth have ripped the already fractionated community asunder."[91]

Due in part to the decline of transportation links to the larger Pittsburgh metropolitan region, the economic dislocation of the 1980s hit the more rural communities of the Upper Ohio Valley particularly hard. While Steubenville's air was cleaner than in the mid-1970s when its coal-fired power plants and steel mills were still in full swing, the decline of heavy industry fueled an exodus that left the community at the very bottom of national census rankings for population loss during the 1980s and 1990s.[92] While less than forty miles away from Pittsburgh, a lack of funds to blast a bypass through the hills above Weirton and build a new bridge across the Ohio River had delayed a proposed highway project for more than two decades.[93] The lack of highways further complicated urban redevelopment initiatives in local communities that already suffered from ethnic and religious fragmentation and a history of weak civic administration.[94] "It was very hard getting an audience initially [for] new highways tying us to the Pittsburgh metro area and then the bridge across the river," concluded Steubenville city manager Gary Dufour. "They were struggles that went on for over forty years."[95]

Becoming the "Burb of the 'Burgh"

The groundbreaking for the final phase of upgrading Route 22 between Steubenville and Pittsburgh in May 1991 was thus heralded as a glimmer of hope in a community going through some of its most difficult days. The four-lane expansion of the highway had reached the Pennsylvania border in 1971, but it was not until 1990 that West Virginia's Robert C. Byrd became chair of the Senate Appropriations Committee and secured nearly $100 million from federal coffers to complete the project.[96] With the long-awaited completion of the Veterans Memorial Bridge, which had taken nearly thirty years since the preliminary engineering report in 1961 to the opening of the bridge to traffic in 1990, Steubenville residents were finally reconnected to the region's metropolitan core.[97] Observing of the highway named in his honor that a community with "a future must have modern, efficient transportation," the senator predicted the new Byrd Expressway would provide access to the economic opportunities of southwestern Pennsylvania.[98]

The opportunities to which Byrd referred were not mere abstractions, but could be found just thirty miles away in the tremendous growth of the so-called Airport Corridor surrounding Pittsburgh International Airport.[99] During the 1980s, a reformed progrowth coalition between the Allegheny Conference, local political leaders and administrators at the University of Pittsburgh's two research universities looked toward the construction of a new $700 million Midfield Terminal at the airport as both a symbol of "postindustrial" progress and an economic generator for the entire region.[100] The new "Airport of the Future," as it was dubbed by boosters, opened to tremendous fanfare in September 1992. "The airport means far more than transportation," declared

Figure 3.5. View from Steubenville across Veterans Memorial Bridge. The span opened on May 1, 1990 and provided a four-lane limited access highway route to Metropolitan Pittsburgh.

Photo by Ron Smith. Courtesy of World Radio Telecommunications, Inc.

the regional marketing firm Penn's Southwest. "It means jobs, development, growth." Allegheny County Commission chairman Tom Forester added, "I think whole new cities will grow up around the airport."[101]

Creating a modern airport had long been an important component of the Pittsburgh Renaissance vision for remaking southwestern Pennsylvania's image and economy.[102] The dedication of the Greater Pittsburgh International Airport in 1952 provided the western anchor of the Penn-Lincoln Parkway extending through Pittsburgh to the Pennsylvania Turnpike in the east.[103] Progrowth boosters envisioned the new airport as complementing downtown redevelopment, but during the 1950s and 1960s the Airport Corridor itself emerged as one of the region's most significant commercial centers. In addition to single-family homes, the area also increasingly played host to multi-family and condominium developments.[104] By 1963, the Airport Corridor formed the region's second largest business center as several large out-of-town firms, including Aetna Insurance and General Electric, chose to locate their regional branch offices along the Parkway rather than in the downtown Golden Triangle.[105]

Airport Corridor development formed a key component of the regional growth strategy promoted by the Allegheny Conference in the wake of rapid declines in the region's traditional industries.[106] In 1979, the publicly subsidized RIDC [Industrial] Park West opened just south of the airport and development officials went so far as to declare that the area offered "unlimited potential in terms of industrial and office development."[107] Private developers, too, flocked to the Airport Corridor, even as the region's industrialized river valleys faced the shock of steel's collapse.[108] Local officials had difficulty leasing the colossal, interconnected mills abandoned in the river valleys, but the new industrial parks met the demands for the small- and medium-sized firms driving regional growth during the 1970s and 1980s. A 1982 industrial site survey found that while purchases of existing manufacturing sites had dropped by 50 percent from the previous year, sales of more modern facilities, found predominantly in suburban industrial parks, rose 35 percent.[109]

Allegheny County commissioners began planning for an airport upgrade during the late 1960s, but political wrangling and a declining local economy stalled the project for over a decade.[110] In January 1985, state representative Tom Murphy (D-North Side) broke the log jam over airport expansion and other economic development initiatives by persuading officials in Pittsburgh, Allegheny County and the region's two major research universities to coordinate their requests for state funding.[111] The *Strategy 21* report, overseen by the Allegheny Conference, argued that airport construction "would have a dramatic effect on the region's economy" by creating 18,000 jobs over the next fifteen years. "It would strengthen the region's attraction as a corporate headquarters and convert seriously underutilized land to diverse, new business purposes with heavy job creation potential."[112] Construction on the airport began in 1987, with the $700 million Midfield Terminal and the seven-mile Southern Expressway opening in 1992. "The new airport," declared county commissioners, "represents our collective efforts to pull ourselves up by our economic bootstraps and prepare to assume our proper place in the emerging world economy.[113]

State and local investment in the Airport of the Future quickly appeared to pay off in millions of dollars in private development nearby. Shortly after the start of terminal construction, work began on the Airport Corridor's largest project to date, the Robinson Towne Center, a mixed-use development fifteen miles west of downtown and two miles east of the airport, which included a 435,000-square-foot strip center, a large enclosed shopping mall, and more than 1.5 million square feet of office space with facilities for research and development. "We felt that the road system combined with the growth projects due to construction of the new Midfield Terminal made Robinson Towne Center viable," explained developer Michael Zamagias.[114]

Residents and officials in nearby Washington and Beaver Counties (Pennsylvania) hard hit by declines in heavy industry also worked to tap into the growth of the Airport Corridor, with results that provided a clear contrast to Steubenville. In 1930, travel time by rail between Pittsburgh and Washington was roughly the same as to Steubenville—eighty minutes for forty miles to Steubenville and sixty minutes for thirty miles to Washington.[115] While Steubenville residents continued to travel on "substandard two-lane" Route 22 through the mid-1990s, however, Interstate 79 was completed between Pittsburgh and Washington in 1972. In 1987, the Washington County Redevelopment Authority began planning a massive mixed-use development twelve miles southwest of the airport that was projected to generate $500 million in private investment and create 4,000 new jobs. By 1993, two housing projects, a golf course, and office buildings for a precision tool manufacturer, an engineering firm, and Mitsubishi's Rotary Nozzle Division were already open at the 600-acre "Southpointe" development.[116]

Similarly, the start of construction on the Beaver Valley Expressway (BVE) in the late 1970s resulted in more than 1,800 employees of U.S. Airways alone living in that county by 1986.[117] State senator Tim Shaffer (R-Butler) and other local officials helped pass a legislative initiative that provided for the completion of the BVE, which opened in 1991 as a toll road.[118] "All of us are disturbed about what has happened to the steel industry, but I think we can't look back," declared state representative Nick

Figure 3.6. Cover page of a special supplement to the *Beaver County Times* for September 13, 1992 celebrating the opening of Pittsburgh International Airport's new Midfield Terminal.

Courtesy of the *Beaver County Times*

Colafella (D-Aliquippa) in 1986.[119] Beaver County native Jay Aldridge, the influential director of regional marketing agency Penn's Southwest, mirrored this optimism. "If you look at the employment figures today," Aldridge reported in 1988, "they exceed the numbers we had 10 years ago." New jobs, he added, "are not from J&L [Steel] like they used to be. They are from the new job generator—the airport."[120]

Steubenville's "Burb of the 'Burgh" campaign can thus best be set into a context of older industrial communities in the Steel Valley working to reshape their communities, both symbolically and physically, into a form suitable for the "postindustrial" economy. Even before the opening of the Byrd Expressway, community leaders in Steubenville had begun to organize and local leaders were determined to capitalize on their new highway link. Uniting under the Alliance 2000 coalition, public officials and businessmen sought to transform the image and reality of their community as a polluted, deindustrialized, dead-end into a progressive, postindustrial alternative to the "traditional" suburbs. Through an advertising campaign targeting southwestern Pennsylvania residents and businesses, Alliance 2000, subsequently renamed the Progress Alliance, emphasized low taxes, opportunities for outdoor recreation, culture, and proximity to Pittsburgh, less than forty miles away. According to one Alliance member, the campaign focused on reaching out to Pittsburgh's civic and business leaders, with the message that, "Hey we're right here. We're not all this distance, two states away from you. We're just a few miles down the road."[121]

The decision to focus marketing efforts on greater Pittsburgh involved an important shift in the regional vision of local leaders. In part, the postwar decline in the relationship between the Upper Ohio Valley and their neighbors in southwestern Pennsylvania was rooted in political and administrative policies that deemphasized the social and cultural bonds between local communities in favor of development projects organized on the state level. Consequently, from the 1960s through the 1980s public officials in Ohio and West Virginia largely looked to more distant cities such as Cleveland, Youngstown, and Charleston as potential economic partners.[122] The 1990s, then, were a period of "rediscovery" for local residents who suddenly found themselves within easy commuting distance of the universities, hospitals, shopping malls, and industrial parks of the metropolitan core.[123] "We do not see ourselves as raiders," declared Progress Alliance director Rick Platt. "We want a strong Pittsburgh, and if it comes down to cheering for some other part of Ohio and Pittsburgh, we will cheer for Pittsburgh just like we cheer for the Steelers over the Browns."[124]

While the creation of new jobs was a welcome relief for local communities suffering from high unemployment and out-migration, Progress Alliance leaders recognized that the strategy of promoting themselves as a low-cost alternative to suburban locations could not make up for the loss of high-paying industrial and coal mining jobs. Efforts to remake the Upper Ohio Valley did have a number of important victories, including the opening of a major Walmart distribution center near Steubenville in 2001 and a mammoth Cabela's retail store and distribution center east of Wheeling in 2004.[125] Nevertheless, the Upper Ohio Valley remained a junior partner in the process of metropolitan development, with little choice but to compete for those employment opportunities available as local communities continued to lose population in the face of ongoing plant closures.[126] Indeed, Steubenville's low-tax strategy of luring investment actually contributed to a stall in housing growth in the Airport Corridor itself during the late 1990s.[127] "When it comes to homes in the $200,000 to $350,000 price range, you can drive another 20 minutes [to Weirton or Steubenville] to save $300 to $500 a month (in taxes)," explained the owner of a Pennsylvania construction company. "There has been some growth there, but not what you think," added Ron Croushore, CEO of Prudential Preferred Realty. "Lots of people still come from the north and south. The malls and shopping centers are drawing from all over. The traffic has been unbelievable, but the housing has not been ahead of the other parts of the city."[128]

The suburban strategy of economic development both complemented and reinforced the rapid growth of peripheral communities that occurred even as the Steel Valley's overall population declined. The efforts of local and regional boosters also implicitly acknowledged the failure of earlier redevelopment campaigns to substantially change the Upper Ohio Valley's declining urban centers.[129] "Right now we're . . . looking at reutilization strategies for brownfields," explained Weirton City Manager Gary Dufour in August 2004. "I think one of the things that has sort of evolved is the understanding that the entire community advances, not just a piece. . . . We're judged by the quality of the total community, not just a piece."[130] Despite the attempts of local officials, however, little new construction actually took place within Steubenville itself, as employers instead flocked to an expansive hilltop industrial park just off Route 22.[131] Even the early promise of state and federal subsidies for brownfield development along the riverfront has faded in recent years from a lack of matching private funds for the removal of toxic wastes.[132]

Conclusion

During the postwar period, the metropolitan regional bonds forged in the late nineteenth century between metropolitan Pittsburgh and the Upper Ohio Valley slowly unraveled. Over time, outlying communities in Ohio and West Virginia lost population and actually grew more isolated from the cultural and economic activities of the metropolis. That is, in effect, they became *more* rural. Eventually this left residents of Steubenville and other local communities to face the collapse of heavy industry without access to the economic and institutional resources of their larger neighbor. Indeed, the process of postwar economic decline went hand in hand with Steubenville's growing isolation from the larger metropolitan region. "You [still] had a two-lane road," recalled Dufour of transportation links in the 1970s and 1980s, and "in Pittsburgh they would say, 'Oh, you're over in Weirton, West Virginia or Steubenville, Ohio. You're clear over there?'"[133]

Though the towns and small cities along the Ohio River continued to produce steel and mine coal, they did not share in the economic transformation that helped Pittsburgh and select suburbs refashion themselves into "postindustrial" centers of high-tech manufacturing and service provision. When Steubenville officials did begin to reimagine their community as part of the greater Pittsburgh region, like most other rural communities they did so as junior partners promoting a low-cost/low-wage alternative to suburban locations. Adopting a suburban strategy for metropolitan growth implicitly acknowledged the failure of earlier urban redevelopment campaigns to substantially change decaying central business districts and urban neighborhoods.[134] Ironically, when considering the historical role of transportation infrastructure in uniting the Steel Valley region, the desire of local boosters to increase accessibility to the metropolitan core also put Steubenville's postindustrial vision of community into conflict with anti-sprawl organizations in Pittsburgh. Steubenville officials, for example, joined the call for better access to the Airport Corridor, a project Progress Alliance director Tom Bayuzik described as "the single most important highway project for this area." This led sustainability activist Cort Gould to opine that "with so much going for our region, we must now ditch old-economy delusions of pavement as the only road to prosperity."[135]

The shifting relationship between the Upper Ohio Valley and metropolitan Pittsburgh raises important questions about the nature of "rust belt" deindustrialization as well as the linear narrative of metropolitan expansion. The case of Steubenville demonstrates that hinterland residents retained agency in the face of overall economic change. Steubenville was not simply incorporated into the metropolitan region as a "natural" part of Pittsburgh's evolution, but rather in response to the actions of boosters who drew federal infrastructure and other resources that made reincorporation possible, albeit in a limited way. On the other hand, metropolitan expansion clearly affected the politics and political economies of the regional hinterland. In Steubenville, this eventually meant a turn away from urban redevelopment and the pursuit of industrial production to a suburban strategy of low taxes, new home construction, and service sector employment that could not provide the same local employment and wage levels that the community had seen in the midst of the industrial era.

In the end, Steubenville's efforts are past of a broader transition whereby industrial small cities have struggled to find a place for themselves within a new economic and spatial reality. The development of new transportation links allowed residents to sell themselves in much the same way local boosters had cast the community in the industrial era—as a small town with easy access to big city amenities. In the process, locals once again refashioned a common physical and cultural landscape into an identity that embraced the commonalities shared with their larger neighbor upriver. "If proximity is a measure of being part of the Pittsburgh area, Steubenville has it," declared one local official. "We proudly call ourselves the "Burb of the 'Burgh." Steubenville is just 10 miles from the Post-Gazette Pavilion and just 30 minutes from Pittsburgh International Airport. How much more 'Pittsburgh area' can a city be than that?"[136]

Notes

I would like to thank Ted Muller, Joel Tarr, Michael Glass and the members of the Pittsburgh History Roundtable for their thoughtful suggestions on an earlier version of this essay. John McCarthy's insightful comments proved very useful in revising the essay for publication.

1. Brendan Sager, "Steubenville's Alliance 2000 Targets Pittsburgh," *Pittsburgh Post Gazette*, November 20, 1998, D-8.

2. Author's interview with Gary Dufour, August 2004. Hereafter cited as Dufour Interview.

3. "Steubenville: Coal and Steel Town Sees Rebirth," Expansion Magazine Online, January 1, 1998 (copy in author's possession); Committee on Environment and Public Works, Subcommittee on Transportation and Infrastructure. Testimony of Richard J. Platt of Alliance 2000 in Steubenville, Ohio, August 8, 2000.

4. Sam Bass Warner, *Streetcar Suburbs: The Process of Growth in Boston, 1870–1900* (Cambridge, MA: Harvard University Press, 1962); Owen D. Gutfreund, *Twentieth-Century Sprawl: Highways and the Reshaping of the American Landscape* (New York: Oxford University Press, 2004).

5. On pollution in Steubenville, see William Stevens, "Ohio is Crucial Testing Ground in U.S. Pollution Fight," *New York Times*, February 10, 1976; Janet Raloff, "Dust to Dust: A Particularly Lethal Legacy," *Science News*, April 6, 1991, 212.

6. David Javersak, A Historical Perspective, recorded on December 15, 1994, Wheeling Area Historical Database, wheeling.weirton.lib.wv.us/history.htm (accessed April 15, 2009).

7. For a useful overview of this literature, see Jefferson R. Cowie and Joseph Heathcott, *Beyond the Ruins: The Meanings of Deindustrialization* (Ithaca: ILR Press, 2003).

8. Howard Gillette, *Camden after the Fall: Decline and Renewal in a Post-Industrial City* (Philadelphia: University of Pennsylvania Press, 2005).

9. Robert Self, *American Babylon: Race and the Struggle for Postwar Oakland* (Princeton: Princeton University Press, 2003); Bruce J. Schulman, *From Cotton Belt to Sunbelt: Federal Policy, Economic Development, and the Transformation of the South, 1938–1980* (New York: Oxford University Press, 1991); Matthew Lassiter, *Silent Majority: Suburban Politics in the Sunbelt South* (Princeton: Princeton University Press, 2007).

10. The notion of "space" as an analytical category has gained a great deal of scholarly attention in recent years. For an overview, see Gyan Prakash and Kevin Kruse, eds., *The Spaces of the Modern City: Imaginaries, Politics, and Everyday Life* (Princeton, N.J.: Princeton University Press, 2008).

11. For an overview of recent trends in suburban historiography, see "Introduction—The New Suburban History," in eds. Kevin M. Kruse and Thomas J. Sugrue, *The New Suburban History* (Chicago: University of Chicago Press, 2006).

12. This oversight stems, in part, from the overriding emphasis of the new metropolitan history on the issue of racial inequality. Even Robert Self's excellent synthesis of urban decline and suburban growth is used primarily as a context for exploring uneven development along racial lines. Race is clearly important for explaining urban development in any community, but this analytical framework does not always fully engage with other aspects of spatial inequality and metropolitan change. The singular focus on race presents a particular problem in understanding Pittsburgh and its hinterlands, which did not receive the influx of African Americans following World War II typical of northern industrial cities and had one of the lowest percentages of nonwhite residents of any major metropolitan region in the United States.

13. Unlike urban scholars who have emphasized the decentralization of the city and the rise of the suburbs, the dominant theme of rural history has been the increasing "interdependence between rural places and people, on the one hand, and the economic activities in metropolitan America, and in the global marketplace, on the other." Emery Castle, "Rural Diversity: An American Asset," *Annals of the American Academy of Political and Social Science* 529 (September 1993): 12–13.

14 In his research on nineteenth-century Chicago, Cronon demonstrated that urban growth manifested itself not merely as changes within the city or in the expansion of residential landscapes, but in far-ranging linkages between metropolitan centers, satellite communities, and rural hinterlands. William Cronon, *Nature's Metropolis: Chicago and the Great West* (New York: W.W. Norton, 1991).

15. Edward K. Muller, "Industrial Suburbs and the Growth of Metropolitan Pittsburgh, 1870–1920" in ed. Robert D. Lewis, *Manufacturing Suburbs: Building Work and Home on the Metropolitan Fringe* (Philadelphia: Temple University Press, 2004).

16. For an expanding version of this call for a "metropolitan regional" history, see Andrew Needham and Allen Dieterich-Ward, "Beyond the Metropolis: Metropolitan Growth and Regional Transformation in Postwar America," *Journal of Urban History* 35, No. 7 (November 2009): 943–69.

17. I use the term Steel Valley when referring to Pittsburgh and its hinterlands in Pennsylvania, Ohio, and West Virginia. I use the term Upper Ohio Valley to refer to the portion of this broader region in West Virginia and Ohio. I use the term metropolitan Pittsburgh to refer to the southwestern Pennsylvania portion of the region.

18. For an overview of urban development in Pittsburgh, see Roy Lubove, *Twentieth Century Pittsburgh, Volume One: Government, Business, and Environmental Change* (Pittsburgh: University of Pittsburgh Press, 1995); Roy Lubove, *Twentieth Century Pittsburgh, Volume Two: The Post Steel Era* (Pittsburgh: University of Pittsburgh Press, 1996).

19. Ernest T. Weir as quoted in David T. Javersak, *History of Weirton, West Virginia* (Virginia Beach, VA: The Donning Company, 1999), 74.

20. In 1916, *The Wheeling Intelligencer* described Sinclair as "the dominant factor . . . in inducing industries to locate at Steubenville, Weirton, and Follansbee." Quoted in Javersak, *History of Weirton*, 68.

21. Dufour Interview.

22. For another example of a "model" industrial community in the Steel Valley, see Anne E. Mosher, *Capital's Utopia: Vandergrift, Pennsylvania, 1855–1916* (Baltimore: Johns Hopkins University Press, 2004).

23. Joel A. Tarr, *Transportation Innovation and Changing Spatial Patterns in Pittsburgh, 1850–1934*, (Chicago: University of Chicago Press, 1978); Muller, "Industrial Suburbs." My analysis of the relationship between Pittsburgh and its hinterlands owes a great deal to the conceptual model put forward by Edward Muller in "Metropolis and Region: A Framework for Enquiry into Western Pennsylvania" in Samuel P. Hays, ed., *City at the Point: Essays on the Social History of Pittsburgh* (Pittsburgh: University of Pittsburgh Press, 1989).

24. On the early economic development of the Pittsburgh region, see Catherine Elizabeth Reiser, *Pittsburgh's Commercial Development, 1800–1850* (Harrisburg: Pennsylvania Historical and Museum Commission, 1951).

25. Letter from Nelson C. Hubbard to Andrew Carnegie, May 12, 1899. Thanks to Dr. Charles Julian of the Robert C. Byrd National Technology Transfer Center for bringing this source to the author's attention.

26. Muller, "Industrial Suburbs."

27. There is an excellent and growing literature on the changing form and function of late nineteenth- and early twentieth-century mill towns and industrial "satellite" cities. See Richard Harris and P. J. Larkham, eds., *Changing Suburbs: Foundation, Form and Function* (New York: Routledge, 1999); Lewis, *Manufacturing Suburbs*.

28. Richard Harris and Robert Lewis, "Constructing a Fault(y) Zone: Misrepresentations of American Cities and Suburbs, 1900–1950," *Annals of the Association of American Geographers* 88, no. 4 (1988): 622–39; Andrew Wiese, "Stubborn Diversity: A Commentary on Middle-Class Influence in Working-Class Suburbs, 1900–1940," *Journal of Urban History* 27, no. 3 (2001): 348–54.

29. Becky M. Nicolaides, *My Blue Heaven: Life and Politics in the Working-Class Suburbs of Los Angeles, 1920–1965* (Chicago: University of Chicago Press, 2002);

Andrew Wiese, *Places of Their Own: African American Suburbanization in the Twentieth Century* (Chicago: University of Chicago Press, 2004).

30. Muller, "Industrial Suburbs," 68.

31. Author's interview with Nicholas Kaschak, July 2004. Hereafter cited as Kaschak Interview.

32. On the role of ethnicity in shaping community life in the Steel Valley, see Franklin Toker, *Pittsburgh: An Urban Portrait* (University Park: Pennsylvania State University Press, 1986).

33. Regional Industrial Development Corporation, *A Community of Interest between the Pittsburgh Metropolitan Area and the Upper Ohio Valley: A Preliminary Analysis* (Pittsburgh: RIDC, 1959), i.

34. For the most comprehensive account of the role of the Allegheny Conference in creating the Pittsburgh Renaissance, see Sherie R. Mershon, "Corporate Social Responsibility and Urban Revitalization: The Allegheny Conference on Community Development, 1943–1968" (Ph.D. diss., Carnegie Mellon University, 2004). See also Lubove, *Twentieth Century Pittsburgh, Volume One.*

35. On the role of the Allegheny Conference in supporting regional parks in western Pennsylvania, see M. Graham Netting, *50 Years of the Western Pennsylvania Conservancy: The Early Years* (Pittsburgh: The Conservancy, 1982).

36. On Pittsburgh's growing reputation as a research center, see David K. Willis, "Pittsburgh Quickens Economic Stride," *Christian Science Monitor*, December 15, 1964, 9; Neal Stanford, "Industrial Fallout" Garnered from U.S. Space Program, June 22, 1965; "Pittsburgh Area a Research Center," *New York Times*, October 27, 1968, F17; Marylin Bender, "An Elite Brain Factory," *New York Times*, October 17, 1971, F3; Bill Zlatos, "Posvar Pushed Economic Rebirth at Pitt, Growing Pains and All," *Pittsburgh Press*, May 13, 1990.

37. Ralph R. Widner, "The Regional City: An Approach to Planning Our Future Urban Growth, an Address to the Annual Meeting of the Allegheny Conference on Community Development," November 26, 1973, 15–16.

38. Widner, "The Regional City," 23.

39. Max Nurnberg, *Economic Study of the Pittsburgh Region, Vol. III: Region with a Future* (Pittsburgh: University of Pittsburgh Press, 1963), 267.

40. Mershon, "Corporate Social Responsibility and Urban Revitalization"; Lubove, *Twentieth Century Pittsburgh Volume One*; Gregory J. Crowley, *The Politics of Place: Contentious Urban Redevelopment in Pittsburgh* (Pittsburgh: University of Pittsburgh Press, 2005).

41. Stefan Lorant, *Pittsburgh: The Story of an American City* (Pittsburgh: Esselmont Books, 1964, revised and expanded editions in 1975, 1980, 1988 and 1999), 373. Quotation is from the 1999 edition.

42. Eileen Foley, "For Monroeville the Bloom is Not Off the 30-Year Boom," *Pittsburgh Post-Gazette*, March 20, 1980.

43. "When We Brag About Our Area's Growth, We Mean White Oaks and Mountain Laurel, Too," *Wall Street Journal*, March 22, 1972.

44. Pennsylvania State Planning Board, *Regional Development Reconnaissance: Region 12 [a Staff Working Paper]* (Harrisburg: The Board, 1966), 62. See also Southwestern Pennsylvania Regional Planning Commission, *Issues in a Region of Contrasts* (Pittsburgh: SWPRPA, 1968).

45. On the development of the Allegheny Valley Expressway, see the "Sunday Alle-Kiski Press" edition of the *Pittsburgh Press* for Sunday August 4, 1985. On the development and evolution of Northpointe, see Armstrong County Industrial Development Council, "Northpointe. A Business and Lifestyle Community for the 21st Century," 2002; Mitch Fryer, "Building the County's Future," *Kittanning Leader Times*, April 15, 2005. On marketing Armstrong County, see Mullin & Lonergan Associates, "Armstrong County Comprehensive Plan," Armstrong County Planning Commission, 2005.

46. Suzanne Elliott, "Armstrong Gains, Loses Trying to Strengthen Economy," *Pittsburgh Business Times*, April 23, 2004.

47. Javersak, *A Historical Perspective*.

48. Author's interviews with Donald Myers, July 2004. Hereafter cited as Myers Interviews.

49. On pollution in Steubenville during the period, see Harry Krause, "Tri-State Conference Finishes with Decision that Pollution Harms Health," *Wheeling News Register*, July, 26, 1968, 22. Robert DeFrancis, "Air Pollution Watchdogs Raise Cry for Ohio Edison Shutdown," *Wheeling Intelligencer*, July 24, 1969, 1. See also Joel A. Tarr, ed., *Devastation and Renewal: An Environmental History of Pittsburgh and Its Region* (Pittsburgh: University of Pittsburgh Press, 2003).

50. United States Bureau of the Census and Inter-University Consortium for Political and Social Research, *County and City Data Book* (Ann Arbor: ICPSR, 1947, 1956, 1962, 1972, 1977, 1983).

51. Myers Interviews.

52. Simonds and Simonds, *Steubenville Central Business District Study* (Steubenville: Steubenville Metropolitan Planning and Redevelopment Commission, 1968), 1.

53. Francis F. Brown, *A History of the Roman Catholic Diocese of Steubenville, Ohio, Volume I, the Mussio Years (1945–1977)* (Lewiston, NY: Edwin Mellen Press, 1994), 374–75.

54. Mussio's crowning achievement had come less than five years earlier with the dedication of a $1.5 million Diocesan Community Arena, the largest in the Steel Valley outside of Pittsburgh.

55. Kaschak Interview; Dufour Interview.

56. For an overview of the Great Society and War on Poverty, see John A. Andrew, *Lyndon Johnson and the Great Society* (Chicago: Ivan R. Dee, 1998); Walter I. Trattner, *From Poor Law to Welfare State: A History of Social Welfare in America*, sixth ed. (New York: The Free Press, 1999), 304–62.

57. On the origins of comprehensive urban planning in the United States, see Jon A. Peterson, *The Birth of City Planning in the United States, 1840–1917* (Baltimore: Johns Hopkins University Press, 2003). On the growth of planning in Pittsburgh,

see John F. Bauman and Edward K. Muller, *Before Renaissance: Planning in Pittsburgh, 1889–1943* (Pittsburgh: University of Pittsburgh Press, 2006).

58. Kaschak Interview.

59. Ted Hacquard, "Field Visit to Jefferson County Community Action," April 11, 1968 in Folder Jefferson County, Box 52039, Series 629, Records of the Ohio Department of Development, Ohio Office of Opportunity, Community Action Files, 1965–1969, Archives/Library, Ohio Historical Society, Columbus, OH. Collection hereafter cited as ODOD.

60. Hal Maggied, "Report on Official Travel to Steubenville, OH," December 10, 1972, Binder Second Progress Report, Box 55526, ODOD.

61. Therese M. Sagun, "Steubenville: Will It Survive?" (Honors thesis, Kent State University, 1983), 42.

62. On pollution in the Upper Ohio Valley, see "Area Conference's Activity Revealed: Air Pollution Fight Exceeds Expectations"; "Court Action Sought Against Koppers Co for Alleged Pollution," *Wall Street Journal*, February 19, 1971, 3; Joe McLaughlin, (reporter), "Transcript of Proceedings of the Conference in the Matter of Pollution of the Interstate Waters of the Ohio River and its Tributaries in the Wheeling, West Virginia Area," October 13, 1971; William K. Stevens, "Ohio is Crucial Testing Ground in U.S. Pollution Fight," *New York Times*, February 10, 1976; Janet Raloff, "Dust to Dust: A Particularly Lethal Legacy," *Science News*, April 6, 1991, 212.

63. Brown, *History of the Roman Catholic Diocese*, 51–54, 155–58.

64. Kaschak Interview.

65. On the role of racism in federal housing policy, see Kenneth T. Jackson, *Crabgrass Frontier: The Suburbanization of America* (New York: Oxford University Press, 1985). On grassroots racism in neighborhood housing markets, see Thomas J. Sugrue, *The Origins of the Urban Crisis: Race and Inequality in Postwar Detroit* (Princeton, NJ: Princeton University Press, 1990), 209–58. On African American suburbanization, see Wiese, *Places of their Own: African American Suburbanization in the Twentieth Century*.

66. Brown, *History of the Roman Catholic Diocese*, 328; Daniel Greene, "Steubenville's Black Ghetto," *National Observer*, April 1, 1968.

67. Kaschak Interview.

68. For the role of transportation in shaping the social and physical landscape in the Steel Valley, see Tarr, *Transportation Innovation*; Muller, Edward and Joel Tarr, "The Interaction of Natural and Built Environments in the Pittsburgh Landscape" in Tarr, *Devastation and Renewal*, 11–40.

69. "Transcript of Hearings in Cambridge, Ohio," August 23, 1973, 132–41. Records of the Ohio Department of Transportation, Series 2610, Box 54329. Archives/Library, Ohio Historical Society.

70. Wallace Richards, "A Fifty-Seven-Million-Dollar Program," *Allegheny Conference Digest*, December 1945, Allegheny Conference on Community Development

Records, Box 129, Folder 5. Archives/Library, Historical Society of Western Pennsylvania.

71. Edwin Beachler, *Growing Pains in the Suburbs: The Story of Metropolitan Pittsburgh's Building Boom* (Pittsburgh: The Pittsburgh Press Company, 1951).

72. The construction of Interstate 70 through Wheeling between the mid-1950s and the early 1970s was the greatest postwar change in the Upper Ohio Valley's highway system. Even before the Federal-Aid Highway Act of 1956, work had begun on the route that would become Interstate 70, which crossed the Ohio River at Wheeling and replaced US 40 through the southern part of the region. However, I-70 was designed by state and federal officials for through traffic and only served a small portion of the Upper Ohio Valley.

73. Kaschak Interview. Even federal funds flowed from different regional offices located in Chicago and Philadelphia.

74. Myers Interviews; Alexander P. Lamis and Mary Anne Sharkey, *Ohio Politics* (Kent, OH: Kent State University Press, 1994).

75. Author's interviews with Charles Steele, July 2004. Herafter cited as Steele Interviews; Roger W. Haigh, *Wheeling, West Virginia: A Community Profile* (Wheeling, WV: Center for Wheeling Area Studies, 1969).

76. Author's interview with Robert Wirgau, August 2004. Hereafter cited as Wirgau Interview. See also Javersak, *History of Weirton*.

77. Ohio Department of Economic and Community Development, "Community Attitude Survey: Steubenville," Feb. 19, 1972, Binder Second Progress Report, Box 55526, ODOD; Wilbur Smith and Associates, *U.S. Route 22 Feasibility Study, Steubenville-Weirton Area* (New Haven, CT: The Company, 1970), 93.

78. Wirgau Interview.

79. Edward Weiner, *Urban Transportation Planning in the United States: An Historical Overview* (Westport, CT: Praeger Publishers, 1999).

80. The two new planning commissions grew out of earlier highway studies mandated for federal highway projects. Highway officials divided responsibility in the Upper Ohio Valley between the Steubenville-Weirton Area to the north and the Belmont-Ohio-Marshall metropolitan area. Before 1950, the entire area had been part of the Wheeling-Steubenville Standard Metropolitan Statistical Area. The division of the region by the Census Bureau and the formation of separate regional planning commissions was a further example of the fragmentation of regional resources.

81. Virginia Ann Randolph Grottendieck, *Problems of Administration in a Bi-State Metropolitan Region* (Master's thesis, West Virginia University, 1970), 85.

82. Grottendieck, *Problems of Administration in a Bi-State Metropolitan Region*, 61.

83. Kaschak Interview.

84. Brooke-Hancock-Jefferson Metropolitan Planning Commission, "A Way to the Future: A Long-Range Look at the Future of Downtown Weirton" (Weirton, WV: The Commission, 1971).

85. Wirgau Interview.

86. Kaschak Interview.

87. Hays was rumored to be one of the most powerful men in Washington before being censured and removed from the House of Representatives in 1976 due to a sex scandal. A former schoolteacher, much of his power reputedly stemmed from his ruthless tactics and acerbic wit. Nicholas M. Horrock, "U.S. Investigating Charges on Hays," *New York Times*, May 26, 1976.

88. Ted Hacquard, "Report of Field Visit: Jefferson County Community Action," April 11, 1969, Folder Jefferson County, Box 52039, ODOD; Myers Interviews; Steele Interviews.

89. Author's interviews with James Weaver, July 2004.

90. On the postwar role of industry in Ohio Valley politics, see Elizabeth Fones-Wolf and Ken Fones-Wolf, "Cold War Americanism: Business, Pageantry, and Antiunionism in Weirton, West Virginia," *Business History Review 77*, no. 1 (2003) and Javersak, *History of Weirton*. There is also some evidence that business leaders were concerned about the effect of regional economic diversification, often presented as part and parcel of highway development, on the local labor pool.

91. "Community Attitude Survey: Steubenville."

92. Felicity Barringer, "Drifting Air Pollution Beginning to Pit States against Their Neighbors," *Washington Post*, October 24, 1983; Felicity Barringer, "Steubenville Journal: As a Test Lab on Dirty Air, an Ohio Town Has Changed," *New York Times*, September 27, 2006.

93. On the Pennsylvania portion of the route, known as the William Penn Highway, see Jeffrey J. Kitsko, "US 22: William Penn Highway," www.pahighways.com/us/US22.html (accessed May 7, 2010).

94. On urban redevelopment in the Steel Valley, see Crowley, *The Politics of Place*.

95. Dufour Interview.

96. Robert C. Byrd, *Robert C. Byrd: Child of the Appalachian Coalfields* (Morgantown, WV: West Virginia University Press, 2005), 495, 515. The $100 million quote includes money earmarked for both the Weirton Bypass (Byrd Expressway) and the Steubenville-Weirton Veterans Memorial Bridge. According to a group opposing government subsidies to the steel industry, a provision of the Surface Transportation and Uniform Relocation Assistance Act of 1987 gave West Virginia highway officials discretion in transferring federal highway money to benefit the Route 22 bypass. At the time, the highway was "characterized as "integral to the continued vitality" of Weirton Steel." American Institute for International Steel, Inc., "Report on U.S. Government Subsidies to the U.S. Steel Industry," November 15, 1999, www.aiis.org/default.asp?contentID=37 (accessed May 7, 2010).

97. West Virginia Division of Highways, "Featured Bridge—Weirton Steubenville Bridge," www.transportation.wv.gov/communications/bridge_facts/Modern-Bridges/Pages/VeteransMemorial(Weirton-Steubenville).aspx (accessed May 7, 2010).

98. Byrd, *Robert C. Byrd*, 515.

99. The Airport Corridor eventually consisted of twenty-four municipalities, including rural Moon, Robinson, and Findlay Townships, as well as the boroughs of Coraopolis, Greentree, and Crafton.

100. Tom Foerster, Pete Flaherty, and Lawrence W. Dunn, "The Allegheny County Commissioners Welcome You to the Airport of the Future—the New Pittsburgh International Airport," *Beaver County Times* (*Special Supplement*), September 13, 1992, 1. The $700 million price tag also included access to the terminal via a new seven-mile "Southern Expressway."

101. Michael Marriott, "Pittsburgh Airport of Future Being Built," *New York Times*, November 12, 1991, A16.

102. Edward R. Weidlein, "Allegheny Conference Progress," *Allegheny Conference Digest* 2, no. 1 (June 1947), 3, Allegheny Conference on Community Development Records, Box 129, Folder 5. Allegheny Conference on Community Development, "Allegheny Conference on Community Development . . . Presents" (Pittsburgh: Allegheny Conference, 1956), 14. Archives/Library, Historical Society of Western Pennsylvania. In May 1946, Allegheny residents approved an Allegheny Conference on Community Development-backed bond issue for highway construction, which earmarked $6 million for converting a military airport in rural Moon Township to civilian use. Of the total cost of the airport, the county provided $24.7 million, the federal government contributed $7.6 million, and the state added $600,000.

103. "Pittsburgh's Airport Has Come a Long Way, Baby," *Beaver County Times* (Special Supplement), September 13, 1992.

104. "Robinson Eyes Borough Status," *Pittsburgh Post-Gazette*, June 7, 1977. One development, Pennbury Hills, featured the highest density in Allegheny County at fourteen thousand residents on forty-nine acres.

105. Ira S. Lowry, *Economic Study of the Pittsburgh Region, Vol. II Portrait of a Region* (Pittsburgh: University of Pittsburgh Press, 1963), 92.

106. City of Pittsburgh, County of Allegheny, University of Pittsburgh, and Carnegie Mellon University, "Strategy 21: Pittsburgh/Allegheny Economic Development Strategy to Begin the 21st Century. A Proposal to the Commonwealth of Pennsylvania," June 1985, 1–2.

107. Michael Baker Jr. Inc., *Allegheny County: Overall Economic Development Plan* (Pittsburgh: Allegheny County Overall Economic Development Program Committee, 1977), 91. Thomas J. Porter, Jr., "RIDC West Park Gets Office, Lab Complex," *Pittsburgh Post-Gazette*, October 24, 1979. According to L.R. Love, an executive at energy and environmental consulting firm National Utility Service (NUS), one of the site's first tenants, the "RIDC West Park site helps combine our activities here making them more efficient. . . . Our work involves a lot of air travel [and] we can reach the airport (Greater Pittsburgh) in a few minutes."

108. Sam Spatter, "Small Industries Taking over Steel's Role Here," *Pittsburgh Press*, July 8, 1982. The thirty-nine-acre Vista Industrial Park off the Parkway West in Robinson Township had nine buildings containing more than 400,000 square feet of space, while construction of a fifteenth building in the adjacent Parkway West Industrial Park provided a total of about 540,000 square feet of industrial space.

109. "Hi-Tech Sites Give Realtors a Boost in Industrial Sales," *Pittsburgh Press*, November 28, 1982.

110. Richardson, Gordon and Associates, Tippetts-Abbett-McCarthy-Stratton, and Allegheny County Board of Commissioners, "Terminal Site Selection Study Greater Pittsburgh Airport" (Pittsburgh: Allegheny County Board of Commissioners, 1967). Tasso Katselas Associates Inc., *Greater Pittsburgh International Airport Expansion Program, New Terminal Complex, Concept Development Phase: Final Report* (Pittsburgh: Tasso Katselas Associates Inc., 1981).

111. Thomas J. Murphy, "Economic Development Activities in Allegheny County," January 14, 1985. Thomas J. Murphy, Papers, 1989–1993, MG 444, Box 3. Pennsylvania State Archives, Harrisburg, PA.

112. City of Pittsburgh et al., "Strategy 21: Pittsburgh/Allegheny Economic Development Strategy to Begin the 21st Century. A Proposal to the Commonwealth of Pennsylvania," June 1985, 1–2. Of the $495 million in state funds requested in the proposal, officials earmarked $173 million for airport expansion.

113. Tom Foerster, Pete Flaherty, and Lawrence W. Dunn, "The Allegheny County Commissioners Welcome You to the Airport of the Future—the New Pittsburgh International Airport," *Beaver County Times (Special Supplement)*, September 13, 1992, 1.

114. Richard Stouffer, "A $500 Million Suburban Mix," *New York Times*, October 16, 1988.

115. I am in debt to Scott Becker, executive director of the Pennsylvania Trolley Museum for information on rail travel times in the region. The city of Washington is the county seat of Washington County.

116. Chriss Swaney, "Mixed Uses on a Farm Site," *New York Times*, February 7, 1993.

117. Pennsylvania Turnpike Commission, "Beaver Valley Expressway: An Overview of Toll 60: The James E. Ross Highway," September 1991, Casey Papers, unprocessed materials, ACCN #3117, Level 2, Slot 2667. Pennsylvania State Archives, Harrisburg, Pa.

118. Jeffrey Kitsko, "Toll Road 60: Beaver Valley Expressway," www.pahighways.com/toll/PATurnpike60.html (accessed May 7, 2010).

119. Debra Utterback, "Outlook Optimistic, Colafella Says," *Beaver County Times*, February 3, 1986.

120. John Barker, "Beaver County Economic Position a Matter of Outsider Perception," *Beaver County Times*, October 14, 1988.

121. Dufour Interview.

122. On urban and economic redevelopment efforts in Pittsburgh and the Upper Ohio Valley, see Allen Dieterich-Ward, "Mines, Mills and Malls: Regional Development in the Steel Valley" (Ph.D. diss., University of Michigan, 2006).

123. A number of newspaper articles appeared during the late 1990s and early 2000s "revealing" the proximity of the Upper Ohio Valley, and especially Steubenville, to Pittsburgh. See, for example, Stephanie Alarcon, "Smiles of a Summer Night; Who Says There's Nothing to Do in Pittsburgh Late at Night? If You Keep Your Eyes Open, There's Plenty," *Pittsburgh Post-Gazette*, August 6, 1996, D-1; Catherine Rizzo,

"Steubenville's Road to Prosperity May Be Route 22." *The Associated Press State & Local Wire*, February 17, 1999; "Charity Comes Every Thursday on Market Square," *Pittsburgh Post-Gazette*, November 22, 2001, B1; Suzanne Elliott, "Outlet Heaven? Developer Banking on Retail Concept to Revitalize Wheeling." *Pittsburgh Business Times*, November 4, 2002; John McCabe, "Officials Seek to 'Dove-Tail' Businesses from Pittsburgh," *Wheeling Intelligencer*, July 30, 1998.

124. "If Pittsburgh Site Doesn't Work, Steubenville Ready for Heinz," *The Associated Press State & Local Wire*, July 30, 1999. On Steubenville's efforts to attract investment based on its proximity to Pittsburgh, see Dan Fitzpatrick, "Alliance 2000 to Heinz: You've Got a Friend in Ohio," *Pittsburgh Post-Gazette*, July 30, 1999, B-1; "On the Map, Watch Out, Pittsburgh. Steubenville, Ohio, Is on the Move," *Pittsburgh Business Times*, May 28, 1999; Brendan Sager, "Steubenville's Alliance 2000 Targets Pittsburgh," *Pittsburgh Post Gazette*, November 20, 1998, D-8; Patty Tascarella, "Steubenville, Ohio, Casts Itself as New, Cheap Pittsburgh Suburb, Effort Has Attracted Local Executives as Pitchmen," *Pittsburgh Business Times*, May 21, 1999.

125. Jack Lyne, 600-Worker Wal-Mart Center Could Hold Steubenville, Ohio's Entire CBD (Conway Delta, 2001), www.siteselection.com/ssinsider/bbdeal/bd011008.htm (accessed May 7, 2010); Teresa F. Lindeman, "Wal-Mart Distribution Center in Wintersville, Ohio, Covers a Lot of Ground," *Pittsburgh Post-Gazette*, July 16, 2003; George Hohmann, "What's Next for Wheeling?" Charleston Daily Mail, July 15, 2003; "Cabela's Planning to Build Mega-Store in East Rutherford, New Jersey," News Release (October 5, 2004), www.cabelas.com/retail-2/--cabelas--en--content--community--aboutus--retail--retail_stores--eastrutherford--erutherford_press.html.shtml (accessed May 17, 2010).

126. Mike Lafferty, "10-Month Job Action Is Costly; Steel Strike's Legacy: Lost Homes, Hopes," *Columbus Dispatch*, August 14, 1997, 1A.

127. "Heal(Th) of Airport Corridor Property Reflected in Big 50 Hotels Ranking," *Pittsburgh Business Times*, August 18, 2000; "Still Waiting for Takeoff: Why Has Development on County-Owned Land Surrounding Pittsburgh International Airport Been So Slow?" *Pittsburgh Post-Gazette*, August 27, 2000. In 1999, only Moon Township, out of all Airport Corridor communities, placed in the top ten in the region for the number of building permits issued for housing construction.

128. Suzanne Elliott, "Airport Area Balancing Boom, Bust, Home Builders Lag Commercial Developers," *Pittsburgh Business Times*, May 19, 2000.

129. U.S. Census Bureau and IUCPSR, *County and City Data Book*.

130. Dufour Interview.

131. "Coal and Steel Town Sees Rebirth"; Fitzpatrick, "Alliance 2000 to Heinz"

132. Spencer Hunt, "Blue Smoke, Tainted Water: Seeing Green in Brownfields," *Columbus Dispatch*, December 6, 2005. Brownfields development is a complex and still-evolving process in the Upper Ohio Valley and the rest of the Steel Valley. For an overview of recent issues, see Paul Giannamore, "Brownfields Funding to Be Used in Jefferson County," *Wheeling News-Register* (Online Edition), Dec. 4, 2009.

133. Dufour Interview.

134. Little new construction actually took place within Steubenville, for example, as employers instead flocked to an expansive hilltop industrial park just off Route 22. Similarly, over the last decade Wheeling has lost many of its remaining downtown businesses to The Highlands, a new hilltop mixed-use development centered on the mammoth Cabela's site.

135. Paul Giannamore, "Progress Alliance Exec Establishes Ground Rules of Future," *Steubenville Herald-Star*, July 23, 2006, D1.

136. William Chesson, "Making the Case for Steubenville," *Pittsburgh Business Times*, December 28, 2001.

∼

CHAPTER FOUR

Creating an "Image Center"

Reimagining Omaha's Downtown and Riverfront, 1986–2003

Janet R. Daly Bednarek

In July 2001, the city of Omaha officially dedicated a new city park. The twenty-three-acre riverfront site was formerly the home of the Asarco lead refinery, an enterprise with roots in the 1870s and a symbol of Omaha's early industrial development. Initially, the city council approved the name "Union Labor Plaza." However, after an election in May 2001, which witnessed the ousting of the incumbent mayor and five city council members, the new mayor and council decided to review the earlier choice. After asking for public input, the council decided on "Lewis and Clark Landing."[1] In many ways the new name was perhaps more fitting given the decided transformation of Omaha's downtown and riverfront involving not only the new park, but a host of other developments from the ConAgra headquarters project in the late 1980s to a burst of large-scale corporate, civic, and residential projects in the late 1990s and early 2000s. Omaha's leaders had first promoted "back to the river" ideas in the late 1960s and early 1970s. By the early twenty-first century, those ideas witnessed a full flowering.

Omaha's return to the river, though, involved not just massive physical transformation, but an extensive reconceptualization of the downtown and riverfront. Omaha's historic downtown riverfront had been home to commerce, transportation and industry. Omaha's new downtown riverfront was home to open space, recreation, leisure and cultural amenities. "Union Labor Plaza" would evoke the historic, somewhat gritty downtown riverfront. "Lewis and Clark Landing," on the other hand, harkened back to a past that pre-dated Omaha itself by a half-century and evoked more pristine images of frontier, wilderness and adventure. Though the plaza eventually held a statue dedicated to Omaha's working people, the choice of name to a certain extent suggested the degree to which Omaha's civic leadership had reconceptualized and transformed the downtown and riverfront to serve as a new "image center" for the city.

Though certainly no longer functioning as *the* center of America's urban areas, downtowns still command a great deal of the attention, energy, and imagination of those concerned with the future of America's cities. Downtown history has also proved of interest to urban historians. The last decade in particular has witnessed the publication of two major works on the history of this crucial urban area. Robert M. Fogelson's work is essentially a political history of the downtown, focused, as he said, on power—who held it, how they exercised it, and how that shaped downtowns from the 1880s to the 1950s.[2] Alison Isenberg, on the other hand, has produced a social and cultural history of the nation's downtowns, taking the story into the 1960s.[3]

Both works ended in the first decades following World War II. By that time, both argued, downtowns had ceased to serve their traditional function as the central place within cities and were being redefined and rebuilt—with varying degrees of success[4]—for a new role or roles in the future. Carl Abbott focused on the issue of the redefinition of downtowns. He noted that since World War II and through the 1980s the very idea of the downtown had changed multiple times and, as a result, planning strategies for the area had changed as well. He identified five different conceptualizations of the downtown and the planning strategies associated with them. From 1945 until 1955, downtown was still regarded as the "unitary" center of the city. The planning strategies employed—mostly involving transportation—aimed at preserving the downtown in that role. By 1955, however, there was a growing realization that downtown no longer functioned as the retail center. To make the downtown accessible and inviting to shoppers once more, planners emphasized urban clearance to, among other goals, clean up "blighted" downtown areas and provide parking. The next major shift came in the mid-1960s as planners began to think of downtown not as a unitary center, but as a "federation of sub-districts," a conceptualization of downtowns that remains to the present. During this period, planners placed emphasis on the variety of experiences provided by downtowns and pushed for conservation, the preservation of historic structures, and efforts to make the downtown a pedestrian-friendly environment. By the mid-1970s, though still interested in the pedestrian, emphasis shifted to issues of design and the provision of cultural facilities, open space and other "urban" amenities. Since the mid-

1980s, however, focus has shifted from the pedestrian to plans that serve the needs of headquarters personnel and other office workers. By that time, downtown had been redefined once more, this time as the "command post" of not just the urban economy, but the emerging global economy.[5]

Robert Fogelson emphasized in his work that the "downtown of the past is gone—and gone for good."[6] Perhaps the most striking evidence of that in Omaha was the fact that as its leaders sought to revitalize the downtown and its riverfront, they actually created something new. The traditional center of downtown was 16th Street. In many ways the new center of the new downtown is 10th Street. Omaha's "new downtown," in going "back to the river" has involved, therefore, a shift in the center of gravity from 16th to 10th Street. Furthermore, as suggested, the downtown's riverfront has been completely reconceptualized. As with most cities in the United States, Omaha began on the river. The riverfront hosted docks, manufacturing, and transportation uses. The river itself served as both a means of transportation and as a convenient sewer.[7] In reclaiming the riverfront, Omaha's civic leadership reconceived and rebuilt it as a center of open space, recreation, leisure, and suburban-like office parks. And what had been the oldest part of the downtown is now the newest, with a new function as "image center" for the city.[8]

Omaha's civic leadership, public and private, has repeatedly addressed the issues that have faced downtown Omaha. To a certain extent since the late 1950s and certainly since the 1960s, various plans were developed to first preserve the central place of downtown and later to re-imagine the downtown as one of many centers in the city.[9] The latest period in downtown planning, that since the late 1980s and continuing into the early twenty-first century, witnessed a significant physical transformation of much of the downtown and riverfront area.[10] Though Carl Abbott suggested a certain level of discontinuity between planning strategies shaping downtowns from 1975 to 1985 and those since 1985, the planning for downtown in Omaha would suggest a certain level of continuity between the two periods. While much of the physical transformation of downtown involved the construction of new corporate headquarters and other office structures, those projects developed within a planning framework that also anticipated the further realization of plans from the 1970s to "return to the river" and provide downtown with open space and recreational amenities, as well as cultural facilities.[11]

This article will trace the major components involved in the transformation of downtown Omaha and its riverfront from the late 1980s through about 2003. First, by all accounts, the key event initiating the actions resulting in the rebuilding began with the 1986 announcement that Enron was moving its corporate headquarters from Omaha to Houston. In many ways, the Enron decision and its aftermath provided the context and momentum for a number of related actions and events—the announcement that ConAgra would build its new headquarters in downtown Omaha, passage of tax reform at the state level, and the successful negotiations by public and private entities that resulted in the clearance of a large historic district near downtown's riverfront, Jobbers Canyon. The late 1980s and early 1990s then witnessed a private sector effort to complete the "back to the river" plans first developed in the 1970s, but largely unfulfilled, as well as city initiatives including development of a new master plan and the designation of the entire downtown as blighted. The pivotal events in the reconstruction of the riverfront, however, came between 1995 and 2003— the mayoral terms of Hal Daub, the decisions of other Omaha companies to headquarter downtown, and the successful efforts to bring new corporate facilities to the downtown, clean-up the riverfront all along the downtown and north to the airport, and build new cultural/recreational facilities in downtown, including a new arena/convention center, a new performing arts center, and riverside parks and trails. The article will end with an examination of the degree to which Omaha's downtown and riverfront have been rebuilt, transformed and reconceptualized to serve as an "image center" for the city and to what extent 10th Street has supplanted 16th Street as the main street of the downtown.

Enron Leaves

In 1985 Omaha-based InterNorth (formerly Northern Natural Gas—a natural gas pipeline company) merged with Houston Natural Gas. Within a year, the new company renamed itself Enron. At the time of the merger, InterNorth was by far the larger of the two companies. However, by the 1986 name change, a number of key individuals with Omaha ties had retired from the board, replaced by Houston-based people. In addition, though executives from InterNorth had originally headed the new company, following their departure, the former head of Houston Natural Gas, Kenneth Lay, assumed the role of chairman and chief executive officer. By the time of its annual meeting in May 1986, rumors abounded that Enron would move its headquarters from Omaha to Houston. Though Lay had announced after the meeting that Enron had "no plans now," he added that the company would have to "evaluate everything."[12]

The bad news came barely a month later. On May 12, 1986, Enron announced it would move its headquarters out of its virtually new building on the eastern edge of downtown Omaha to Houston, Texas. Although the announcement focused just on the 200 people directly involved with the headquarters move, it soon became clear that many more jobs would be lost over the following year. Instead of 200 jobs, estimates were that Enron would cut up to 1,000 jobs in Omaha, which, at the time of the announcement, had approximately 1,900 Enron employees.[13]

Though many local civic and governmental leaders attempted to put the best "spin" possible on the news—declaring that the move was more about the nature of the natural gas industry than anything about Omaha—nonetheless many began to criticize the business climate, especially the tax structure, in the city and the state. And over the following months public declarations varied between minimizing the impact of the loss of jobs and calling for action, primarily tax reform, economic diversification, and better local leadership.[14] Meanwhile, the Enron presence in the city continued to diminish. By May 1988, the local newspaper reported that most of the 400 remaining Enron employees in Omaha would be let go or offered transfers to Houston.[15] Meanwhile in the wake of the Enron departure, civic leaders, determined not to have history repeat itself, responded to another corporate headquarters decision-making process with a series of actions that would mark the beginning of a new phase in the development and transformation of downtown Omaha.

ConAgra Stays, LB 775 Passes, Jobbers Canyon Falls

Barely six months after Enron decided to move to Houston, another Omaha-based company, with its headquarters in downtown, ConAgra, a packaged food company in the Fortune 500, announced plans that included the construction of a new food products laboratory (in Omaha or perhaps elsewhere) and the possibility of a move of its headquarters to another city. In contrast to Enron, a little over a year later, ConAgra unveiled plans for a new downtown Omaha riverfront corporate complex.[16] Between the two announcements, several key pieces had to be put in place to bring about the desired result. First was the passage of new tax legislation at the state level, LB775. Second, city leaders—public and private—had to come together to acquire the riverfront site indentified as the best location for the proposed complex. Adding to the complexity of that task, the preferred site was a nineteenth century warehouse district called Jobbers Canyon, listed on the National Register of Historic Places. Both pieces were put in place in large part through the concerted effort of civic leaders, local and state, determined to keep ConAgra—and other important companies—from leaving Omaha and Nebraska. The ConAgra complex, even before its completion, sparked great optimism and new enthusiasm for downtown redevelopment.

When ConAgra announced plans for its new laboratory and possible headquarters move, its chairman, Charles M. "Mike" Harper, bluntly told state officials that they needed to restructure the tax system or his company would leave.[17] The entire restructuring package that the state then proposed included four pieces of legislation. By far the most controversial was LB775, the Employment and Investment Growth Act. LB775 gave "a company a tax credit worth 5 percent of the additional payroll it creates if it adds at least thirty new jobs and invests at least $3 million." Additionally, a company could receive "tax credit equal to 10 percent of a capital investment of at least $20 million."[18]

LB775 faced strong opposition in the Nebraska legislature. Many there argued that the proposed law was specifically designed for ConAgra and that the state was being pressured by the company's threatened actions. In the end, the bill survived attempts at unfriendly amendments and even a filibuster by Omaha state senator Ernie Chambers. The bill finally passed by a vote of 37–11 in late May 1987. As Governor Kay Orr announced she would sign the bill, Mike Harper announced ConAgra would stay in Omaha and build its new food product laboratory in the city.[19]

Equally controversial was the proposed site for the new ConAgra complex, Jobbers Canyon. In 1986, the Nebraska State Historic Preservation Board recommended a number of properties for inclusion on the National Register of Historic Places, including the city's Jobbers Canyon Historic District, a collection of nineteenth-century warehouses on Omaha's waterfront, east of 10th Street. Only a year after this successful nomination, city officials and representatives from the Chamber of Commerce were working with ConAgra to identify a downtown riverfront site for its proposed complex. Eventually, the company decided on Jobbers Canyon. For the ConAgra project to go forward, Jobbers Canyon had to go.[20]

By late 1987, the Omaha Development Foundation, the development arm of the Omaha Chamber of Commerce, had begun negotiations with property owners in Jobbers Canyon. Though property owners were receptive, strong opposition to the purchase and demolition of the warehouses came from Omaha's historic preservation community. Throughout the lengthy process of purchase and clearance, historic preservationists waged a determined, but ultimately futile, effort to prevent the demolition.[21] Late on the date set by ConAgra for final resolution of the Jobbers Canyon land deal, January 4, 1988, the Omaha Development Foundation announced it had reached an agreement to purchase all the Jobbers Canyon properties. On January 5, 1988, ConAgra formally announced its plans for the site.[22]

ConAgra's decision to build its new corporate complex on Omaha's downtown riverfront was immediately hailed as a "new chapter" for downtown Omaha. The project, according to local sources, potentially could spark up to $175 million in private construction spending. Indeed, following the ConAgra announcement, the Union Pacific Railroad announced it would renovate its freight house, located adjacent to the ConAgra site, into a state-of-the-art dispatch center. The mayor and chamber officials all predicted tremendous gains for the area as a result of the ConAgra decision. The final details between the city, county, and ConAgra were worked out by March 1988 and included a commitment by the county to build a thirty-acre park with a fifteen-acre lake, named Heartland of America Park, just north of the ConAgra property, along the Missouri River.[23]

Refocusing on Downtown and the Riverfront: City Plans and Private Plans, 1988–1995

ConAgra's decision to locate its new complex along Omaha's riverfront prompted a new round of planning—public and private—for downtown Omaha. Much of it harkened back to the ideas from the 1970s that had envisioned a revitalized downtown, reconnected with the river. The centerpiece of the 1970s era return-to-the-river planning was the Central Park (now Gene Leahy) Mall, a block-wide green space carved out of the downtown from 15th Street to near the river (8th Street), between Farnam and Douglas Streets.[24] Construction began in 1975 and the city officially took possession in 1982. Though construction ended, the mall was not yet complete. The last two blocks, between 10th and 8th Streets, remained unfinished for another thirteen years [25]

City officials had hoped that the Central Park Mall would serve as a catalyst for downtown redevelopment. And there were some notable construction projects along or very near the mall—the W. Dale Clark Public Library, the Peter Kiewit Conference Center-State Office Building, the Central Park Plaza (which housed ConAgra's headquarters until the move to the new riverfront complex), and the Northwestern Bell (now World-Herald/ Qwest) building.[26] There were also notable failures, including an attempt to rekindle retail activity along 16th Street—the historic retail "heart" of downtown. The Omaha Development Foundation spearheaded the effort to build a small retail complex just one block west of the Central Park Mall (on the west side of the Central Park Plaza) and the city redesigned 16th Street as a pedestrian-friendly mall with fewer lanes of traffic and attractive transit stops. The heated bus shelters, however, acquired the reputation not for commuter comfort but as gathering places for the homeless. Youth "gangs" congregated at and near the small ParkFair Mall, adding to the negative image of the area. As of 2008, the bus shelters were still in place, but the Park FairMall has been transformed into indoor parking for tenants of the Central Park Plaza. Very little retail activity remains along 16th Street.[27]

Following the ConAgra decision, both city and private developers seized upon the enthusiasm generated by the project to begin to draw up new plans that each hoped would finally result in the dynamic revitalization of the downtown promised, but never fully realized, in the 1970s plans. First, to speed redevelopment projects—and potentially the ConAgra project in particular should private negotiations with property owners fail—the city council in late December 1987 declared the entire downtown area as blighted. Under Nebraska law, the designation paved the way for the city to create redevelopment plans, to use the power of condemnation, and allow tax-increment financing.[28] The city could also create special redevelopment districts within the blighted areas. That action allowed land assembled by the city through purchase or condemnation to be turned over to private developers as long as the project was identified as having a public benefit.[29] Although the city did not need to use its powers of condemnation for the ConAgra project, the ability to create special redevelopment districts proved very important later.[30]

Then in 1988, the city planning department, city council, and the office of the mayor began work on a new city development plan, approved in June 1990. The development plan, though designed for the entire city, included language defining the downtown and policies directed specifically at the area. First, the plan declared that downtown Omaha was "a special place for Omaha" and called for "its comprehensive revitalization." It pointed out that the downtown was "geographically remote from newly developing parts of Omaha" but a healthy downtown was "especially important to all parts of the city." It emphasized the "unique built environment" and the fact that it was still "a critical part of the city's view of itself" as well as "the city's single biggest concentrated employment center" and "the center of Omaha's civic and cultural life."[31]

As the city developed its own plans, a group of local civic and corporate leaders (in fact among the most prominent and powerful) proposed its own set of ideas, eventually labeled "Gateway" and focused on the riverfront north of the ConAgra complex. The Gateway project centered on a proposal to transform the Union Pacific repair shops/yard on the northern edge of downtown into a $150 million (later $500 million) 235-acre development with office buildings, apartments, condominiums, a marina, hotel, botanical center, and parkland. Full realization of the plan depended upon not only the cooperation of the Union Pacific Railroad, which backed the plan, but also the relocation of a number of industrial operations along the river including a lead refinery, a scrap metal yard, and a barge terminal. The need to relocate those activities prompted strong and determined opposition from some of the companies involved. Though the Union Pacific pledged to donate land and several city and county officials pledged support, the Gateway plan remained on the drawing board as long as the private interests behind it struggled to deal with the companies determined not to make way.[32]

The Pieces Come Together: The Transformation of Downtown Omaha, 1995–2003

Though ideas and plans for downtown and the riverfront appeared periodically between 1988 and the early 1990s, most projects remained on the drawing board until the mid-1990s. Between 1995 and 2001, during the mayoral terms of Hal Daub, a new city plan involving the downtown was approved and a number of major projects were started or announced that together formed the foundation for the physical transformation of much of the eastern downtown area. Three companies—the Union Pacific Railroad, the First National Bank, and the Omaha World-Herald—all announced major construction projects. Another company—the Gallup Organization—announced it would move its headquarters to Omaha. The National Park Service decided to build a new regional headquarters building. And Omaha's voters approved a bond issue to build a new arena/convention center. Few of these would have been possible absent a dynamic public-private partnership between city leaders, especially Daub, along with state and federal officials and local civic leaders.[33] And in many ways the key action taken by this partnership involved the clearance of the riverfront area, a process that involved the demolition of the Union Pacific yards, the removal of a lead refinery and a scrap metal operation, and the relocation of the municipal river port. All this was in place by 2001.

By far the easiest piece of the riverfront puzzle was the Union Pacific's shuttered repair shops and rail yards. The Union Pacific had supported the private Gateway project in the early 1990s and even offered to donate land. As that effort languished, the Union Pacific made plans to prepare its 235-acre property for redevelopment. The original Gateway project had envisioned the refurbishing and reuse of some of the buildings, However, by 1995, the Union Pacific had decided to demolish the structures and clear the area in order to prepare it for redevelopment. At that time, though, the railroad had no buyers for the property.[34] Another piece fell in place in 2001 when the city developed a plan to move the municipal port to a location north of the airport.[35] Far more difficult were the negotiations involving Asarco and Aaron Ferer & Sons.

Asarco Inc. owned and operated a lead refinery along the riverfront at 500 Douglas Street, near the northeastern boundary of the Central Park Mall and Heartland Park. The company had been under pressure to clean up its operations, particularly the release of lead into the atmosphere, for a number of years. In 1989 the company spent $6.7 million to install a new facility to improve the recovery of precious metals during the refining process and to reduce lead emissions. Immediately following the opening of the new facility, lead levels measured in the downtown area dropped, but in 1990 the U.S. Environmental Protection Agency reported that lead levels in the downtown area again exceeded federal standards. The blame was placed not on Asarco, but on demolition work around an old battery plant.[36] Nonetheless, the continued high lead levels resulted in renewed efforts by state and federal environmental agencies to reduce lead emissions.

The Nebraska Council of Environmental Quality issued a July 6, 1993 deadline for the company to cut lead emissions. As that deadline approached, the company requested a six-month extension. It argued that without the extension, it would have to close its Omaha operations, which had 220 employees. Following a series of negotiations, the company agreed to spend $25.8 million on plant improvements and $1.9 million per year on operations to bring lead emissions down to healthy limits. The state then extended the deadline to January 6, 1997.[37] Just as it seemed the company had put its environmental problems behind it, in March 1994 two residents of Bellevue, Nebraska, a community just south of Omaha on the Missouri River, filed suit against Asarco. Their concern was not air pollution, but water pollution. This action came one day after the company filed suit against the Nebraska Council of Environmental Quality, arguing that it had a valid permit to discharge wastes into the river. The following month the U.S. Environmental Protection Agency filed suit to halt discharges into the river.[38] As the various suits made their way through the court system, a number of Omaha and Nebraska politicians began negotiations with the company. Their aim was to convince the company to move rather than improve.

About a year after the first lawsuits were filed, Senator Bob Kerrey (D-NE) confirmed in March 1995 that he was leading negotiations between Asarco and other local officials including Governor Ben Nelson (D) and newly elected Mayor Hal Daub.[39] Kerrey was interested in the creation of a park that would stretch along the Missouri River from the Heartland of America Park north along the river to near the airport. This park would be part of a larger complex of riverfront trails envisioned to stretch from the city of Tekamah to just south of Bellevue. The creation of such a riverfront park, it was suggested, would aid in the commercial development of the Union Pacific property. Kerrey strongly suggested that Asarco could spend the money it planned to use to meet environmental standards at its current location to instead fund a move to a new location.[40]

As determined negotiations with Asarco proceeded, in June 1995, Mayor Hal Daub announced his own vision for the downtown riverfront. Looking more to the major projects that might be inspired should a riverfront park be realized than to the scenic trails system emphasized by Kerrey, Daub spoke of a downtown riverfront that would include "a 35,000-seat domed stadium, a 250,000-square-foot convention center, two major hotels, apartments, restaurants, shops and a monorail." He estimated the price tag at "$600 million to $1 billion." He also estimated that the project could take seven years to complete—three years to plan and four years to build. He admitted that the plan was ambitious, responding: "But if you don't stick your neck out, you're never going to make any progress. . . . There are risks involved in this . . . It will take persistence, determination and a commitment to cooperate instead of figuring out some little nit-picky thing that they want to hang up on and become a naysayer."[41] An examination of the plan in the local newspaper, the *Omaha World-Herald,* the following month noted the similarities (in spirit especially as well as in a few details) between Daub's vision and the Gateway plan of the early 1990s as well as with the riverfront plans developed in the early 1970s.

Before any of those visions could be realized, however, local, state, and federal officials needed to work out a plan to move Asarco from its riverfront location. Negotiations continued through 1995 and into 1996. Finally, following a settlement of the federal lawsuit concerning discharge into the river, the city and Asarco announced an agreement. Though the company suggested that it might build a new plant somewhere near the city, the agreement announced in April 1996 did not specify when or where. Instead, it simply stated that the company would close the refinery, demolish its buildings, and perform an environmental clean-up so that by the end of 1998 the city would be presented with a twenty-three-acre grassy area that could be developed as a park. However, negotiations over some details of the plan, especially concerning clean-up and future liability, continued through 1998.

The company came to final agreement with the state in September 1997; the city and the company signed a final deal on June 10, 1998. Operations of the refinery ended in July 1997 and demolition began in August 1998. The company turned the property, now known as Lewis and Clark Landing, over to the city in 2000.[42]

The final piece fell into place in 2001. Aaron Ferer & Sons, a scrap metal business had resisted plans to force it to move since the early 1990s and the initial announcement of the Gateway plan. In September 1996, Mayor Daub indicated that talks were underway with the company.[43] Following the Asarco deal and the clean-up of the Union Pacific property, the momentum behind the riverfront idea put additional pressure on Aaron Ferer & Sons. In early June 1998, company officials still voiced strong opposition to any plan to relocate the firm. Later that same month, Matthew Ferer, company president, gave an interview to the Omaha World-Herald in which he emphasized the value of the recycling done by the company. He also noted that the city had approached the company about riverfront plans as early as 1995, but then nothing happened. In the meantime, the company purchased a new $2 million machine to shred metal into "pieces that steel foundries or other customers can throw into their furnaces." A move, he argued, would cause "irreparable harm." When asked if his statements meant that any attempt by the city to move the company would cost a considerable sum of money, Ferer responded, "Oh, yes."[44] Eventually, though, in March 2001 a deal was struck following the news that the Gallup Organization wanted to move its headquarters to Omaha and build a new complex along the riverfront (see below). The Greater Omaha Chamber of Commerce spearheaded a private fundraising effort to purchase the property. The company received $6 million for the land and $8 million to cover relocation costs. With the city's agreement to clean up the refinery property, as well as the former municipal port area, the entire riverfront area was available for redevelopment.[45]

The projects constructed in the eastern part of the downtown and along the waterfront reflected ideas expressed by the mayor and in a city planning document produced in 1995. That document was a follow-up to the city's development plan approved in 1990. Following the approval of that plan, Mayor P. J. Morgan appointed a fifty-member citizen task force to work with the city planning department to develop a new city master plan. The committee first met in July 1991 and completed its work in 1995. The new master plan included a number of sections or reports including a "concept element" and one on "land use." The "concept element" of the master plan contained a vision statement: "Omaha must be a community committed to promoting and maintaining a high quality of life for all of its people." To realize that vision, the document included a number of goals, two of which were extremely important for the downtown. The first goal declared that the city must "manage the growth of the city." To achieve that goal, the document asserted that the city must "be pro-active rather than reactive regarding development." The second goal said that the city must "develop and maintain a positive city image." To achieve that goal, the document called for the city to take action to "strengthen the CBD [Central Business District] as the City's 'image center.'"[46] Over the next several years, city leaders took both goals very much to heart.

Another section of the plan, the "land use element," further articulated the idea of the downtown as the "image center" of the city declaring:

> Omaha's downtown will be the clear and positive "image center" for the City. The Downtown/Riverfront area should contain a wide variety of activities and facilities, but should focus on being the location for major governmental offices, major corporate offices, major culture/entertainment facilities, major public open spaces and attractions, major convention/hotel facilities, educational facilities, and specialty retail and residential facilities.[47]

In addition to more fully defining the idea of the downtown as the "image center," this part of the plan also included a number of other important ideas. First, it clearly linked the downtown and the riverfront as a focus of land use planning. Second, it articulated a desire to bring certain specific land uses to the downtown and riverfront, stating: "Public funds must not be used to construct . . . facilities outside of the Downtown unless it has been determined that the proposed facility does not fit within the overall plans for Downtown and it is clear the development of the amenity elsewhere would not detract from the effort to establish the Downtown/Riverfront area as the City's 'image center.'"[48] In many ways, whether in response to this new city plan or due to other factors, the projects constructed within the downtown and on the riverfront reflected the vision and goals of the new city master plan.

As noted, three important components of the ultimate redevelopment of the downtown and riverfront involved the decisions by three locally headquartered companies to build new facilities in the eastern half of the downtown. Following a major corporate merger that sparked rumors of its imminent departure, the Union Pacific Railroad, long headquartered in the city, announced in 1997 that it would remain in the city. While that cheered local leaders, in some ways even better news came two years later.[49] The Union Pacific Corporation, a holding company formed in 1969 and, from that point on, the parent company of the Union Pacific Railroad, initially established its headquarters in New York City. In 1987, the Union Pacific Corporation moved to Bethlehem, Pennsylvania and then in 1997, to Dallas, Texas. However, that same year the corporation moved its chief financial officer and those reporting to him to Omaha, leaving only nineteen headquarters employees in Dallas. Finally, in April 1999, the Union Pacific Corporation announced plans to move its headquarters to Omaha. Though few jobs came with the move, the relocation put the headquarters of another Fortune 500 company (the others at the time being ConAgra, Berkshire Hathaway, IBP, Inacom, Mutual of Omaha, and Peter Kiewit Sons Inc.) in Omaha.[50]

Almost immediately speculation on a new headquarters building began. Behind the scenes the city and the Chamber of Commerce held negotiations with the company. Attention focused on the city block between 14th and 15th Streets, Douglas and Dodge Streets. The city—having created within the "blighted downtown" a special redevelopment district (see below)— agreed to handle the acquisition of the site and to purchase the company's old headquarters building. The agreement between the city and the Union Pacific Corporation was finalized with a city council vote in April 2001. The company unveiled the plans for the new building the following June. The new headquarters building opened three years later in June 2004.[51]

The same special redevelopment area containing the new headquarters of the Union Pacific Corporation also included building projects by First National Bank and The World-Herald Corporation. In October 23, 1996, city leaders unveiled an extensive downtown redevelopment plan that included the creation of a Downtown Northeast Redevelopment Area, a thirty-two-block area bounded by Douglas Street to the south, Interstate 480 to the north, 8th Street to the east and 17th Street to the west. Only twenty-three of the thirty-two blocks, though, would be targeted for redevelopment. The creation of the redevelopment area allowed for government assistance to the companies for the projects including the use of tax-increment financing, the issuance of redevelopment bonds, and the use of eminent domain to acquire properties. The city also agreed to build a number of new parking garages. Just over a year after the completion of the new city master plan committee's work and the call for transforming the downtown into the "image center" of the city, the planning board approved the downtown redevelopment project in November 1996.[52]

In response, First National Bank first announced a plan to construct a new data operations center at 16th and Capitol. That project was scheduled to begin in 1997 and be completed by 1998. Additionally, the bank announced plans for a new headquarters building. The bank stated that initially it had considered building its new headquarters on land it owned in the western part of the city. However, the aid from the city, plus the symbolic advantages of locating in the center city, caused it to reconsider. The bank unveiled the final plans for its headquarters building in September 1998. The bank's new headquarters would soar to forty stories (638 feet) above street level, making it the tallest building in the city. As designed, the First National Center was estimated to cost $200 million (actual cost: $208 million), and included a privately owned, public-access park with fountains and sculptures on about one quarter of the city block occupied by the building and an indoor, glass-enclosed "winter garden" at the base of the tower. The First National Center, designed to help promote the downtown as the city's "image center," opened in September 2002.[53]

At the same October 1996 press conference announcing the bank's plans, the parent company of the local newspaper, The World-Herald Corporation, declared that when it built its new production facility and if it built a new headquarters building, both would be located downtown. Though president and CEO of The World-Herald, John Gottschalk, stated bluntly that it was not clear that downtown would be the best location and that it might be economically disadvantageous to build there instead of at a vacant suburban location, he went on to say that the company did have a "civic responsibility to keep downtown healthy." In October 1996, Gottschalk further declared that "the company is committed to downtown."[54]

Indeed, the company decided on a downtown location at 14th and Capital Streets for its new $125 million production plant and broke ground on May 1, 1999. The new building opened in 2001. On the other hand, the World-Herald decided not to build a new headquarters building. Instead, in April 2006 it announced that it would buy the Qwest Communications building at 13th and Douglas. Northwestern Bell Telephone built the structure in 1980 and it was one of a group of building projects credited to the construction of the Central Park Mall. Through mergers in the phone business, what had been Northwestern Bell first became part of U.S. West Communications and finally Qwest Communications. When Northwestern Bell occupied the building it had 2,000 employees working in it. In 2006, Qwest had only 700–800. Under the terms of the sale, Qwest would continue to occupy half the building and the World-Herald would occupy the other half.[55]

The Union Pacific, First National Bank, and World-Herald projects all came from companies with long ties to the city. Another important piece of the downtown redevelopment came when the city successfully persuaded the Gallup Organization to move its headquarters to Omaha and to build its new facility on the soon-to-be fully cleared riverfront. The Gallup Organization bluntly told the city that it was looking for both a site and incentives to move to Omaha. In June 2000, Mayor Daub revealed that the city and Gallup had been in negotiations for several months and were ready to come to a final deal. That deal basically was struck by late September 2000 and the site selected was a sixty-acre tract along Abbott Drive (the road between the downtown and the nearby airport). It included land occupied by Aaron Ferer & Sons (still in negotiations with the city) and the Port of Omaha (soon to move). Gallup's planned new complex included a headquarters building and a leadership training center called Gallup University. Final negotiations between the city, the Chamber of Commerce, and Gallup continued into 2001. The big remaining issue involved who would be responsible for the estimated $62 million cost of land acquisition and clearance. The plan was to have everything in place so that Gallup could begin construction Spring 2002. As noted above, the final details with Aaron Ferer & Sons were in place by March 2001 and by April 2001 the last details had been worked out with Gallup and the decision finalized shortly thereafter. The city and county took responsibility for footing the bill for land acquisition and clearance. The full development package also included a donation of land which the county owned within the riverfront redevelopment area for a new headquarters for the National Park Service.[56]

As important as the deal to move Aaron Ferer & Sons was to the final clearance of the riverfront to make way for the Gallup organization's new buildings and the Park Service headquarters, Mayor Daub asserted that Gallup finalized its decision at least in part following voter approval in May 2001 of bonds to build an arena-convention center on the soon-to-be cleared riverfront. That project, resulting in the construction of what is now known as the Qwest Center, was viewed as the most important of all the projects aimed at transforming the downtown/riverfront and the image of Omaha.

The idea of replacing the 1950s-era municipal auditorium with a new arena-convention center had been floating since the 1970s. A certain degree of urgency was injected into the lingering discussion in the late 1980s. Douglas County was proposing to purchase the Ak-Sar-Ben property, a 300-acre site northwest of 63rd and Center Streets.[57] The proposal included a request that the city build a new convention center and arena there. In January 1989 City Council President Fred Conley responded by arguing that any new arena-convention center must be built downtown. Though discussions between the city and the county over the issue continued, the next month the city council voted to support the idea of constructing an arena-convention center downtown, pending the availability of funds.[58] Mayor P. J. Morgan, elected in June 1989, on the other hand, favored and pushed forward a renovation of the existing municipal auditorium rather than incurring the expense of building a new facility anywhere.[59]

The arena-convention center project, thus, remained in the talking phase for another seven years. However, shortly after the announcement of the First National Bank and World-Herald construction projects, the *World-Herald* printed an editorial calling on the mayor to support a new downtown arena-convention center. By early 1997, Mayor Hal Daub, who had announced his expansive vision for riverfront development in June 1995, was ready to fully back the idea. In his State of the City address in January 1997, Daub declared that Omaha needed both a new convention center and a new sports stadium. He believed that such projects, located in the downtown/riverfront, could inspire a number of other possibilities, such as a science center, an outdoor amphitheater, and a new symphony hall. All those facilities were needed, but particularly the convention center and sports stadium to promote economic development. Though initially more local leaders voiced support for the sports stadium than the convention center, attention soon focused on the latter as a Chamber of Commerce study released in May 1997 called for the construction of a $200 million arena-convention center as well as the creation of a special authority to manage the planning and construction of the complex.[60]

Despite strong support voiced by local leaders in specially commissioned report on the arena and convention center idea, the convention center campaign did not begin immediately.[61] Debate still centered on location— downtown, Ak-Sar-Ben, or some other site. By early summer 1998, Mayor Daub vowed to work to get the process moving and pushed again for the downtown site. He also proposed the creation of an authority, the Metropolitan Entertainment & Convention Authority (MECA), to manage the new convention center.[62] By the end of 1998, Daub presented a $300 million development plan for the riverfront to city council that included "a convention center-arena complex, a new 400-room hotel" as well as "a science education center, an expanded marina, condominiums, and a cluster of shops on the banks of the Missouri River."[63] In 1999 Daub won the approval of the city council and the city made plans for a $198 million bond issue to finance the convention center part of the plan. He also renewed his call for the creation of an authority to manage the facility.[64] The civic leadership got behind the effort. In January 2000, the Chamber of Commerce declared that passage of the bond issue would be "their top priority for this year."[65] In a May 2000 election, voters approved the bonds by a margin of 63 percent to 37 percent and the creation of MECA by 60 percent to 40 percent.[66]

As the city prepared to break ground on the new convention center, the momentum that had been building since the mid-1990s for downtown/riverfront development seems to have reached a high point. A number of dramatic, visible changes were already in place—the World-Herald Freedom Center printing facility was open; the First National data center was up and running, and the First National Tower was under construction. Most impressively, the riverfront was cleared awaiting the construction of not just the convention center, but the new Gallup complex and the new headquarters for the National Park Service. Abbott Drive, the route from downtown to the airport, and 10th Street were both scheduled for major improvements, with the latter becoming "the new main route into downtown Omaha." Starting with the arena and other downtown projects, city planners anticipated a wave of development that would "dwarf the last twenty years of downtown redevelopment."[67] By the time the Qwest Center opened in September 2003, the First National Tower was finished, the Union Pacific was building a new headquarters building, and a new $90 performing arts center was under construction. Gallup had begun construction on the riverfront and a number of high-rise condominium projects were either underway or soon to be approved.[68]

Downtown Since 2003: Shifting Center of Gravity and "Image Center"

By 2003, Omaha's downtown and riverfront had undergone a remarkable transformation. For the most part the warehouses, railroad facilities, and industrial plants that had marked the historic downtown and riverfront had been replaced by modern, and often glittering, corporate headquarters, a convention center, hotels, condominium projects, and open space. Up through the 1960s, for most in Omaha, going downtown meant going to the retail core on 16th Street. By the early twenty-first century, going downtown increasingly involved visiting the Qwest Center, Heartland of America Park, Lewis and Clark Landing, the Old Market, or the Western Heritage Museum (the former Union Pacific Station) all on or near 10th street.

In the early 1970s, Omaha's civic leadership dreamed of a "return to the river." Though the Gene Leahy Mall was constructed and several other major projects completed, the expansive vision remained largely unrealized into the early 1990s. With the clearance of the riverfront and the many corporate and civic projects constructed there, Omaha's downtown finally had connected to its long neglected riverfront. Many of the projects reflected the latest trends and ideas in downtown and riverfront revitalization. Critics, however, decried the loss of many historic properties, especially those in Jobbers Canyon.[69] In fact, Omaha's return to the riverfront involved not so much an embrace of an historic area, but an extensive reconceptualization of it. The historic riverfront had been a location of commerce, industry and transportation facilities. The new downtown riverfront—stripped of its warehouse district, industry, and railyards—instead emphasized recreation, leisure, and open spaces. The headquarters for both ConAgra and the Gallup Organization recalled not so much the compact and vertical downtown of the past, but more the horizontal suburban office park.

The revitalization along Omaha's riverfront has also in many ways shifted the center of gravity in the downtown from the traditional retail corridor on 16th Street to the new "front door" on 10th Street.[70] Visitors coming to Omaha via its airport travel into the city center via Abbott Drive and can first enter the downtown at 10th Street. Nearly all of the downtown attractions drawing locals and tourists to the area are located on or near 10th Street and/or east of 16th Street. Most of the new residential developments planned, underway, or just completed are also located in or adjacent to this eastern part of the downtown. And the bold architecture of many of the projects, including the Qwest Center and the recently completed pedestrian bridge across the Missouri River, have been used to give Omaha a new, modern image. When Omaha's civic leadership first developed plans for its downtown in the early 1960s, they focused on maintaining it in its traditional role as the center of the city. In the late twentieth century, the civic leadership—an engaged business community and an energetic mayor[71]—guided a remarkable physical transformation of the area. No longer considered the single center of Omaha, the transformed and reconceptualized downtown and riverfront, emphasizing recreation, leisure and open space, nonetheless now serve as the city's new "image" center.

Notes

1. Lawrence H. Larsen, Barbara J. Cottrell, Harl A. Dalstrom, and Kay Calame Dalstron, *Upstream Metropolis: An Urban Biography of Omaha & Council Bluffs* (Lincoln and London: University of Nebraska Press, 2007), p. 409; Rick Ruggles, "Its Official: Riverfront Park is Lewis and Clark Landing," *Omaha World-Herald*, July 23, 2001, p. 11.

2. Robert M. Fogelson, *Downtown: Its Rise and Fall, 1880-1950* (New Haven: Yale University Press, 2001).

3. Alison Isenberg, *Downtown America: A History of the Place and the People Who Made It* (Chicago: The University of Chicago Press, 2004).

4. For an assessment of both success and failure in rebuilding downtowns from the 1940s through the early 1980s, see Jon C. Teaford, *The Rough Road to Renaissance:*

Urban Revitalization in America, 1940-1985 (Baltimore: The Johns Hopkins University Press, 1990).

5. Carl Abbott, "Five Downtown Strategies: Policy Discourse and Downtown Planning Since 1945," in ed. Martin V. Melosi, *Urban Public Policy: Historical Modes and Methods*, (University Park: The Pennsylvania State University Press, 1993).

6. Fogelson, *Downtown*, p. 6.

7. For a brief discussion of the traditional view of the city's downtown and riverfront and the early steps toward transforming their image, see Janet R. Daly-Bednarek, *Changing Image of the City: Planning for Downtown Omaha, 1945-1973* (Lincoln: The University of Nebraska Press), pp. 73-76.

8. For a discussion of the perceived problems with Omaha's image—or lack thereof—and efforts to address it see Larsen et al., *Upstream Metropolis*, pp. 399-402.

9. For a detailed look at planning for downtown Omaha through the 1970s, see Daly-Bednarek, *The Changing Image of the City*.

10. Omaha is not unique in focusing renewal efforts on its riverfront. For additional examples of recent efforts to use riverfront projects to promote urban revitalization, see Paul Stanton Kibel, ed., *Rivertown: Rethinking Urban Rivers* (Cambridge, MA: The MIT Press, 2007). An early post-war and highly influential example of combined downtown and riverfront redevelopment can be found in Portland, Oregon. For a overview of the riverfront and downtown redevelopment process in Portland see Carl Abbott, *Portland: Planning Politics, and Growth in a Twentieth-Century City* (Lincoln: University of Nebraska Press, 1983), pp. 207–28.

11. For a discussion of the perceived problems with Omaha's image—or lack thereof—and efforts to address it, see Larsen et al., *Upstream Metropolis*, pp. 399–402.

12. Alan Gersten, "'Cost Efficiency is Goal' Enron Chief: No Moving Plans, but Evaluation a Possibility," *Omaha World-Herald*, April 10, 1986, p. 1; "Some Debate Enron Corp. Home Office," *Omaha World-Herald*, April 13, 1986, p. 1.

13. Doug Gollin, "Houston Move Clouds a Sunny Morning," *Omaha World-Herald*, May 12, 1986, p. 1; Robert Dorr and Steve Jordan, "Enron to Keep Gas Division in City, but Move 200 Jobs," *Omaha World-Herald*, May 12, 1986, p. 1.

14. Steve Jordan, "Executives Say Omaha Should Work to Improve Business Climate," *Omaha World-Herald*, May 25, 1986, p. 1; Jeff Gauger, "Enron Job Loss 'Not Serious,'" *Omaha World-Herald*, August 7, 1986, p. 1; Alan Gerstein, "Omaha Must Not Stand Still, Says Commerce Official," *Omaha World-Herald*, September 12, 1986, p. 1; Nick Schinker, "Diversification Is Seen as the Key to Future of Omaha's Job Market," *Omaha World-Herald*, January 4, 1987, p. 1.

15. "Steve Jordan, "Physicians Mutual to Buy New Enron Office Center," *Omaha World-Herald*, December 10, 1986, p. 1; Jim Baker, "Enron Puts Omaha Building on Sale," *Omaha World-Herald*, October 14, 1987, p. 1; Jack Phinney, "Enron Sells East Annex, Scoular Planning $4 Million to Renovate Its New Home," *Omaha World-Herald*, December 23, 1987, p. 1; John Taylor, "Enron Reported Ready to Sever Most Ties Here," *Omaha World-Herald*, March 8, 1988, p. 1.

16. "ConAgra Decision Chronology," *Omaha World Herald*, January 5, 1988, p. 1.

17. Robert Dorr, "Hard-Driving ConAgra Chairman Doesn't Shy Away From Conflict," *Omaha World Herald*, May 31, 1987, p. 1.

18. "Growth Bill Passed, 37–11," *Omaha World-Herald*, May 27, 1987, p. 1. LB 775 was effectively replaced by a "next generation" incentives bill, LB 312 (Nebraska Advantage Act), passed in 2005 and effective January 1, 2006.

19. "Gov. Orr Sees Bigger Picture on ConAgra," *Omaha World-Herald*, May 19, 1987, p.1; "Sen. Schmidt Display Skills in Brining Issue to a Vote," *Omaha World-Herald*, May 21, 1987, p. 1; Gabriella Stern, "Gov. Orr, ConAgra Are Optimistic," *Omaha World-Herald*, May 21, 1987, p. 1; "Growth Bill Passed, 37–11," *Omaha World-Herald*, May 27, 1987, p. 1; "Gabriella Stern, "ConAgra Says It'll Stay as Gov. Orr Sign Bill, Laboratory to Be Built In Metro Area," *Omaha World-Herald*, May 27, 1987, p. 1.

20. "12 Properties Might Join Historic Places," *Omaha World-Herald*, October 9, 1986, p. 1; Kevin Collison, Robert Dorr, and Alan Gersten, "Simon Hopes to Lure Two to Riverfront," *Omaha World-Herald*, August 26, 1987, p. 1.; Robert Dorr, "ConAgra's Plans Praised at Ceremony," *Omaha World-Herald*, August 31, 1988, p. 19; Kevin Collison, "Harper Says Progress Being Made, ConAgra, City Make Waves on Riverfront Site," *Omaha World-Herald*, September 11, 1987, p. 1; Kevin Collison, "Negotiations On For Warehouses In Riverfront Site," *Omaha World-Herald*, September 28, 1987, p. 1.

21. For a sense of the battle over the demolition of Jobbers Canyon, see "Views Conflict on Future of Omaha's Jobbers Canyon," *Omaha World-Herald*, December 6, 1987, p. 1; Kevin Collison, "It Helped Fuel Growth, He Says, Preservationist Defends Jobbers Canyon," *Omaha World-Herald*, December 16, 1987, p. 1; Kevin Collison, "Jobbers Canyon Demolition Work May Start In April," *Omaha World-Herald*, March 16, 1988, p. 1; Nick Schinker, "Shukert Calls Riverfront Plan 'Best Option,'" *Omaha World-Herald*, July 12, 1988; Nick Shinker, "Magistrate to Accept Only part of Paper in Riverfront Dispute," *Omaha World-Herald*, July 12, 1988, p. 12.

22. Kevin Collison, "Toast at 11th Hour Sealed Canyon Deal," *Omaha World-Herald*, January 5, 1988, p. 1; Kevin Collison, "ConAgra Drops Anchor At Omaha's Riverfront, 'New Chapter' Is Predicted for Downtown," *Omaha World-Herald*, January 5, 1988, p. 1.

23. Kevin Collison, "ConAgra Drops Anchor At Omaha's Riverfront, 'New Chapter' Is Predicted for Downtown," *Omaha World-Herald*, January 5, 1988, p. 1; Kevin Collison and Paul Goodsell, "Riverfront Interests More than ConAgra, Park May Lure $175 Million," *Omaha World-Herald*, January 6, 1988, p. 1; Kevin, Collison, "Mayor Simon Predicts Boom in Development," *Omaha World-Herald*, January 8, 1988, p. 1; "Officials Hope for Snowball Effect," *Omaha World-Herald*, January 10, 1988, p. 1; Kevin Collison, "Agreement Sets Blueprint for Riverfront," *Omaha World-Herald*, March 2, 1988, p. 1; Cindy Gonzalez, "County Board Gives Riverfront Go-Ahead," *Omaha World-Herald*, March 15, 1988, p. 1; Kevin Collison, "Council OKs Riverfront Agreement," *Omaha World-Herald*, March 15, 1988, p. 1.

24. For greater detail on the riverfront initiatives of the 1970s and the Central Park mall, see Daly-Bednarek, *The Changing Image of the City*, pp. 208–25.

25. "1954–1979: Growth, The Mall's Evolution," *Omaha World-Herald Magazine*, June 13, 2004, p. 101. Construction of Heartland of America Park in many ways set the stage for the completion of the mall and its connection to the river.

26. Jena Janovy, "Omaha's Doorstep Mall Began Downtown Renaissance That Could Continue on the Riverfront Part of a Vision History of the Mall," *Omaha World Herald*, October 25, 1995, p. 12.

27. For a sense of the "rise and fall" of the ParkFair Mall and retailing on 16th Street, see Steve Jordon, "Park Fair (sic) Likened to Endowment, Retail Mall called 'Vital Step,'" *Omaha World-Herald*, November 14, 1983, p. 1; "ParkFair Merchants See Sunny Outlook," *Omaha World-Herald*, June 23, 1985, p. 1; Mike Reilly, "Morgan to Write of ParkFair Loan," *Omaha World-Herald*, December 8, 1990, p. 1; Deborah Alexander, "16th Street Faces Exodus of Businesses, FedEx Kinko's, Blimpie Are the Latest Retailers to Pull Out of the Downtown Area," *Omaha World-Herald*, December 9, 2004, p. 1D; Deborah Shanahan, "Retail Spot a Parking Lot, Parkfair [sic] Becomes a Garage; Downtown Full of Empty Offices, Chronology of Buildings," *Omaha World-Herald*, March 1, 2005, p. 1D.

28. Tax increment financing is an economic development tool. It allows municipalities to finance improvements (demolition, environmental remediation, utilities and so on) associated with economic development projects within defined tax increment districts based on the projected tax revenue increases produced by the improvements and subsequent development within the district.

29. For information on tax increment financing as related to urban redevelopment, see the webpage of the Nebraska Department of Economic Development-Tax Increment Financing www.neded.org/content/view/100/232 (accessed September 4, 2008).

30. "Omaha Downtown Area Declared Blighted," *Omaha World-Herald*, December 30, 1987, p. 1; Leslie Reed, "'Blight' Label Might be Dropped, Voters on Nov. 7 Will Decide Fate of a Designation that has Often Been Stretched to Promote Development. High-Profile 'Blighted' Sites," *Omaha World-Herald*, October 14, 2006, p. 1A.

31. City of Omaha, "City Development Plan: A Comprehensive Plan for the City of Omaha," P. J. Morgan, Mayor, June 1990, p. 7.

32. Steve Jordon, "Downtown's Riverfront Project Moves Toward Gateway Phase," *Omaha World-Herald*, November 22, 1990, p. 47; Steve Jordon, "Problems Not Conceded as Insurmountable, Gateway Plan Has Obstacles," *Omaha World-Herald*, January 13, 1991, p. 1M; Jim Rasmussen, "Riverfront Plan Backers Urge Big Thinking," *Omaha World-Herald*, January 30, 1991, p. 17; Jim Rasmussen, "U.P. to Offer Land to Build Riverfront Site," *Omaha World-Herald*, March 10, 1991, p. 1B; Jim Rasmussen, "$500 Million River Plan Is Endorsed, Project Would Rise North of Downtown," *Omaha World-Herald*, September 24, 1991, p. 1.

33. While Omaha's civic leadership has generally been quite strong and active over the years, particularly through the Greater Omaha Chamber of Commerce, leadership from city hall has been somewhat less consistent. Between 1973 (the end

of the term of Mayor Eugene Leahy who pushed for the original riverfront development plans) and 2003, Omaha had twelve different mayors—six of whom served as acting or interim mayors for terms ranging from one week to a little over a year. Of the other six, Edward Zorinksy, a very popular major and Leahy's immediate successor, resigned after a little more than three years into his four-year term upon election to the U.S. Senate. Al Veys, after being elected as a write-in candidate, served only one term. His successor, Mike Boyle, was elected to a second term, but removed from office less than three years into that term as the result of a recall election. P. J. Morgan resigned shortly after being elected to a second term in order to accept a job in the private sector. Hal Daub was first elected in a special election to fill Morgan's unexpired term. He was then elected to one full term, but voted out of office in 2001. His successor, Mike Fahey, was elected to a second term in 2005. He did not seek a third term in 2009. Fahey was first mayor in nearly a half-century to serve two full terms in office.

34. Fred Thomas, "'Big Stuff' Comes Down at U.P. Shops," *Omaha World-Herald*, March 22, 1995, p. 13.

35. Chris Burbach, "Omaha's Port Rollin' on the River, A City Plan to be Unveiled Today Would Move the Dock Northwest of Eppley Airfield to Make Way For Redevelopment," *Omaha World-Herald*, July 11, 2001, p. 13.

36. Alan Gersten, "ASARCO has Omaha Plans, $6.7 Million on Tap For Improvements," *Omaha World-Herald*, March 22, 1989, p. 43; Fred Thomas, "Lead Level in Air Rises Downtown; EPA Says Lower It, Clean Air Act's Passage to Bring Nebraska Money," *Omaha World-Herald*, June 29, 1990, p. 13.

37. Fred Thomas, "Asarco Expects to Close Unless Deadline Eased," *Omaha World-Herald*, May 22, 1993, p. 49; Fred Thomas, "Refinery Plans Strategy to Cut Lead Emissions, Parks Director Says Riverfront Will be Safer, ASARCO Lead Output," *Omaha World-Herald*, June 17, 1993, p. 13; Fred Thomas, "State Says Refinery on Track, ASARCO Cleanup Discussed at Hearing," *Omaha World-Herald*, p. 19.

38. Fred Thomas, "Suit Filed Against Asarco; Company Sues State Agency," *Omaha World-Herald*, March 15, 1994, p. 12; Fred Thomas, "EPA Files Suit to Prevent Discharges From Asarco," *Omaha World-Herald*, April 5, 1994, p. 18.

39. Kelley and Nelson were both Democrats. Even though elected mayor on a nonpartisan ballot, Daub was a well-known Republican, having served as a Republican in the U.S. House of Representatives during the 1980s. Daub came to office following a special election in January 1995 to fill term of Mayor P. J. Morgan who resigned as mayor to take a job in the private sector.

40. Fred Thomas, "Riverfront Plan Would Move Asarco, Riverfront Businesses," *Omaha World-Herald*, March 8, 1995, p. 1; Fred Thomas, "Park Viewed as Jewel In Plans for Riverfront, Riverfront Businesses," *Omaha World-Herald*, March 9, 1995, p. 1; Fred Thomas, "Park Supporter Says Plans Could Mesh," *Omaha World-Herald*, March 10, 1995, p. 21.

41. Jena Janovy, "Daub Fleshes Out Riverfront Dream," *Omaha World-Herald*, June 25, 1995, p. 1A.

42. For a sense of the course of the lawsuits, the various negotiations, and the final deals, see Joy Powell, "Arsarco, Government Propose Agreement, Deal Would Impose Fines, Settle Claims Asarco Case," *Omaha World-Herald*, June 29, 1995, p. 1; Julie Anderson and Joy Powell, "Suit Settled, Asarco Looks at Relocation," *Omaha World-Herald*, January 9, 1996, p. 11; Julie Anderson, "City, Asarco Reach Agreement on Site, Firm to Vacate Refinery; Area To Be Park," *Omaha World-Herald*, April 13, 1996, p. 1; "Asarco Agreement Clears the Way," *Omaha World-Herald*, April 18, 1996, p. 24; Jena Janovy and Julie Anderson, "Council Get Behind Asarco Cleanup Plan, Amendment Born of Concern Over City's Liability," *Omaha World-Herald*, July 31, 1996, p. 1; Julie Anderson, "Asarco Accelerates Plan, Will Close July 1," *Omaha World-Herald*, February 15, 1997, p. A-1; Jennifer Dukes Lee, "Asarco Cleanup Plan Wins State Approval; The Ruling Requires that the Property be Turned Over to the City or a 'City-Created Entity' After the Site is Cleaned." *Omaha World-Herald*, September 5, 1997, p. 13; "The Asarco Plan Opens Door to Better Times on Riverfront," *Omaha World-Herald*, June 4, 1998, p. 12; Kendrick Blackwood, "City, Asarco Sign Deal To Turn Plant to Park; Asarco Park Plan; Asarco Liability Amendment," *Omaha World-Herald*, June 10, 1998, p. 1; "Asarco, Omaha Negotiators Did Well," *Omaha World-Herald*, June 10, 1998, p. 8; Julie Anderson, "Asarco Hires Firm to Demolish Refinery Site," *Omaha World-Herald*, August 13, 1998, p. 17.

43. Steve Jordon, "Problems Not Conceded as Insurmountable, Gateway Plan Has Obstacles," *Omaha World-Herald*, January 13, 1991, p. 1M; Fred Thomas, "Things Taking Shape Along the Riverfront," *Omaha World-Herald*, September 1, 1996, p. 10B.

44. Christopher Burbach and Todd Cooper," River Not Just a Place to Play, Busy Firms Have Roots Where Daub Wants New 'Front Yard,'" *Omaha World-Herald*, June 14, 1998, p. 1a.

45. C. David Kotok, "Gallup Project's Path Is Cleared, Omaha Obtains the Key Aaron Ferer & Sons Scrap-Metal Property along Missouri River," *Omaha World-Herald*, March 21, 2001, p. 1; Robert Dorr, "Ferer Land Price Tag: $14 million, If the City Council Approves the Deal, Construction of the Gallup Riverfront Campus Would Be Assured, Daub Says, Riverfront Area," *Omaha World-Herald*, March 23, 2001, p. 1; Rick Ruggles and Tom Shaw, "Gallup Plan Gets Council's OK," *Omaha World-Herald*, April 11, 2001, p. 17.

46. Omaha Planning Department, "Omaha Master Plan Report No. 264 (revised): Concept Element," (City of Omaha, September 1995), pp. 2, 7.

47. Omaha Planning Department, "Omaha Master Plan Report No. 272: Land Use Element," (City of Omaha, September 1995), p. 12. The emphasis on the downtown and the idea that downtown must house amenities aimed at attracting people to the area in many ways built on earlier plans for the downtown promoted in the late 1960s and early 1970s, thus demonstrating a certain level of continuity between plans produced before and after 1985. For more on the history of planning the downtown as a location for cultural and recreational amenities see Daly-Bednarek, *The Changing Image of the City*, pp. 200–25. This also details the development of the Old

Market, another key in the redevelopment of the downtown but outside the precise scope of this work.

48. Omaha Planning Department, 1995.

49. Matt Kelley and Stephen Buttry, "Merger Raises Question: Where Will Home Be?" *Omaha World-Herald*, August 6, 1995, p. 1A; Matt Kelley and Stephen Buttry, "Enron Left; ConAgra Stayed: U.P. Factors Invite Comparison," *Omaha World-Herald*, August 6, 1995, p. 12A; Matt Kelley, "U.P. to Stay in Omaha After Merger, City Pressing for Building of a New HQ," *Omaha World-Herald*, p. 1A; Matt Kelley, "U.P. Leader: New Building Not in Plans, City Officials Had Pushed Riverfront Site," *Omaha World-Herald*, July 11, 1996, p. 1; Matt Kelley, "Chamber Holds Hope for U.P. Offices," *Omaha World-Herald*, July 12, 1996, p. 17; Matt Kelley, "U.P.: Any New Site to Be Downtown." *Omaha World-Herald*, November 1, 1996, p. 1; Chris Olson, "U.P. Decides It Will Lease Office Space, Nothing's Final on Construction of New Building," *Omaha World-Herald*, January 9, 1997, p. 1.

50. Jim Rasmussen, "U.P. Corp. Eyes Move to Omaha," *Omaha World-Herald*, September 25, 1998, p. 1; "Homecoming for the U.P.," *Omaha World-Herald*, April 17, 1999, p. 14; "It's Official: Omaha Is U.P. Headquarters," *Omaha World-Herald*, July 1, 1999, p. 22.

51. Grace Shim, "City May Buy Building From U.P," *Omaha World-Herald*, October 31, 2000, p. 1; Grace Shim, "U.P. Selects Site Downtown, The rail giant will build its new headquarters across the street from its present location," *Omaha World-Herald*, November 1, 2000, p. 1; Rick Ruggles and Grace Shim, "Building's Future Use Still Open After U.P. Constructs a New Headquarters, the City Plans to Acquire its Current Building and Turn it Over to a Developer," *Omaha World-Herald*, November 2, 2000, p. 2; Grace Shim, "U.P. Building Plan Moves Forward, The City Council Approves an Agreement for the Railroad's New Downtown Headquarters," *Omaha World-Herald*, April 18, 2001, p. 13; Grace Shim, "U.P. Gives Thumbs Up to Building, The Railroad Will Unveil More Details Today About a New 19-Story Headquarters Downtown," *Omaha World-Herald*, June 1, 2001, p. 1; "U.P. Opens Up, New Office Headquarters Adds to City's Increasing Shine," *Omaha World-Herald*, June 6, 2004, p. 12B. The city tried for years to find a developer to take over the old Union Pacific headquarters building, but in 2005, having failed to do so, decided to demolish the building in hopes of finding a developer for the vacant lot. Tom Shaw, "Demolition Likely End for U.P. Building, No One Has Come Forward with a Place to Restore the Railroad's Historic Headquarters," *Omaha World-Herald*, March 30, 2005, p. 2B.

52. Steve Jordan, Alva James-Johnson, "Big Project Bubbling in Downtown Omaha," *Omaha World-Herald*, May 12, 1996, 1A; Steven Jordan and Jena Janovy, "Announcement Expected On Downtown Project, *Omaha World-Herald*, October 22, 1996, p. 1; Steve Jordan, "Office Park to Reshape Downtown, Bank, World-Herald Plan Major Projects , Downtown Projects," *Omaha World-Herald*, October 23, 1996, p. 1; Steven Jordan and Jena Janovy, "A Vibrant Downtown Called Vital, Revitalization Plan Seen as Partnership," *Omaha World-Herald*, October 24, 1996,

p. 1; Fred Mogul, "Planning Board Approves Downtown Development," *Omaha World-Herald*, November 7, 1996, p. 27.

53. Steven Jordon, "Office Park to Reshape Downtown, Bank, World-Herald Plan Major Projects, Downtown Projects," *Omaha World-Herald*, October 23, 1996, p. 1; Chris Olson, "Omaha Skyline Climbs, first National Bank to Build 40 Stories of Glass, Granite, First National Center Coming Thursday," *Omaha World-Herald*, September 23, 1998, p. 1; Steve Jordan, "Park, Plaza to Take Flight, First National's Downtown Oasis Will Enliven Street Outside Tower with Fountains, Sculpture, Park Facts, First National Tower," *Omaha World-Herald*, September 18, 2002, p. 1D.

54. Steve Jordan and Alva James-Johnson, "Big Project Bubbling in Downtown Omaha," *Omaha World-Herald*, May 12, 1996, p. 1A; Steve Jordan, "Office Park to Reshape Downtown, Bank, World-Herald Plan Major Projects, Downtown Projects," *Omaha World-Herald*, October 23, 1996, p.1.

55. Robert Dorr, "The World-Herald Freedom Center Press Facility Invests in Future, Newspapers and Downtown Freedom Center," *Omaha World-Herald*, May 1, 1999, p. 1: Deborah Shanahan, "World-Herald Buying Quest Office Building, Newspaper Offices to Move Across Street," *Omaha World-Herald*, April 3, 2006, p. 1A; Virgil Larson, "Building has Weathered Phone Business Changes, Quest Sells Predecessor's Former Headquarters," *Omaha World-Herald*, April 4, 2006, p. 1D; Steven Jordan and Deborah Shanahan, "Another Boost for Downtown, The World-Herald's Move Shows Commitment to City's Heart," *Omaha World-Herald*, April 4, 2006, p. 1A; Steve Jordan and Deborah Shanahan, "Corporate Support for Downtown is Up, The World-Herald's Purchase of a Major Building is Seen as a Commitment to the Commercial Core," *Omaha World-Herald*, April 5, 2006, p. 1D.

56. Victor Epstein, "City Works to Lure Gallup Headquarters, The Polling Firm Wants to Secure a 50-Acre Site and Financial Incentives Before it Moves its Operational Base Here," *Omaha World-Herald*, July 29, 2000, p. 1; Victor Epstein, "Gallup's Headquarters To Be Built in Omaha," *Omaha World-Herald*, September 27, 2000, p. 1; Steve Jordan, "Gallup Negotiations Called Complex, The City, and Company and the Chamber of Commerce Officials Try to Figure Out How to Split Costs, Gallup Riverfront Campus," *Omaha World-Herald*, February 18, 2001, p. 1M; C. David Kotok, "Gallup Project's Path Is Cleared, Omaha Obtains the Key Aaron Ferer & Sons Scrap-Metal Property Along Missouri River," *Omaha World-Herald*, March 21, 2001, p. 1; Rick Ruggles and Tom Shaw, "Gallup Plan Gets Council's OK," *Omaha World-Herald*, April 11, 2001, p. 17.

57. Ak-Sar-Ben is a civic/social organization. Its property included an arena with an ice rink and a horse-racing track.

58. Paul Goodsell, "Officials Say They See Erosion In Plan for River Front Center," *Omaha World-Herald*, May 18, 1986, p. 1; Cindy Gonzalez, "Conley: Put New Arena Downtown, Says City Should Act Before Ak Is Bought," *Omaha World-Herald*, January 12, 1989, p. 1; "A Variety of Options Available, Too Soon to End Debate On Convention Center, "*Omaha World-Herald*, January 27, 1989, p. 40;

Cindy Gonzalez, "Downtown Site for Center Gets Council Backing," *Omaha World-Herald*, February 1, 1989, p. 1.

59. "Morgan's Good Grades as Mayor Tempered by His Early Departure," *Omaha World-Herald*, September 18, 1994, p. 24A.

60. Matt Kelley, "Daub: Omaha Must Plan for Stadium, Competitive Edge Depends on It, He Says," *Omaha World-Herald*, January 8, 1997, p. 1; "Focus on City Arena Question Comes at an Appropriate Time," *Omaha World-Herald*, May 26, 1997, p. 10b.

61. See Metropolitan Omaha Convention Sports & Entertainment Authority, "Report to the Citizens of the Omaha Metropolitan Area and Their Governmental Representatives on the Feasibility of a Convention Center and Arena Facility" (December 29, 1997).

62. "Daub Eyes Arena Prize," *Omaha World-Herald*, June 5, 1998, p. 41.

63. Jason Gertzen, "A Billion-Dollar Maybe Arena Is 'Crown Jewel' of Daub Plan, Plan Highlights," *Omaha World-Herald*, November 9, 1998, p. 1.

64. Robert Dorr, "Daub Projects Subsidizing Center-Arena for 5 Years," *Omaha World-Herald*, September 21, 1999, p. 13.

65. Ed Russo, "Top Priority; Chamber to Back Convention Center In Ad Campaign," *Omaha World-Herald*, January 29, 2000, p. 57.

66. Robert Dorr, "Arena Work to Start Fast, Voter-Blessed Project Aims to Open in 2003," *Omaha World-Herald*, May 10, 2000, p. 1.

67. Chris Burbach, "Arena Could Usher In Lively New Downtown, Omaha's Front Door, from Iowa and Eppley Airfield, Is Opening to Dramatic Changes," *Omaha World-Herald*, June 11, 2000, p. 1a.

68. "New Center is Symbol of Change," *Omaha World-Herald*, August 10, 2003, p. 2ss. For a sense of the residential developments sparked by the riverfront redevelopment, see Grace Shim, "Developers Say Demand is Strong, Downtown Omaha Area is Conducive to Condos, New Projects," *Omaha World-Herald*, November 23, 2002, p. 1D; C. David Kotok, "Condo Competition by the River, The Developer of a Bluffs Project Isn't Fazed by Plan Unveiled for the Omaha Side," *Omaha World-Herald*, November 10, 2003, p. 1B; C. David Kotok, "Riverfront Place Project Moving Toward Reality, Construction to Being in the Spring on the Condo Community South of the Gallup University Campus," *Omaha World-Herald*, August 30, 2004, p. 1B; Deborah Shanahan, "New Life for a Landmark, A Developer Will Convert Omaha's Brandeis Building into Condos," *Omaha World-Herald*, December 9, 2004, p. 1A; Karen Sloan, "Council Approves Condo Plan for Former U.P. Site, A Redevelopment Agreement Calls for City to Provide $15.6 Million in Tax-Increment Financing, but It Won't Have to Pay for the Demolition of the Old Building," *Omaha World-Herald*, December 20, 2006, p. 1D. For details on the performing arts center see Ashley Hasselbroek, "Omaha's Arts Center Named after Hollands," *Omaha World-Herald*, September 22, 2004, p. 1A.

69. For examples of critiques leveled at downtown/riverfront development by those objecting to the loss of historic structures, see "Razing Tears City's Heart,"

Omaha World-Herald, May 5, 1997, p. 27; Robert Dorr, "Should History Give Way to the Future? Arena Touches A Sore Spot," *Omaha World-Herald*, November 18, 1997, p.1; "Razing of Past Limits Future," *Omaha World-Herald*, October 27, 1999, p. 45.

70. For a sense of the centrality of 10th Street to downtown and the revitalized riverfront, see Jeffrey Robb, "Opening of 10th Street Revives Hopes for Glory, The Omaha Convention Center and Arena will Begin Greeting Visitors Up Close as the New 10th Street Beckons. The Corridor is Prominent in Omaha's History and is a Connection Between Some of the City's Major Attractions," *Omaha World-Herald*, September 10, 2003, p. 1a; Chase Davis, "Fun Will Flow on Revamped Riverfront, The Area where Omaha Got Started Looks Better Than Ever, and It's a Key Part of the City's 150th Birthday Plans," *Omaha World-Herald*, July 14, 2004, p. 1A.

71. Daub lost his bid for a second full term in 2001. However, he was credited with bringing great, if sometimes controversial, leadership to the revitalization of downtown and the riverfront. See Henry J. Cordes, "Daub Will Leave His Imprint On the Downtown Landscape, Significant Events in Hal Daub's Mayoral Career," *Omaha World-Herald*, May 20, 2001, p. 1a.

CHAPTER FIVE

~

The Gravity of Capital

Spatial and Economic Transformation in Muncie, Indiana, 1917–1940

LaDale Winling

With a phone call and a lunch meeting spaced a few months apart in 1917 and 1918, two brothers of the Ball family in Muncie, Indiana, arranged for the creation of a normal school that became a major Midwestern teaching university and now serves as the heart of the Muncie economy. The episode began when George Ball, member of a leading manufacturing family, empowered his attorney in the fall of 1917 to purchase the property of a failed private teaching school on the edge of town during a court-administrated auction. Later, at a winter meeting of the Muncie Rotary Club, Charles Mc-Gonagle, the city's state legislative representative, struck up a conversation with Frank Ball offering to negotiate with Indiana's governor to accept donation of the institution's campus by the state. In the spring of 1918 the state created a new public institution on the site and by June 1918 the Muncie campus of the Indiana State Normal School held its first classes.[1]

Considering this negotiation and the establishment of a college in this way, as part of a set of transformative capital investments in the physical, economic and social landscape of Muncie, frames the enterprise of higher education in a very different way from what we have come to expect. Rather than being an "ivory tower," an institution removed from the messy concerns of modern life, urban politics, and economic growth, Ball State Teachers College, as it came to be known, was part of a broad agenda to advance the economic base and prestige of the city—to concentrate the gains of industrial production, extracted from consumers across the nation, in multiple forms

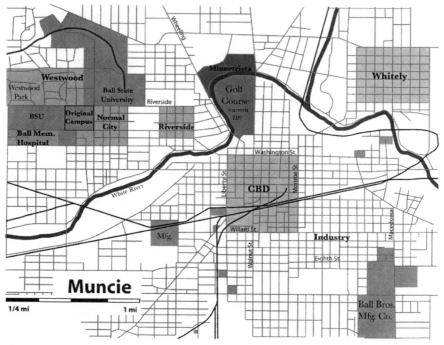

Figure 5.1. Central Muncie.
Map by the author.

on the Muncie landscape. Not only was it an urban institution, the college was an *urbanizing* institution, one capable of catalyzing changes in land and population development; social, cultural, and economic opportunity; as well as increasing the value of real estate, human labor, and community prestige.[2]

This institution and these investments, however, were not evenly shared throughout the Indiana city. The creation of the college, among other efforts, both expanded the privilege of the business class and catalyzed a transformation of urban geography, by mid-century turning Muncie into a community that turn-of-the-century residents would not have been able to recognize. So significant was the scale of change, shifting the broad pattern of urban investment dramatically in favor of the northwest quadrant of the city, that investment on the city's east end stagnated.[3] The physical growth of Ball State Teachers College in this era illuminates the role of institutions such as colleges and universities in the political economy of metropolitan regions and their effects on the urban landscape as far back as the 1910s. Urban historians and sociologists have long studied the political economy of industrial transformation and metropolitan stratification, but have located the origins of urban disinvestment in the World War II era.[4]

As this chapter shows, the alliances between educational leaders and urban elites date even from the founding of such institutions, and predated mobilization for World War II substantially.[5] Indeed, the expansion of federal capacity in the New Deal and during and after the war, so often named as the necessary or sufficient condition for urban transformation, in Muncie only intensified a process that had been initiated years earlier by the city's industrial leaders.[6]

Colleges and universities, when used forcefully as instruments of the local metropolitan elite, have the power to change patterns of urban development. The Ball family espoused an agenda of urban and regional development through the creation of educational institutions and the teachers' college was one of a set of allied efforts in pursuit of that agenda, including a health care facility and an art museum. After the Balls' investments in northwest Muncie spurred building on the outskirts of the city, investment on the east side of the city stagnated even while Muncie developed into a leading Indiana city and a node in the Midwestern networks of education, health care, cultural production, and finance, in addition to its already robust industrial position. The business and professional class withdrew from their traditional residential neighborhoods in the East End and left deterioration and declining property values in their wake.[7] The Balls' geographically concentrated investments and ongoing civic philanthropy exerted their own force, a kind of gravity of capital, that drew other investments toward itself, profoundly influencing the future of Muncie, Indiana, in ways that were both intentional and unforeseen.[8]

Perhaps more importantly, the myriad community investments the Ball coalition made in Muncie helped create a postindustrial economic basis for the city. Even as Robert and Helen Lynd were studying and writing about the industrial transformation of the Indiana community in the pioneering study *Middletown* and their follow-up, *Middletown in Transition*, Muncie was undergoing profound economic and social changes that the sociologists failed to appreciate.[9] Among them were the incorporation of several emerging institutions in American society, those of higher education and health care, into the Fordist order of consumer capitalism by creating and helping govern a public college that would bear an industrialist family's name. However, the mid-century growth of the American state and its investment in infrastructure and scientific knowledge, along with a shift in labor development, undermined organized labor and heavy industry in favor of knowledge workers and a service economy, which intensified the transformation of Muncie. This was part of a national process in which industry fled from unionized, domestic production centers and metropolitan economic growth relied upon federal subsidies and the development of a productionless consumption economy in place of a productive industrial economy.[10]

However, the Ball family's role as local leaders and as patrons of a growing educational institution in Muncie also illustrates the limits of philanthropy and the waning influence of local industrial elites as the twentieth century progressed. These local elites were later surpassed by the growing power of the federal government and the integration of regional, national, and global capital. In Muncie, too, the power of local industrial capital diminished over time as production grew less concentrated and corporations like Ball Brothers transitioned to a geographically diffuse knowledge economy, one that itself increasingly relied upon the patronage of the federal government, at the expense of Midwestern cities like Muncie.[11]

A Company Town

For more than a century, the identity and development of Muncie, located sixty miles northeast of Indianapolis, was entwined with the Ball family and the Ball Brothers manufacturing companies. The discovery of natural gas in east central Indiana in the 1880s created an economic boom for the city in which the population more than doubled from 5,200 in 1880 to 11,300 in 1890.[12] Entrepreneurs and migrants flocked to Muncie to take advantage of the abundant natural resource, a useful energy source for the industrial revolution that was transforming the American economy in the latter half of the nineteenth century. Though the Muncie population was largely composed of white Protestants, before the turn of the century business interests were diverse and relatively small-scale.[13]

Ball Brothers Glass Manufacturing Company was a transplant to Muncie, attracted by the financial support and booster rhetoric of business leaders in 1886. Two brothers, Frank C. Ball and Edmund B. Ball, had founded the company in Buffalo, New York, and managed a growing enterprise creating the glass jars that rural and small town families used to preserve fruits and vegetables throughout the winter. When their Buffalo factory burned down in 1886, the brothers began a search for and found a site in east central Indiana where gas for their glass blowing furnaces was plentiful and cheap. Muncie's business leaders offered Frank Ball free land and free gas for five years if the Balls moved their concern to Muncie. Frank struck a deal and he and Edmund moved the company to the Midwest the next year, including two of their remaining three brothers.[14] Ball Brothers glass jars soon came to dominate the canning market owing to high quality and reliability, to the point where, by the turn of the century, the Balls were among the state's wealthiest individuals and their glass jars comprised more than a third of the national output.[15]

Foundations

In 1898, a group of regional businessmen formed an association to create a private, for-profit normal school that was a harbinger of the city's changing economic condition. Though Muncie was clearly a growing, industrial city, by the turn of the century the underground gas stores that had precipitated the economic boom were exhausted and growth could no longer depend on this cheap energy source. The end of the region's resource economy did nothing to stop the arrival of mass industrialization, but it led to a decline in small manufacturing throughout the city, which made the rise of a non-industrial economy a more attractive basis for Muncie's future. As they had a generation earlier, the city's business leaders stepped into the breach.

Higher education provided a means for dealing with this economic crisis. Education advocates around the country had argued for the integration of higher education into the growing industrial economy in the late nineteenth century.[16] Academic leaders at leading universities including Michigan and Harvard had advanced ideas and pursued reforms of the classical curriculum in favor of scientific training and the elective system, while the federal Morrill Acts had established engineering and agricultural schools throughout the United States.[17] Indeed, the second half of the nineteenth century saw an expansion and proliferation of colleges and universities that was unmatched in American history, developing and incorporating new lines of professional training and intellectual acquisition into college curricula.[18] Mining, engineering, and scientific schools aided industry in extracting, making efficient use of, and even synthesizing the natural resources that enabled the American industrial revolution, while increasingly training the expanding ranks of clerks, managers, middlemen, and entrepreneurs of the middle class. In this age of growing access to and demand for higher education, education schools, including public and private normal schools, were but one of many new types of institutions that both increased the availability of higher education to the middle classes and helped expand the professional classes.[19]

The normal school in northwest Muncie was founded on real estate development. In 1898 a group of investors bundled a land deal with a new education enterprise to finance the development of the school's campus. Members of the Eastern Indiana Normal University Association optioned a tract of agricultural land beyond the northwest borders of Muncie. The businessmen subdivided the land into three hundred lots and platted a development they called Normal City.[20] Announcing the foundation of the normal school, a private, for-profit institute that would train young men and women to be teachers in rural schools, the investors announced that sales of the residential lots would finance construction of the campus physical plant.[21] (See figure 5.1.)

The unorthodox financing of the normal institute presaged twenty years of economic uncertainty for higher education in Muncie. The Eastern Indiana Normal University (EINU) opened with a flourish and began classes in 1899 with an impressive neoclassical building for instruction and administration. (See figure 5.2.) Local and regional students attending the school lived in Muncie rooming houses and patronized local businesses for meals, fulfilling the community business rationale for the school.[22] However, the institution fell into financial difficulties and was forced to close for lack of students in 1901, reopening as Palmer University with the promise of aid from New York financier Francis Asbury Palmer in 1902.[23] Palmer died before finalizing the gift and the school closed again, to reopen three years later.

Figure 5.2. The Administration Building at Ball State, the structure that housed the Eastern Indiana Normal University when it opened in 1899.
Courtesy of Ball State University Archives and Special Collections

A new education association, numbering Frank Ball among its member-ship, directed the normal school and tried to merge with several established Indiana schools such as Taylor University. Financial troubles doomed the third institution and a new set of businessmen formed a fourth venture, the Muncie Normal Institute, in 1912. Later named the Muncie National Institute, em-phasizing training in hotel management as much as education, the seemingly star-crossed school accrued such significant debts that, when it failed, an Indi-ana court ordered asset liquidation to repay the school's creditors.[24]

Like their contemporaries in cities around the country, Muncie business elites took vigorous action to secure the future of their higher education institution. Major universities throughout the country—the University of Michigan, the University of California–Los Angeles, and Duke University, to name just a few—were founded or provided campus land by local civic and commercial leaders, many with an eye toward urban development.[25] The Ball brothers were especially forceful, intervening as part of a strategy to physically develop the real estate of northwest Muncie and to economically develop the east central region of Indiana. The normal school's assets for sale included the original administration building, a wood frame dormitory, and about seventy acres of land, appraised at $409,492.[26] A representative of the school's creditors participated in the bidding, announcing the intention to break up the property and sell parcels individually in hopes of recouping their investments, while a Chicago auction house also bid on the property.[27]

The Ball family, classically liberal in their economics, had allowed the normal schools to fail repeatedly over two decades, but when the entre-preneurial churn of creative destruction threatened to break up the private institute's campus lands near their homes northwest of the city, the Balls would not allow it.[28] Frank Ball secretly arranged for a local attorney to bid for the property on his family's behalf. The judge set bidding rules so that half the amount would be paid immediately and the balance cleared by the end of the week. When the bids came in, the judge accepted the Balls' $35,100 offer for the property—slightly lower than the auction house's bid—because their cash was available immediately.[29] George A. Ball, who approved the deal over the telephone, off-handedly remarked to his brothers at lunch, "[I] just bought a college."[30]

That acquisition accomplished, colleagues in the political community provided the means of disposition of the Ball property. The Muncie Rotary Club—where George and Frank C. Ball of the first generation were members, and Edmund A. and Frank E. Ball of the second generation would become members—comprised the civic and business leadership of the community.[31] Among their Rotary colleagues was Charles McGonagle, a state representative, longtime Muncie politician and government administrator. McGonagle was chair of the state's Ways and Means committee and an ally of both the state's governor, James Goodrich, and the Balls. The Indiana legislature had passed a law early in 1917 empowering the state to accept donations on behalf of colleges and universities in order to improve state park resources.[32] At a Rotary meeting in early 1918, McGonagle suggested that the governor and legislature would be willing to accept a donation of the campus property under the law and operate a normal school as a branch of the Indiana State Normal School (ISNS, now Indiana State University) based in Terre Haute. When McGonagle discussed the issue with Governor Goodrich, the idea of state-sponsored higher education in east central Indiana appealed to the politician from nearby Winchester, Indiana.[33] Establishment of a new public institution in their home region would serve the area's business and political interests, while strengthening the three men's individual influence and the collaboration of private enterprise and the state.[34] Together, McGonagle, Goodrich, and the Balls collaborated on the agreement that enabled a state takeover of the Ball campus property. State acceptance of the donation represented the assumption of private liability by public institutions. This donation was especially important to the Ball interests because the state's assumption of ownership relieved the family of liabilities acquired from the school in the course of its failure. Several creditors, irate at debts redeemed at less than ten cents on the dollar, threatened lawsuits to mitigate their losses. Under the agreement with the state, the lawsuits would then be directed at and defended by the state of Indiana.[35]

The new division of the Indiana State Normal School early on exhibited the enduring influence of the Ball family. The ISNS board of trustees had ratified the governor's bargain—provided Frank Ball agreed to serve as a trustee for the school, assuring his continued interest in the institution. Ball served as a steady advocate of the Muncie institution, pushing for independence from Terre Haute, while he contributed to a conservatism on campus that reflected in microcosm the ideals and power structure of the broader Muncie community. So robust and sustained was Frank Ball's and the Ball brothers' commitment to the college, lobbying for state funds and participating in campus planning, that in 1922 the board of trustees moved to name the Muncie institution after its chief benefactors, changing the school's moniker to Ball Teachers College, the Eastern Division of ISNS.[36]

Muncie Politics

The development of the northwest edge of Muncie became a city-wide political issue as the normal school was taken over by the state. The new residential areas of Normal City and Riverside, surrounding the normal school, had been built outside the urban boundaries of Muncie, and thus these valuable and desirable neighborhoods escaped municipal taxation but received city services by contracting with the city.

During the 1917 campaign for mayor, the Progressive Republican challenger, businessman Charles Grafton, made taxation and metropolitan equity a centerpiece of his classic good government campaign against Democratic incumbent Rollin "Doc" Bunch. Bunch was a physician and an old-style Democratic ward boss. He drew strong support from the northeast and southeast areas of the city where many black and white working class residents lived. Owing to his patronage machine, he presided over a city payroll tens of thousands dollars larger than that of any of his predecessors.[37] Grafton, an officer of a clay pot manufacturing company, pledged that he would not allow the new educated and professional class of the northwest suburbs to enjoy Muncie's urban amenities without contributing tax revenue.[38] Indeed, much of the city's industrial south side had been annexed into the city in 1909 and industrial workers owning homes in the industry neighborhood near the manufacturing plants paid more in property taxes than did residents in the subdivision of Normal City.[39] Grafton claimed that the mayor could have annexed the suburbs at any point in the preceding four years, but Bunch benefited electorally from the annexation of wet, Democratic south side industrial workers. Likewise, by not bringing the dry, Republican, professional-class suburbanites into the city's electorate via annexation, the mayor had mitigated the difficulties of establishing and consolidating political power in the midst of metropolitan growth.

Prompted by his challenger, the mayor recognized the political volatility of these geographic inequities and adopted policy positions that both recognized and advanced the spatial transformation of the city. Pledging to capture taxes from the development going on outside the northwest boundaries of the city, including the Normal City and Riverside neighborhoods, Bunch initiated the annexation of the wealthier areas the city. In doing so, the mayor attempted to reaffirm his populist credentials by declaring that he would not tolerate geographic inequality in metropolitan tax policy. The mayor's move assuaged residents in working class parts of the city who picked up on the rhetoric of northwest Muncie free riders and Bunch coasted to another term leading the city. The city completed the annexation in 1919.[40]

As this political issue illustrated, Muncie had become increasingly segregated by class and the new educational institution played a significant part in this geographic transformation.[41] The paucity of student residences south of the rail lines illustrates the re-inscription of the city's class distinctions upon the Muncie landscape and implicates the college in this process. Few working class families from south of the tracks sent their children to college as the students and their parents found difficulty in paying for advanced schooling, while also suffering from low educational expectations.[42] Even as early as the mid-1920s members of the industrial community believed that education was a key to social and economic advancement and the Lynds noted that working class families realized that higher education provided a means of escaping lives of manual labor and marginal economic means. "A boy without an education today just ain't *anywhere!*" lamented one Muncie father.[43] However, the city's industrial families were largely unable to enjoy the economic mobility that could empower them to change the class geography of the city or to serve as a counterweight to the investments of the Muncie business class near Normal City. Indeed, the normal school had served both obliquely as an instrument for the enrichment and protection of the business elites in the northwest part of the city—the anchor to a real estate endeavor—and directly as a means of class mobility and professional training unevenly shared by the business class and working class segments of the population living in neighborhoods around the city.[44]

Campus Expansion

The Ball family continued to support the institution that bore their name through philanthropic efforts that increased the college's educational capacity, including donating a gymnasium and a women's dormitory.[45] In the final phase of building in the 1920s, the college abandoned the formula of private capital and public operational expenses in favor of wholly public expenditures to create a new laboratory school directed by the college and the Muncie school district. BTC administrators lobbied the state for appropriations for the school, which would provide progressive education for Muncie students from kindergarten through senior high school and gave future teachers opportunities to gain experience through the practice teaching required by the college curriculum.[46] BTC leaders arranged with Muncie school officials to close a nearby grade school and have the Burris School, named for a state education official and former BTC president, serve the population of northwest Muncie. The school's individualist curriculum produced stellar graduates and Burris became renowned for successful athletic teams in sports-hungry Muncie.[47]

Progressive education, like tax policy, was implicated in the city's political economy and proved politically controversial, as Muncie residents recognized the inequities of urban investments in the city. From the school's completion in 1929, college officials battled charges of elitism at the school. BTC administrators defended the arrangement against accusations that it served only the wealthy business class by noting the Burris School also aided a group of poor families living near the college. Further, they characterized the sons and daughters of Muncie's professional class as "average" and "typical" students who benefited from the principal's strict discipline.[48] However, the Burris school's geographic district boundaries served, in combination with the teacher's college, as a significant amenity attracting business and professional class families to move to northwest Muncie. In 1937, the Lynds reported that the curricular experimentation and individuation, modeled on John Dewey's education principles, proved somewhat controversial but ultimately desirable to residents, noting "if some parents leave the district because of the school, more move in to gain the combined educational and social advantages of the West End."[49] The school's location was no accident and its academic quality was only part of its value and demand, which was inextricably tied to the new patterns of Muncie development and concentration of capital.[50]

Founding a Hospital

The Balls continued their development of economic, educational, and real estate interests in northwest Muncie by providing the resources to found a new, modern hospital. Lucius Ball, the eldest brother and the least interested in the operations of the glass jar company, had pursued a profession in medicine, eventually joining the manufacturing concern as the company physician. Ball had helped found a modest, community-run hospital in 1905, the Muncie Home Hospital, and along with his brother, Edmund, had long promoted the idea of a major regional hospital in Muncie.[51] After two decades with only a single, small care facility located downtown, city leaders led by Edmund Ball began promoting the idea of a new, larger hospital rather than an expansion of the aging Muncie Home Hospital.[52]

Again the Balls used the power of the state to realize their vision for the city, catalyzed by their own financial contributions. As they had done with the normal school, members of the Ball family provided the capital to create the hospital as part of an agreement that a government unit would take over and operate the hospital once it was built. Edmund Ball negotiated with members of the state assembly to authorize Delaware County to create a new hospital to serve east central Indiana. Prior to his death in 1925, Edmund provided in his will for the establishment of a charitable foundation—now the Ball Brothers Foundation—to continue his philanthropic activities in

Muncie, chief among them funding for the coming hospital. His surviving brothers, along with other medically minded civic leaders, formed an organization to create the hospital he had envisioned, the Ball Memorial Hospital Association (BMHA). Ball Memorial Hospital was to be operated by the county after the Balls provided funding for design and construction of the hospital.[53] Frank Ball, one of the directors of the BMHA, convinced the board to locate the hospital adjacent to the college that bore the family name, arguing that each institution would benefit from close proximity to the other.[54] Much additional land south and west of the teachers' college quadrangle was owned by BTC from the original auction and donation but was restricted for educational purposes, subsequently going unused as a result. However, the hospital was to include a nurses training program, satisfying the educational requirements of the gift, and Frank Ball arranged for the college to transfer dozens of acres of land for the hospital to build upon.[55]

As with the college, the Balls put their own aesthetic and moral stamp upon the hospital. The hospital association hired Muncie architect Cuno Kibele, the designer of choice for the Balls' private commissions and several Ball State buildings, to design Ball Memorial Hospital.[56] In keeping with his and the college's historicist designs, Kibele designed the façade in the Tudor Gothic style, symbolically lending the new institution age and authority, even as it contributed to the modernization of health care, higher education, and the economy in Muncie. (See figure 5.3.) In creating the hospital, the city's leading industrial family characteristically combined philanthropy, economic development, and special attention to women's opportunities, all embedded within the real estate regime that began to concentrate investment profit and Muncie's population of knowledge workers in the northwest quadrant of the city. The Balls provided funds for the design and construction of Maria Bingham Hall, a women's dormitory for nurses in training at the hospital, built in 1930 and named after their mother. (See figure 5.4.) In sum, the complex cost $2 million to build, paid for by the foundation and the manufacturing company.[57]

Ball Memorial Hospital opened in August of 1929 and continued the economic transformation of northwest Muncie. The hospital employed numerous physicians and trained scores of nurses annually in the course of its operations, many of whom eventually came to populate the subdivisions of northwest Muncie.[58] By mid-century, Muncie outstripped comparable or larger Indiana cities such as Hammond and Terre Haute in number of physicians, nurses, and even educators in the workforce, though lagging in positions such as chemists and engineers.[59]

Figure 5.3. Ball Memorial Hospital, opened in 1929.
Courtesy of Ball State University Archives and Special Collections

Figure 5.4. Maria Bingham Hall, a dormitory for female nursing students training at BMH, opened in 1930.
Courtesy of Ball State University Archives and Special Collections

The Gravity of Capital

These investments in the educational landscape of Muncie rendered spatial changes in the city's metropolitan order. The shift from agricultural land to education enterprises required municipal infrastructure, from roads to power to water and sanitation. Where once these civic investments had been made exclusively south of the White River, increasingly they were required in the northwest part of the city, which enabled other opportunities for real estate investment.

Real estate continued to dominate the relationship between the Ball family, their city, and the institution that bore their name as the second generation of Ball men sought ways to make their names. These men—E. Arthur, Elliot, and Frank A. Ball—grew up exceedingly wealthy but, due to the long and vigorous careers of their fathers, were largely shut out of leadership of the glass manufacturing company. Several sons turned to other civic and entrepreneurial activities, including politics and real estate development. Both national and local trends contributed to the growing real estate market in northwest Muncie. The city's industrial growth provided a demand-side impetus for investments in real estate. The city's population increased by half—12,500 people—between 1910 and 1920, while growth in industrial employment created manufacturing jobs as well as expanding the managerial and professional class. National monetary policy and the loosening of credit standards also aided the growth of suburban development. At both the national and local levels public policy, private enterprise, and consumer demand promoted and relied upon the expansion of credit. The creation of the Federal Reserve Bank in 1913 established a new national banking system to help eliminate panics and manage increases in the money supply. This national framework included regulatory and legislative mandates for banks that would borrow from the Reserve and created national structures governing lending activity. The 1920s saw numerous innovations and expansions of financial products that fueled growing consumerism, including installment financial instruments for such products as automobiles, laundry washing machines, refrigerators, and radios—real estate was no exception.[60]

The Ball family controlled or exerted influence over much of the land in the northwest part of the city. Frank C. Ball held strong influence over the campus grounds proper in his position as a member of the ISNS board of trustees since the founding of the Muncie branch. Members of the Ball family had purchased a large amount of land in the Normal City and Riverside developments around the college in addition to building their own opulent homes overlooking the White River.[61] The Ball Brothers Foundation was the beneficiary of land in northwest Muncie accumulated by Edmund Ball. As the normal school grew and became Ball Teachers College and then Ball State, the next generation of Balls expanded the family land investments.

Residential real estate development in northwest Muncie followed enduring principles of suburban exclusion. E. Arthur Ball, the son of Frank Ball, bought a large tract of the plentiful agricultural land that remained undeveloped north of the college campus in 1923 (see figure 5.1).[62] He and a partner formed a land development company and platted out a residential subdivision they named Westwood in 1923 (see figure 5.5). Purchase of a lot in Westwood obligated new landowners to abide by restrictions that governed nearly every aspect of home building. The mandates established by the real estate company explicitly forbade minority ownership or residence except as domestic servants, reserving the subdivision for "the pure white race" with restrictive covenants.[63] In addition, the community plan included economic and social barriers to the white working class, including a minimum lot size of 7,500 square feet, property setbacks of 7 feet from each lot line (and farther from the front line), and even required approval of architectural plans for

Figure 5.5. The house of E. A. Ball in Westwood, the suburban subdivision he developed adjacent to Ball State Teachers College.
Courtesy of Ball State University Archives and Special Collections

any structures built.[64] The development restrictions and geographical location of the Westwood development made the area exclusive, figuratively and literally. Separated from much of the rest of Muncie by the White River, the subdivision was utterly remote from the working class and industrial southern section of the city and the small black community of Whitely on Muncie's northeast side.[65] The developers drew upon the cachet of Ball Teachers College in their advertising, where education stood in as a class signifier and the college's investments in campus planning provided positive externalities to the surrounding area.[66] E.A. Ball illustrated he was independent of the influence of his father's generation but was more than satisfied to obey the mandates of capitalist accumulation, replicating this process with a new subdivision called Westwood Park adjacent to Westwood in 1939.[67]

In their follow-up inquiry into Muncie life, *Middletown in Transition*, Robert and Helen Lynd observed these spatial changes to the city.

> Since 1925 the X family has literally moved the residential heart of the city. An outstanding change in these ten years is the development of the northwest section of the city, the section where the X's live and the section most remote from local industrial plants, into the outstanding residential section.[68]

Making reference to the Balls' civic investments, the authors noted,

> This shift has been carefully engineered by members of the X family. As a result, the aristocratic old East End, the fine residential section in the pre-motor period when it was an asset to live "close in" and even in the early 1920's, runs a lame second to the two new X subdivisions in the West End to which the ambitious matrons of the city are removing their families.[69]

With the publication of *Middletown in Transition*, LIFE magazine hired photographer Margaret Bourke-White to document the town, illustrating the extremes of poverty and plenty while illuminating the structures of continuity in the urban community. LIFE also emphasized the patterns of metropolitan growth and the geographic implications of economic change amidst this cultural continuity, noting,

> Far across town from the college are homes like these. Depression years have made them shabbier, but the people in them, like all Middletown, have resisted fundamental change. New streets may strike out through the cornfields, new houses arise, new faces emerge. But year in and year out, these earnest midland folk still steer their customary middle course, still cling to their old American dreams.[70]

The Federal Influence

The onset of economic depression and the establishment of a more robust federal apparatus in the New Deal commenced a period of transition in the economic and social transformation of Muncie. Key New Deal investments built upon existing institutions and consolidated, rather than upended, the established metropolitan and spatial order of the city that had been altered by the Ball family and the city's business class.[71] However, these federal actions began a long-term process of national economic restructuring. The political economy of the New Deal created new production centers around the country and created the means for powering them and delivering their goods to markets.[72] In addition, during the 1930s the federal government began to offer more robust support for higher education, a sector that had long been left to state and local authority for financial support and policy development, commencing a mid-century transformation that would lead to the booming colleges and universities that helped signal the new postwar economy of the 1950s and 1960s.[73]

By the mid-1930s, the Muncie workforce and the city's economy suffered from the effects of the Great Depression even more than the nation as a whole. By 1933, industrial employment in the city had declined by more than one-half, more than one-third of retail jobs had been eliminated, and building construction declined by 95 percent, putting the Muncie labor force in greater crisis than the nation overall, which saw a peak of 24.9 percent unemployment in 1933.[74]

Of the many policy developments of the Roosevelt administration, some of most enduring are the Public Works Administration (PWA) and the Works Progress Administration (WPA), which supplied grants and loans for the design, construction, and expansion of numerous forms of public infrastructure, from transportation systems to education buildings. Ironically, these are some of the least understood, as historians have not investigated the spatial implications of these forms of physical investment. Between 1933 and 1939, the Public Works Administration supported the construction of approximately 70 percent of the nation's new school buildings, even while enrollment in higher education institutions declined or stagnated.[75]

Muncie saw its share of these federal proceeds in an unusual set of public and private partnerships in which the federal government joined the Balls in supporting development, again concentrated in the northwest part of the city. The federal government contributed grants and loans to construct one building and expand two others at BSTC, while also providing aid for the expansion of the Burris experimental school in northwest Muncie. At

Ball State, the institution was able to expand Assembly Hall, the library and auditorium building that was also open to the public; Ball gymnasium, the athletics center on campus originally financed by the philanthropy of the industrial family; and to build the Arts Building, a joint instructional and museum building, which was filled with the art collections of the Ball family.[76] The Ball family also provided the necessary local match for the Arts Building that enabled the award of the federal grant to BSTC. In sum, the federal government provided $367,000 in grants that enabled nearly one million dollars of construction, all of which was concentrated in the northwest part of Muncie, a city that had seen a total value of construction of only $111,000 in 1933.[77]

Conclusion

By contributing their art holdings, the Balls had helped create a regional college, a teaching hospital, and finally an art museum for Muncie, making it the economic and cultural capitol of east central Indiana and making northwest Muncie the new residential center and economic, intellectual, and cultural laboratory of the city. However, by the end of the 1930s, Ball philanthropy was no longer the sole source of development financing for college expansion or urban development. Through New Deal programs the federal government became a college benefactor, financing construction, providing financial aid to students, and supporting progressive educational initiatives like the Burris School. The 1944 Servicemen's Readjustment Act would intensify this growth after World War II and begin the national transformation to mass higher education.

All of these sources of aid were part of a much larger shift in the federal government's role in higher education, in many ways beginning to supplant the tradition and expectation of private support and philanthropy at institutions such as Ball State, part of a growing commitment of the state in American life. The federal government had also begun to alter the curricula of institutions of higher education, sponsoring basic research and providing fuel for the engine of technological and economic innovation that colleges and universities would become. The consequences for the American economy and the political economy of American regions would be serious, particularly for cities like Muncie in the Midwest that relied upon heavy manufacturing and the creation of durable goods to sustain its workforce. Throughout the period under discussion, private industrial investment continued, largely concentrated in the southeastern part of the city, developing along existing lines. However, even during the 1930s the city saw a dramatic reduction in industrial employment and growth, a long-term shift toward modest growth and contraction that war mobilization and the national post-war boom could not reverse. And while these Depression-era efforts were part of a broad set of initiatives to provide work relief and to stimulate the national economy, in Muncie they served as much to expand the foundations of what would become the postindustrial economy, especially adding capacity to the higher education sector, which would eventually become a key source of employment in its own right, but would serve as the fundamental catalyst for individual and regional economic development in the postwar era.

Though it profoundly altered the economic basis of the city's growth, federal intervention did not change the fundamental direction of development in Muncie. Instead, it intensified the existing pattern of investments that the Ball family had created, continuing a process of social and economic segregation that privileged the emerging group of knowledge workers—part of the business class of citizens the Lynds first identified and categorized in *Middletown*. Even by the 1920s, this tectonic shift had begun to emerge and was readily apparent in the 1930s. Ball State Teachers College, the institution that joined and enabled these two forms of community transformation—economic restructuring and geographic organization—had its origins in land speculation at the turn of the century and found its footing in the community with the strong intervention of the Ball family, whose members rescued, supported, and profited from its operations, even as the political economy of federal aid began to structure a shift away from manufacturing and towards a knowledge economy.[78]

Notes

The author thanks Bruce Geelhoed for his useful comments, and James Connolly and the Center for Middletown Studies for research support and editorial direction—making this study possible.

1. Anthony O. Edmonds and E. Bruce Geelhoed, *Ball State University: An Interpretive History* (Bloomington: Indiana University Press, 2001), 57–66. Charles Van Cleve, "Beneficence: A History of Ball State Teachers College," (Muncie, IN: Ball State University Archives, 1961), 42–43.

2. In this work I have found the scholarship of critical geographers very useful, especially David Harvey, *The Urbanization of Capital* (Baltimore: Johns Hopkins University Press, 1985).

3. While industrial investments in the southern part of the city continued through the postwar period, the investment trend in residential and retail development and educational expansion in the north and west has been far more durable, consistent with the transformation of the broader American economy.

4. John Logan and Harvey Molotch, *Urban Fortunes: The Political Economy of Place* (Berkeley: University of California Press, 1987). Thomas Sugrue, *The Origins of the Urban Crisis: Race and Inequality in Postwar Detroit*, 2nd ed. (Princeton: Princeton University Press, 2003). Margaret Pugh O'Mara, *Cities of Knowledge: Cold War Science and the Search for the Next Silicon Valley* (Princeton: Princeton University Press, 2005).

5. See Frederick Rudolph, *The American College and University: A History* (New York: Alfred A. Knopf, 1962), 4–5. Daniel Boorstin, *The Americans: The National Experience.* (New York: Random House, 1965), 152–61. LaDale Winling, "Building the Ivory Tower: Campus Planning, University Development, and the Politics of Urban Space" (Ph.D. Dissertation, University of Michigan, 2010).

6. Perhaps the most resounding statement of this discovery comes from Kenneth Jackson, *Crabgrass Frontier: The Suburbanization of the United States* (New York: Oxford University Press, 1985).

7. Robert Staughton Lynd and Helen Merrell Lynd, *Middletown in Transition: A Study in Cultural Conflicts* (New York: Harcourt, Brace & Co., 1937), 82.

8. In this respect, such institutions might be seen as adjuncts to or benefactors of the real estate development industry, whether explicitly, as in the case of the Eastern Indiana Normal University, or implicitly, as in many cases where investors and boosters are backers of education institutions for more general economic development effects. See Winling, "Building the Ivory Tower."

9. Robert Staughton Lynd and Helen Merrell Lynd, *Middletown: A Study in American Culture* (New York: Harcourt Brace, 1929). Lynd and Lynd, *Middletown in Transition.*

10. For evidence of this transformation before World War II, see Alexander Field, "The Most Technologically Progressive Decade of the Century," *American Economic Review* 3, no. 4 (2003). Christopher Loss, "From Democracy to Diversity: The Politics of American Higher Education in the Twentieth Century" (Ph.D. Dissertation, University of Virginia, 2007). On the postwar consequences of this transformation see, for example, Lizabeth Cohen, *A Consumers' Republic: The Politics of Mass Consumption in Postwar America* (New York: Vintage Books, 2003), Robert Collins, *More: The Politics of Economic Growth in Postwar America* (New York: Oxford University Press, 2000). On the effects of such transformation on work and organized labor, see Jefferson Cowie, *Capital Moves: RCA's Seventy-Year Quest for Cheap Labor* (Ithaca: Cornell University Press, 1999). Nelson Lichtenstein, *State of the Union: A Century of American Labor* (Princeton: Princeton University Press, 2002).

11. Considering this framework of economic transformation can also help understand the enduring debate regarding local power raised by the Lynds in *Middletown in Transition.* On behalf of the liberal pluralist interpretation, see Nelson Polsby, "Power in Middletown: Fact and Value in Community Research," *The Canadian Journal of Economics and Political Science* 26, no. 4 (1960). In support of the federalist interpretation, see Carrolyle Frank, "Who Governed Middletown? Community Power in Muncie, Indiana, in the 1930s," *Indiana Magazine of History* 75, no. 4 (1979). For a

review of key scholarship on Muncie after the Lynds' work, see James Connolly, "The Legacies of *Middletown*," *Indiana Magazine of History* 101, no. 3 (September 2005).

12. U.S. Census data, 1880, 1890.

13. In 1900, only 3.6 percent of the population was nonwhite, though this increased to 5.7 percent by 1920. U.S. Census data. Edmonds and Geelhoed, *Ball State University*, 44–45. Part of the premise of *Middletown* is that the White Anglo-Saxon Protestant old stock of 1890 and their values were in decline by the 1920s. Lynd and Lynd, *Middletown*, 5–6.

14. Frank C. Ball, *Memoirs of Frank Clayton Ball* (Muncie, IN: Privately printed, 1937). Edmonds and Geelhoed, *Ball State University*, 48.

15. Edmonds and Geelhoed, *Ball State University*, 49.

16. On the prevalence of mainline public and private colleges in the nineteenth century, see Laurence Veysey, *The Emergence of the American University*. The federal Morrill Land Grant Act of 1862 created a line of federal support for engineering and agricultural schools in northern states, followed by the second Morrill Act of 1890, which extended the provisions to southern states. For examples of leading advocates of the integration of higher education and regional economies, see Henry Philip Tappan, *A Discourse: Delivered by Henry P. Tappan at Ann Arbor, Mich., on the Occasion of His Inauguration as Chancellor of the University of Michigan, December 21, 1852* (Detroit: Advertiser Power Presses, 1852). On the broader intellectual transformation of higher education in this period, see Julie Reuben, *The Making of the Modern University: Intellectual Transformation and the Marginalization of Morality* (Chicago: University of Chicago Press, 1996).

17. John Thelin, *A History of American Higher Education* (Baltimore: Johns Hopkins University Press, 2004), 74–109.

18. Burton Bledstein, *The Culture of Professionalism: The Middle Class and the Development of Higher Education in America* (New York: Norton, 1976).

19. Christine Ogren, *The American State Normal School: An Instrument of Great Good* (New York: Palgrave MacMillan, 2005).

20. Delaware County Plat Book. County Recorder. Muncie, Ind. Edmonds and Geelhoed, *Ball State University*, 56.

21. Edmonds and Geelhoed, *Ball State University*, 51–54. Among the investors was George McCulloch, the city's leading transportation entrepreneur. For classic studies detailing the importance of rail transit in the expansion of urban and suburban development, see Sam Bass Warner Jr., *Streetcar Suburbs: The Process of Growth in Boston, 1870–1900*, 2nd ed. (Cambridge, MA: Harvard University Press, 1978), Robert Fishman, *Bourgeois Utopias: The Rise and Fall of Suburbia* (New York: Basic Books, 1987), Ann Durkin Keating, *Building Chicago: Suburban Developers and the Creation of a Divided Metropolis* (Columbus, OH: Ohio State University Press, 1988), Jackson, *Crabgrass Frontier*.

22. In 1902 EINU built a coeducational frame dormitory housing approximately sixty students. Many community institutions served as boosters of the private normal schools and their public successor, including Muncie newspapers. "Muncie Enters

College Fight." *Muncie Sunday Star*, March 30, 1924. Edmonds and Geelhoed, *Ball State University*, 56.

23. Glenn White, *The Ball State Story: From Normal Institute to University* (Muncie, IN: Ball State University, 1967), 33–34. Various sources indicate Palmer did make a sizeable gift before his death, but it seems unlikely the school would fail given such a significant endowment. "Mrs. Rockwell Cut Off from Palmer Wealth." *New York Times*. November 6, 1902. "F.A. Palmer's Kin Seek to Upset Will." *New York Times*, October 16, 1904.

24. Edmonds and Geelhoed, *Ball State University*, 57.

25. The University of California, Los Angeles, for example, originally a normal school, moved to its current Westwood campus in a land development deal between the state and real estate developers. See also the founding of the University of Michigan, where local business leaders donated fifty acres of undeveloped land, and the University of California, Berkeley, the creation of which entailed several land schemes. Andrew Hamilton and John Jackson, *UCLA on the Move: During Fifty Golden Years 1919–1969* (Los Angeles: University of California, 1969), 39–46. Howard Peckham, *The Making of the University of Michigan, 1817–1992* (Ann Arbor: University of Michigan Press, 1997). Verne Stadtman, *The University of California 1868–1968* (New York: McGraw-Hill, 1970), 19–34. In the same era, tobacco magnate Washington Duke became a patron of Trinity College in Durham, North Carolina, which was subsequently renamed Duke University and heavily endowed by his son, James Duke.

26. White, *The Ball State Story*, 41. $7,000,230 in 2008 dollars. Consumer Price Index Inflation Calculator, http://data.bls.gov (accessed August 9, 2008).

27. Edmonds and Geelhoed, *Ball State University*, 60–61.

28. Several sources attest to the Balls' laissez-faire economic ideology and belief in "rugged individualism," conflict though it might with their frequent public-private efforts on Ball State, Ball Memorial Hospital, and establishment of their own business. Lynd and Lynd, *Middletown in Transition*, 74–101. These actions illustrate Joseph Schumpeter's theory on capitalism's trend toward corporatism and pursuit of stability rather than entrepreneurship and the destruction of wealth and existing assets in pursuit of new forms of wealth and exchange. Joseph Schumpeter, *Capitalism, Socialism, and Democracy* (New York: Harper & Brothers, 1942). One such account of real estate in New York uses this theory to explain the city's development history. Max Page, *The Creative Destruction of Manhattan, 1900–1940* (Chicago: University of Chicago Press, 1999).

29. $600,032 in 2008, less than a tenth of its appraised value. Consumer Price Index Inflation Calculator, http://data.bls.gov (accessed August 9, 2008).

30. Edmund B. Ball, "A Lifetime Investment," quoted in Edmonds and Geelhoed, *Ball State University*, 60.

31. Pamphlet. List of Members of the Muncie Rotary Club, 1932. "Membership Lists 1932–1957." Folder 7, Box 5, Muncie Rotary Collection MSS 125, Stoeckel Archives, BSU Special Collections. For a broad history of organizations such as Rotary, see Jeffrey Charles, *Service Clubs in American Society: Rotary, Kiwanis, and Lions*

(Urbana: University of Illinois Press, 1993). Two significant early studies of such clubs include Charles F. Marden, *Rotary and Its Brothers: An Analysis and Interpretation of the Men's Service Clubs* (Princeton, 1935) and University of Chicago Social Science Survey Committee, *Rotary? A University Group Looks at the Rotary Club of Chicago* (Chicago: University of Chicago, 1934). *Middletown*, however, remains the classic small city study of the influence of such an organization.

32. Lloyd Lieurance. "The History of the Organization, Administration, and Control of the Normal School at Muncie, Indiana." (MSS M.S. Indiana State Normal School, 1926), 172–74. BSU ASC. The Muncie transactions sparked interest around the state in socializing private education institutions, notably including Valparaiso College. Horace Ellis to James Goodrich, December 26, 1918. Box 137. Goodrich Papers, Indiana State Archives.

33. Edmonds and Geelhoed, *Ball State University*, 58. Charles Van Cleve. "Beneficence: History of Ball State Teachers College." Pp. 43–44. MSS, Center for Middletown Studies Archives. Ball State University (Hereafter CMS BSU).

34. Indeed, when state education administrators first arrived in Muncie to inspect the property after acquisition, they were feted by the Muncie Commercial Club with a crowd of 200 strong. Lieurance, "The Normal School," 179.

35. The Balls and Muncie residents had to offer an additional gift to the state to provide for any losses the state would incur. Edmonds and Geelhoed, *Ball State University*, 63. "State Can Take Balls' Gift." *Muncie Morning Star*. March 1, 1918.

36. Edmonds and Geelhoed, *Ball State University*, 42.

37. Thomas Buchanan, "The Life of Rollin "Doc" Bunch, the Boss of Middletown" (Dissertation, Ball State University, 1992), 62–65.

38. "Bunch and Annexation, Etc." *Muncie Evening Press*. October 28, 1917.

39. Buchanan, "The Life of Rollin 'Doc' Bunch," 65. Industry was the location of one of two African American neighborhoods in Muncie before World War I and, in the postwar period, became the site of the Munsyana Homes, a federal low-income housing project.

40. Indiana law did not require a majority affirmative vote of residents within areas proposed for annexation. The northwest side of Muncie voted more heavily Republican and the south side more heavily Democratic—thus, Grafton was alienating his potential base in favor of good government and metropolitan equity in hopes of creating a wedge issue to attract members of the Bunch coalition. In the 1919 municipal annexation, the northeastern industrial suburb of Whitely was added to Muncie along with the Normal City and Riverside communities. This changing political geography would continue to roil city elections, particularly during the rise of the Ku Klux Klan in the 1920s. Frank, "Who Governed Middletown?." Leonard Moore, *Citizen Klansmen: The Ku Klux Klan in Indiana, 1921–1928* (Chapel Hill: University of North Carolina, 1991).

41. Lynd and Lynd, *Middletown*.

42. A 33.3 percent sample of students from 1928 indicates approximately 4.1 percent of BTC students (14 of 344) lived on the south side of the city. BTC

Student Directory, 1928–1929. BSU ASC. In *Middletown*, the Lynds contrast the education planning of the business class, where preparation for college—including family saving and consideration of high school coursework—was nearly universal, to the working class, where preparation for college was rare and, when it did occur, was vague and aspirational rather than concrete and operational. Lynd and Lynd, *Middletown*, 187–89.

43. Lynd and Lynd, *Middletown*, 185–87.

44. See interviews in the Middletown Jewish Oral History Project I, including, for example, R 14, Sherman Zeigler, February 26, 1979.

45. White, *The Ball State Story*, 239. Edmonds and Geelhoed, *Ball State University*, 80.

46. Edmonds and Geelhoed, *Ball State University*, 98.

47. Edmonds and Geelhoed, *Ball State University*, 117–18.

48. Edmonds and Geelhoed, *Ball State University*, 117.

49. Pragmatist philosopher John Dewey became an education reformer and first created the renowned Laboratory School at the University of Chicago. For a key example of his thought, see John Dewey, *The School and Society* (Chicago: University of Chicago Press, 1900). Lynd and Lynd, *Middletown in Transition*, 219.

50. Urban historians have largely neglected the importance of schools in creating and reaffirming metropolitan segregation. See Jack Dougherty, "Bridging the Gap between Urban, Suburban, and Educational History," in William J. Reese and John L. Rury, eds., *Rethinking the History of American Education* (New York: Palgrave Macmillan, 2007).

51. Spurgeon Wiley, *Ball Memorial Hospital, 1929–1989: A Legacy of Caring* (Muncie, IN: Ball Memorial Hospital, 1989).

52. Ball, *Memoirs*, 138.

53. Edmonds and Geelhoed, *Ball State University*, 87–88.

54. Wiley, *Ball Memorial Hospital*, 45.

55. Ball, *Memoirs*, 138.

56. Jena Noll, *The Residential Architecture of Cuno Kibele in Muncie, Indiana, 1905–1927.* (MS Thesis, Ball State University, 1999).

57. Ball, *Memoirs*, 139. $2,010,000 in 1929, the equivalent of $25.9 million in 2008. CPI inflation calculator, http://data.bls.gov (accessed August 25, 2008).

58. In the first years of the Westwood development, industrialists predominated. However, throughout the twentieth century the number and proportion of the industrialist class declined, while the amount of physicians and educators dramatically increased, together far outnumbering industrialists by the end of the century. Frederick Graham and Dawn Lee Patrick, *Westwood: A 75 Year History* (Muncie, IN: Minnetrista Cultural Foundation, 2000).

59. U.S. Bureau of the Census. *1950 Census of the Population* Table 75. Vol. II Characteristics of the Population. Part 14, Indiana.

60. For example, see Frederick Lewis Allen, *Only Yesterday: An Informal History of the 1920s* (New York: Harper and Row, 1964), 139–40. On the impact of Fordism

and its relationship to advertising, see also Susan Strasser, *Satisfaction Guaranteed: The Making of the American Mass Market* (New York: Pantheon, 1989).

61. County land records testify to the active participation of several members of the family in real estate.

62. Graham and Patrick, *Westwood: A 75 Year History*.

63. Plat of Westwood. Delaware County Plat Book, p. 68. County Recorder. Muncie, Ind. See Wendy Plotkin, ""Hemmed In": The Struggle against Racial Restrictive Covenants and Deed Restrictions in Post-WWII Chicago," *Journal of the Illinois State Historical Society* 94, no. 1 (2001). Jackson, *Crabgrass Frontier*.

64. Plat of Westwood. Delaware County Plat Book, pp. 65–68.

65. Whitely was originally planned as a white industrial suburb but the northern migration of African Americans earlier in the century had made it one of the centers of the metropolitan black population. For the first major effort to understand this process of black suburbanization in the United States, see Andrew Wiese, *Places of Their Own: African American Suburbanization in the Twentieth Century* (Chicago: University of Chicago Press, 2004). On the historical geography of industry, see, for example, Robert Lewis, *Chicago Made: Factory Networks in the Industrial Metropolis* (Chicago: University of Chicago Press, 2008).

66. Advertisement. "Westwood—A Residential Park." *Muncie Sunday Star*. October 19, 1924.

67. Plat of Westwood Park. Delaware County Plat Book. County Recorder. Muncie, Ind.

68. Lynd and Lynd, *Middletown in Transition*, 81–82.

69. Lynd and Lynd, *Middletown in Transition*, 82.

70. "Muncie Ind. Is the Great 'U.S. Middletown.'" *LIFE*. May 10, 1937.

71. For broader interpretations of the New Deal investigating the business-friendly nature of these reforms without consideration of the spatial and geographic implications, see Colin Gordon, *New Deals: Business, Labor, and Politics in America, 1920–1935* (New York: Cambridge University Press, 1994). Alan Brinkley, *The End of Reform: New Deal Liberalism in Recession and War* (New York: Knopf, 1995).

72. See especially Bruce Schulman, *From Cotton Belt to Sunbelt: Federal Policy, Economic Development, and the Transformation of the South* (New York: Oxford University Press, 1991). Jason Scott Smith, *Building New Deal Liberalism: The Political Economy of Public Works, 1933–1956* (New York: Oxford University Press, 2006). Robert Leighninger, Jr., *Long Range Public Investment: The Forgotten Legacy of the New Deal* (Columbia: University of South Carolina Press, 2007).

73. Alice Rivlin, *The Role of the Federal Government in Financing Higher Education* (Washington, D.C.: Brookings Institution, 1963). For a key statement of postwar higher education, see Clark Kerr, *The Uses of the University*, Fourth ed. (Cambridge, MA: Harvard University Press, 1963; reprint, 1995). On the postwar knowledge economy, see Stuart Leslie, *The Cold War and American Science* (New York: Columbia University Press, 1994), Rebecca Lowen, *Creating the Cold War*

University: The Transformation of Stanford (Berkeley: University of California Press, 1997), O'Mara, *Cities of Knowledge.*

74. Appendix III, tables 1 and 2. Lynd and Lynd, *Middletown in Transition*, 13, 529–32. John T. Dunlop and Walter Galenson, eds., *Labor in the Twentieth Century* (New York, Academic Press, 1978), 27.

75. William Leuchtenberg, *Franklin D. Roosevelt and the New Deal, 1932–1940* (New York: Harper & Row, 1963), 133. Proportionally, education buildings were the second best-funded PWA project type in terms of both number of projects and project funds after streets and highways. Streets and highways received 15.7 percent of funds while education buildings received 14.0 percent. Smith, *Building New Deal Liberalism*, 90. The PWA could provide 35 to 40 percent of the cost of a project in grants and offer a significant portion of the balance in loans. Leighninger, *Long Range Public Investment.* The institution became known as Ball State Teachers College in 1929. The National Youth Administration helped college-age Americans attend higher education institutions during the Depression by providing scholarships or stipends for hourly work. Richard Reiman, *The New Deal and American Youth: Ideas and Ideals in a Depression Decade* (Athens: University of Georgia Press, 1992). Ball State's enrollment fluctuated between 1,000 and 1,200 during the 1930s, while nationally full-time higher education enrollment grew from 588,000 to 874,000 between 1930 and 1939, 4.8 percent per year, including decreases during 1932 and 1933. Garland Parker, *The Enrollment Explosion: A Half-Century of Attendance in U.S. Colleges and Universities* (New York: School & Society Books, 1971), 28–32.

76. The PWA provided a grant of $128,000 to BSTC and Ball contributed $100,000 to cover the part of the required local match for the building that cost $442,000. The college subsequently received PWA grants of $130,000, $43,000, and $66,000 to expand the Burris teacher training school, Assembly Hall, and Ball Gymnasium, respectively. Letter from A.H. Hinkle to L.A. Pittenger, March 29, 1934. RG 3 President's Papers. Letter from W.E. Wagoner to F.M. Logan, May 29, 1933. "Buildings, Federal Aid" Box 6. RG 3 President's Papers. BSU ASC. Ball, *Memoirs*, 137. Edmonds and Geelhoed, *Ball State University*, 102. Letter from D.R. Kennicott to Lemuel Pittenger, August 25, 1938. Letter from D.R. Kennicott to Lemuel Pittenger. Folder "Buildings 1938" Box 6 RG 3 President's Papers. BSU ASC. Letter from Sherman Minton to Lemuel Pittenger, June 14, 1939. Folder "Federal–National NYA, Dept. of Interior." Box 19. RG 3 President's Papers. Stoeckel Archives. BSU ASC.

77. $367,000 in 1935 inflates to approximately $5.7 million in 2009. CPI Inflation Calculator, http://data.bls.gov (accessed January 17, 2010).

78. The Ball Corporation is itself an illustrative example of this shift. Ball purchased a Colorado firm in 1956, which made a small weighing device useful in transportation. However, this division subsequently came to develop technology for the aerospace industry, NASA, and the Department of Defense, while the Ball Corporation spun off its glass jar divisions. In 1998, the Ball Corporation moved its headquarters to Broomfield, Colorado, and no longer manufactures glass jars or has a presence in Muncie.

~

CHAPTER SIX

Curing the Rust Belt?

Neoliberal Health Care, Class, and Race in Mansfield, Ohio

ALISON D. GOEBEL

In 1966, the Mansfield City Directory boasted that this small north central Ohio city had the second highest average family income in the state.[1] Though smaller than the state capital, Columbus, and the major industrial cities of Cleveland, Cincinnati, Akron, Canton, Toledo, and Youngstown, Mansfielders enjoyed all the benefits of big city living. By 1970, unemployment was at 4.4 percent and over 40 percent of Mansfield's 55,000 working residents labored in manufacturing. Another 25 percent were employed in the banking, real estate, educational, and health professions that developed alongside the factories, and close to 35 percent worked in the retail and service industries that served Mansfield's blue and white collared workers.[2] Mansfield's high income levels sustained numerous department stores, three regional train lines, jazz clubs, bars, restaurants, four movie theaters, rigorous public schools, competitive youth athletic programs, and solid rates of new housing development. Located halfway between Columbus and Cleveland, Mansfield seemed to be the perfect alternative to the volatility of large postwar cities and the conformity found within their growing suburbs. Seeing themselves as a smaller, better paid version of a quintessential metropolis, such facts of prosperity and success were important for Mansfielders in understanding themselves and their small city.

Four decades later, residents struggled to reconcile the image of Mansfield as it once was with what it had become in the new millennium. By 2008, Mansfield was among the poorer cities in Ohio with high rates of unemployment, spiking numbers of housing foreclosures, a shrinking city government budget, public schools in academic emergency, and an aging population.[3] Like many cities in the industrial midwest, Mansfield has struggled to regain its footing since the 1980s and 1990s when factory after factory downsized or closed and thousands of unionized workers were left underemployed and often without any work. Mansfield's recent history hews to the standard story told of deindustrialization which emphasizes the devastating effects of capital withdrawal, declining community wealth, and a decaying built environment. And rightfully so; communities throughout the industrial northeast and midwest have been completely decimated socially and economically by the widespread closure of factories and continue to be further challenged by the imploding auto industry. Yet such a rendering of the post-Fordist economy, particularly as experienced by small cities within the United States and Canada, elides several key developments. New industries have been sprouting in deindustrializing North America even as manufacturing has stagnated and declined in prominence, employment numbers, and revenue returns. Corporate investments—especially in the health care industry—and federal and state assistance programs have been moving into the midwest and northeast, helping to construct a new economy in the rust belt.[4]

Instead of working on factory production lines, many local Mansfielders now labor as medical assistants and technicians. But this reconfigured economy has also brought with it new workers: workers who are mostly college-educated, white-collared, and foreign-born or "imported" from other parts of the United States. Prior to the 1990s, Mansfield was almost 90 percent white and 10 percent African American with miniscule numbers of Native Americans, Latinos, or Asian-descent residents. By 2008, the Census estimated that 73 percent of Mansfielders self-identified as white, 23 percent as African American or black, 1.7 percent as Hispanic or Latino, and 0.6 percent as Asian.[5] Two percent of all residents (no matter race or ethnicity) were foreign-born; most were naturalized citizens.[6]

The influx of highly educated and well-paid "outsiders" during the last two decades has reconstituted class disparities in new multiracial and multicultural ways. As a result, simultaneous trends of economic development and divestment, along with the increasingly marked visibility of race, ethnicity, and class, have indelibly imprinted city life with unresolved tensions. As all Mansfielders strive to understand themselves and their changing city, visions of, and for, the small city compete with one another. Mansfield's situation resonates with hundreds of small cities in North America and underscores the often paradoxical and contentious processes of deindustrialization and neoliberal capitalism.[7] The small city of Mansfield suggests a perspective that is often absent in discussions about urban development and points to larger neoliberal trends that are reconfiguring cities throughout the United States.

This chapter is based on anthropological fieldwork conducted in Mansfield between 2005–2010. I lived in Mansfield for two summers and then a full year from 2008–2009 and I periodically return for follow-up ethnographic research. I am not from Mansfield or Ohio; rather, I grew up in the Chicago suburbs. As a white, middle-class woman and outsider to the city, I primarily learned about Mansfield's history and residents' responses to their changing economy through participant observation. I accepted every invitation offered, attending festivals, high school sporting events, and meetings for many different organizations. I hung out in bars and coffeshops, played poker in people's homes, and went to church weekly. I supplemented my participant observation by recording semi-structured interviews with informants from various age cohorts, racial backgrounds, and class backgrounds. I conducted research in the local history archives to document historical changes my informants talked about in interviews and participant observation. While this chapter is based on ethnographic observations I made while doing fieldwork in Mansfield,[8] I use data from the Bureau of Labor Statistics and the Census Bureau to confirm the trends I found emerging in my qualitative research.

Neoliberalism and the Small City

As the county seat and largest city in the twelve county area, Mansfield serves as the economic hub for the north central Ohio region and takes on the brunt of the county's operating costs and civic responsibilities. When factories began to leave the midwest and northeast for the southern United States and then the global south in the 1980s and 1990s, Mansfield and Bromfield County[9] realized the entire area would be severely impacted. As a small city it had fewer sources of revenue than other, larger, cities.

Despite federal programs designed to help cities weather economic change, Mansfield has had uneven success. One reason it has struggled is because the city fits awkwardly into Housing and Urban Development (HUD) classifications that generate decent relief funds or redevelopment programs. (HUD divides locales into two categories: those with a population of 50,001 and larger, and 50,000 and smaller.) As a result, with its current population of just barely over 50,000 people, Mansfield vies against very large metropolises like Cleveland for funding. In some state and philanthropic programs, Mansfield competes against much smaller locales.[10] Being on the cusp of two drastically different federal (and sometimes state and philanthropic) categories has been a constant concern for city government officials.

Therefore, in the 1980s and 1990s, city and county officials sought to retain existing companies and began courting new businesses and industries to replace the leaving ones. As a testament to Mansfield's infrastructure, pre-existing worker know-how, marketing savviness, and a little bit of luck, man-ufacturing was still (just barely) the largest employer in the city and county in 2008, despite the layoffs during the 1980s and 1990s. In 2008, 22.10 per-cent of all employed Mansfielders worked in manufacturing; 20.6 percent in educational services, health care, and social assistance.[11] Yet manufacturing's prominence and prestige has declined precipitously in Mansfield with many small nonunionized shops taking the place of the large unionized factories which had employed thousands in the postwar period.[12] Union membership has significantly declined in Ohio and Mansfield's membership reductions are presumably similar, or even more severe, than the state's. (Because of its size, union membership information for Mansfield is not enumerated by the Bureau of Labor Statistics or the Census.) Youngstown, Ohio has a similar industrial profile to Mansfield's and can serve as an analogous case. In 1986, 36.6 percent of Youngstown workers were union members. By 2009, 20.4 percent of all workers in Youngstown were members.[13] Organized labor has lost numbers and power because the entire nature of labor within the United States has shifted. As factories fled the industrial United States for Latin America, Asia, and Africa during the 1960s–1980s, industrial unions found they no longer had workplaces to organized, or the ability to effectively maintain their members' rights and protections. Membership in service unions (like SEIU and UNITE-HERE) have seen an increase since the 1980s, but service and health care still remain drastically underorganized.[14]

In the 1970s and 1980s, countries and private corporations began imple-menting a range of economic practices which social scientists and urbanists usually call neoliberal capitalism or, simply, neoliberalism.[15] Neoliberal eco-nomic programs maintain that the global marketplace should determine the costs of services and goods. In the name of increasing efficiency and profit, neoliberal economic policies are marked by deregulation, globalization, the rising use of third party contractors, and the privatization of services and responsibilities that the state formerly assumed.[16] However, the World Trade Organization, the World Bank, and nation-states around the world have legislated and enforced policies to ensure this economic approach works.[17]

Accompanying neoliberal economic policies has been the intensification of social practices which position individuals and organizations (including cities) as entrepreneurs, all equally capable of competing in the marketplace as profitable workers, savvy consumers, and self-regulating citizens.[18] More-over, social neoliberal ideologies suggest that one can, and should, improve one's self in order to be a better economic, political, and cultural citizen; whatever shortcomings one might experience, are the individual's responsibility to rectify.[19] With a premium on maximizing profit, racism and other forms of exclusion are morphing to accommodate into the marketplace, but also take advantage of, previously excluded people. Workplaces, schools, and other institutions are becoming more multiracial, multiethnic, and multicultural even as racism and xenophobia (along with ablism, homophobia, sexism, classism, ageism) continue to shape all peoples' life experiences and opportunities.[20] In the context of late global capitalism, the twin processes of neoliberal capitalism and neoliberal social ideologies now inextricably shape life in Mansfield and all cities within the United States and beyond.

Therefore, as a small city, Mansfield has had little choice if it wants a fighting chance on the global marketplace. For example, to cope with the closing of massive factories, the city used state and federal money to expand the two unionized state prisons and offered tax abatements and free utilities to urge ARM Steel to keep Mansfield's steel mill open.[21] Tax breaks and construction costs for utilities were also taken on by Mansfield, its sister village Linden, and Bromfield County to court multinational big box retailers and service industries like call centers. But these measures, while keeping some jobs in place and generating new low-waged, low-skilled jobs, were not enough, and city officials, regional county planners, and business boosters sought other solutions.

While Mansfield was losing its major factories, the industrial midwest and northeast, like much of the country, was expanding local health care facilities and services. Since the late 1980s, the health care industry has grown exponentially, becoming the largest employing industry within the United States by 2008.[22] Such trends tracked similarly in Mansfield and Bromfield County with health care as an employing industry growing 56 percent since 1990. Health care has become the new, largely unacknowleged, economic darling in Mansfield. I focus on the health care industry because it provides a compelling example of how neoliberal capitalism intersects with small city economics and small city social life. Events occurring in Mansfield are familiar to many other small cities within the United States.

Neoliberal Health Care

In 1996, the Mansfield area hospitals—Mansfield General Hospital located within the city and Magnolia Community Hospital located thirty minutes north in the town of Magnolia—merged and were reincorporated as Sunshine Health System. Citizen's Hospital, located immediate east of Mansfield's city

limits in an unincorporated township, was bought by nearby Rosebud Sa-
maritan in 1997 but was permanently closed the following year. Despite the
continued presence of manufacturing in the area, Sunshine is now the largest
single employer in the six-county area it primarily serves. Sunshine indirectly
employs hundreds more because health care in Mansfield, as elsewhere, now
encompasses much more than just hospitals and doctors' offices.

This industry, what Arnold S. Relman calls the medical industrial complex,[23] includes durable medical equipment suppliers, private ambulance and
ambulette services, home health services, nursing homes, medical transcrip-
tion services, dialysis clinics, occupational therapy offices, oncology treatment centers, outpatient surgery practices, digital imaging facilities, case
workers, and much more.[24] Even though Sunshine Health System is nonprofit (and thus tax exempted), the hospital contracts much of its elite staff
(ex. all emergency room medical personnel, cardiac clinic personnel) from
private companies. The third party contracting system is in keeping with
neoliberal economic practices that encourage public sector programs to use
private sector, for-profit, contractors to deliver services.[25]

As it did for retailers and new manufacturers arriving after 1990, the city
of Mansfield and the county took on the cost of running utility lines out to
private medical developments on the edge of the city where local business
partnerships and Sunshine Health System were building doctors' offices and
outpatient clinics. These office complexes, along South Bricklayers Avenue,
line over a mile of the city's "outer belt" and are located several miles away
from the outpatient clinics and the medical offices which grew around the
centrally located hospital. The South Bricklayers Avenue complexes are
mostly private offices, providing non-emergency and in some cases, non-
essential services. While a women's health practice and a dialysis clinic are
located on South Bricklayers, so are private clinics and a medical spa that
offer colon cleansing, botox injections, and chelation therapy.[26]

These offices are not located "in the city," which would be central for
most of the county and on the limited public transit lines used by Mansfielders without transportation. Instead, the South Bricklayers Avenue developments have reconfigured the city by expanding the municipal boundaries and
carving out a new niche for middle-class and upper-class patient-consumers.
In interviews, informants perceived the city neighborhood around the hospital to be dangerous because it is primarily renter-occupied, with aging
housing stock and is racially mixed. The South Bricklayers Avenue developments enable residents to avoid the hospital neighborhood completely. The
construction of specialty practices on the edge of the municipal limits is
happening in rust-belt cities around the nation.[27]

Small cities heavily court and subsidize niche specializations because the health care market is so fierce. In order to distinguish themselves from regional competitors, local health care systems often target particular consumers. Mansfield's Sunshine Health System boasts that it has the number one best cardiac surgery unit in the state and "cancer treatments, diagnostics procedures, and research protocols are the same as those offered by hospitals in larger cities, without the hassle of daily commuting."[28] Other small rust-belt cities like Richmond, Indiana, advertise that they have the highest quality digital imaging and comprehensive heart center in the area. Decatur, Illinois, has primary stroke center certification.[29] Small cities use financial assistance and tout their pre-existing infrastructure to convince hospitals and health care providers to expand facilities. The relative ease in driving to a small city for health care—health care which is as competent as big city care—enables a place like Mansfield to draw consumer-patients who might otherwise go to Columbus or Cleveland for treatment.

But I contend that it is not just small cities driving the intensification and growth of the health care industry in the rust belt. I believe the medical industrial complex was, and continues to be, interested in former industrial cities precisely because of the industries that previously dominated places like Mansfield. Although many factories downsized or closed in the 1980s and 1990s, plenty of unionized retirees with generous benefit packages and pension plans remained in the city after the plants shuttered. Until recently, it seemed guaranteed that retired workers would have benefits in perpetuity. As it is, almost one fourth of Mansfield's households received retirement income from 2006 to 2008.[30] Strong union contracts and revenue from other worksites were high enough to support early retirees, full-term retirees, and their spouses.[31] Having bought their homes and established roots locally, it was unlikely that many former workers or their spouses would leave the city and take their health care plans with them. Instead these residents were locked into the area, and as their aging bodies required more care (especially likely for those that worked in the dangerous and environmentally hazardous conditions found in and around most manufacturing plants); they would become long-term "clients" of the industry.

Additionally, in Mansfield at least, the prisons, GM, and ARM Steel continue operating,[32] and with these unionized workplaces, workers and some dependents continue to access health insurance. With general trends of downsizing and reduced production in the last two decades, the most junior (and thus usually youngest and healthiest) employees have been let go first, leaving an older unionized workforce in place. In general, these workers need more care due to age and time on the job and have access to health benefits through union contracts that pay for back surgeries, knee replacement surgeries, heart stents, and other major, costly procedures. Although many of the remaining manufacturing shops in Mansfield use long term "temporary" and "contract labor" in order to avoid union demands, and union membership has declined in Mansfield, the number of households drawing retirement benefits is seven percentage points higher in Mansfield than in the United States.[33] Social security pensioners and survivors receiving benefits account for 31.9 percent of all Mansfield households (Medicare reimbursements are not included in this enumeration).[34] Civilian veterans makes up 10.2 percent of the population and often qualify for VA benefits.[35]

Even as GM and other companies have negotiated recent rollbacks in union contracts, which have included the slashing of health benefits for spouses, many workers who retired with enough savings turned that capital into property and stock investments. The landlord/tenant ratio in Mansfield is noticably lopsided vis-à-vis the country at large and reflects both the low cost of property and one common way middle-class and elite Mansfielders generate income. In the 2006–2008 U.S. Census Community Survey, Mansfield's owner/renter ratio was 58.9 percent : 41.1 percent. The nation at large was 67.3 percent : 32.7 percent. While doing research in Mansfield it seemed as though almost every white homeowner over the age of fifty I encountered, and a good number of older black homeowners I met, actually owned more than one home—their primary residence and then their rental property. Although it sometimes felt like every homeowner I was ever introduced to had another property, certainly that was not the case.

However, according to the 2006–2008 Community Survey, 21.4 percent of all households in Mansfield received income through rent income, stock dividends, savings and bond interest, or estate and trust fund payouts (the census does not enumerate median dollar amounts per subcategory, nor does it break down this information by race, age, or sex). Assuming that the vast majority of households receiving interest, dividends, or net rental income own their own home, the proportion is actually 36.4 percent. Nationally, 25.1 percent of all households reported rental or dividend income in 2008.[36] In most cases landlords in Mansfield only own one or two other properties, but income from those rentals is enough to pay for vacations, children's college tuition, save for financial emergencies, indulge in pricy hobbies like car restoration, and in general maintain a middle-class lifestyle. This kind of captive capital, which seemed somewhat assured in the late 1990s and early 2000s, guaranteed that people would pay for medical care, even for care that private insurers or Medicare didn't pay for.

I certainly do not want to suggest that Mansfielders have wonderful health insurance plans, plentiful savings, or that everyone even has access to health care. On the contrary, more and more residents are going without health insurance and many are forgoing medical attention because they can not afford it.[37] The majority of my informants, in fact, were not privately insured, though some had Medicaid, Medicare, Social Security Disability Insurance, or SCHIP (state-sponsored health insurance for children). But in many cases, particularly among working-class, working-poor, and unemployed Mansfielders, basic pain and cold medicines are beyond everyday budgets and people do without, borrow money, or forgo other expenses in order to access rudimentary medical supplies.

Those who are lucky enough to receive medical attention and medication through the public health clinic, emergency room, public assistance programs, or by paying out of pocket, regularly take only part of their prescriptions. One working class family I interviewed saved money by giving their son ADHD medication only during the school year (colleagues in the mental health field tell me this is a common strategy nationwide). Over time I learned that many of my informants saved medication for another bout of illness—either their own or a family member's or friend's. These medications were rarely sold for money, but were exchanged as part of a larger economy of circulating goods, capital, and familial obligation. Such practices are in keeping with the more general economy of neighborliness and reciprocity in low income communities.[38]

The most commonly shared pills—those for pain and for sleep—are certainly attractive to all people, but they are especially prized by sleep-deprived, low-waged workers who may work more than one job, usually on their feet on factory lines, in restaurants, in big box store aisles, or as maintenance and cleaning crews. Inhalers are another often-shared medication and are also sought-after by industrial workers and service workers, many of whom have difficulty breathing after working years with chemicals or in particulate dust. While one prescription might be divided among family members or friends, there is still a large consuming market for these medications in Mansfield and pharmaceutical companies are not losing money, even on shared prescriptions. In fact, peer-to-peer sharing accounts for a fair number of requested prescriptions. Also, the free medical and mental health clinics usually give out samples in order to save patients money; this generosity by pharmaceutical companies works to make Mansfielders familiar with targeted medicines and is written off as a tax-deductible donation by the pharmaceutical company. Surely, health care industries, especially pharmaceutical companies, recognize that they have a captive and receptive pool of potential consumers in the rust belt.

Living and moving through a built environment with many brownfields, older housing stock with asbestos and lead, and a continued presence of air pollution sickens a high number of residents. Mansfielders are also "unhealthy" because many, especially working-class and poor residents, have limited food options. One white woman in her sixties told me in the summer of 2008, "they say everyone's overweight but it's not everyone you know. With the cost of gas going up, how much do you think fresh vegetables and fruits are going to cost this summer? We can't pay for it, even if we wanted good food. Celebrities and you know can afford to stay thin. They have the personal chefs and can buy fresh food. I can't."

Cigarette breaks are still honored in Mansfield and many former industrial cities; drinking is a relatively cheap way to socialize with coworkers, family, and friends.[39] Economic insecurity, and thus insecurity about the future, has also led to a rise in mental illness. Residents struggle with nostalgia for a city as it once was and with the unfulfilled fantasies of the economic and social securities formerly found in the city. The stress of being unable to provide the consumer goods, and sometimes basic necessities, for children, parents, partners, and families troubles many Mansfielders, especially men.[40] The health care industry must be well aware of the rates of respiratory illness, high blood pressure, heart disease, diabetes, and other corporeal marks of the stresses and cultural practices of rust-belt living.

Filc argues that the intensification of the health care industry capitalizes on neoliberal models of care and individualization. These frameworks encourage personal responsibility among patients; in this way individuals self-diagnose and proactively request treatment, or treat themselves. As a result, specialty and designer care has increased, as has the outsourcing of family or community based care to group homes, nursing homes, home health aides and other health experts. Such practices of personal responsibility and outsourcing dovetail with frameworks that emphasize biomedical (versus sociostructural) explanations for health. "The medicalization of everyday life plays a significant role in determining the importance of the health care sector as a field for capital accumulation . . . medicalization contains the potential to make almost any problem appear to be a "health problem," medicine becomes the answer for problems whose origin is social."[41] Entire industries and facilities of expert health knowledge have developed in Mansfield and throughout the rust belt to treat symptoms.

Neither the industry, nor the city that courts the medical industrial complex, acknowledge that many of these health problems are expressions of unaddressed societal problems. Understanding people's obesity or overweightness, smoking, substance use or abuse, and other "unhealthy" activities as individual failings elides societal problems that create a conducive environment for these deviances.[42] Certainly people are making the decision to smoke, drink alcohol, use drugs, and eat unhealthy food despite the presence of public service announcements, media reports, public health campaigns, and medical advice that warn against these potentially self-harming practices. But focusing solely on individuals ignores larger problems like chronic individual and community stress, constrained family budgets for fresh food or preventive medical care, and the lack of state commitment to healthy communities and healthy choices. Even when state agencies work to improve poor and working-class lives, their efforts are partial and benefits uneven as social welfare programs compete with state economic policies that created the need for these programs in the first place.

Reproducing Class in the Small City

As union-secured corporate paternalism disappeared along with factories in the 1990s, the state was forced to address the voids created by capital withdrawal, decimated wages, and contract rollbacks. In response, the Social Security Administration and the Department of Job and Family Services expanded their offices in Mansfield to develop worker retraining programs, GED programs, unemployment benefits, and government assistance programs through food stamps, housing vouchers, and rent assistance. United Way partners like the Area Agency for Aging and the drug and alcohol center also grew as the societal impact of the stresses of unemployment became obvious. Although the Clinton administration sharply curtailed government assistance benefits nationwide, the number of recipients went up within Mansfield.[43]

For those workers who were negatively affected by factory closure, the state attempted to find them new jobs in nonunionized manufacturing, service industries like call centers, or significantly, in the health care fields. Many workers and soon-to-be workers were encouraged to get certificates and associate's degrees at the local technical college. Of the twenty-eight associate's degrees and eighteen certificate programs currently offered, almost half are in health care fields.[44] The technical college also maintains agreements with colleges and universities within Ohio and hosts visiting instructors, two way video conferencing, and online courses for bachelor degree programs. Again, almost half of these bachelor degrees are in health care (primarily nursing) or technical fields like information technology and technical management.[45]

Also indicative of the push toward health services was the establishment of a private college of nursing through Sunshine Health System in 1997.[46]

Perhaps the most obvious evidence of how much the small city is banking on health care (as well as new iterations of manufacturing and production), can be found in the public school district. Within the last decade, the Mansfield City Schools have established a health technologies course series for its high schoolers and in 2008 considered developing a biosciences and health sciences magnet school. Fifty-five percent of public school high schoolers are in "Career Tech" courses, which include the health technologies series, as well as childhood education classes, machine technology, construction and maintenance, CAD, culinary arts, and cosmetology.[47] While these skills are practical and useful, and do indeed help city high schoolers find jobs after graduation, these jobs reproduce class and employment stratifications. Students in these courses are tracked out of liberal arts college preparatory courses and away from the foundational educational resources and requirements needed for professional, white-collared, high-paying jobs.

Of intersectional significance is that many of these career tech students are white Appalachians and people of color of all class backgrounds, and working poor whites. According to many of my informants, the school system has historically tracked these marginalized groups into the "industrial arts" and nonhonor courses. From my observations in the public schools during the 2008–2009 school year, it is clear this kind of tracking is still practiced, though perhaps it is not as obvious today as over half the student body is classified as economically disadvantaged and it is almost equally divided between whites and nonwhites.[48] Tracking racially, culturally, and economically marginalized students into the industrial arts and career tech programs disadvantages precisely the students who would gain the most from preparatory courses and training for liberal arts university degrees.

While renal dialysis technicians and emergency medical technicians can earn more than their peers who work in fast food or at the local plastics factory, these are still extremely low-waged jobs. Even more to the point, medical technician and health care support occupations that are overwhelmingly filled by women (for example, nurses' assistants, home health aides, phlebotomists) are especially low paying, with a national average of $26,340 a year.[49] Mansfielders earn less than the national average at $23,200 a year. The largest subgroups of health care workers in Mansfield—home health aides; and nursing aides, orderlies, and attendants—average $19,380 and $21,200 respectively.[50] The commodification and neoliberalization of health work is in line with enduring modes of capitalism that appropriate and undervalue the important and economically critically work women do.

Although city boosters treat the medical and health care industry as the answer to factory closures, these $7.25–$12 an hour jobs are the new contingent labor workforce. Many jobs are call-in (i.e., as needed) or part time.[51] Ironically, only some of these jobs provide medical benefits to their employees and there is no nurses' union or health care workers' union in Mansfield. Moreover, I know from interviews with workers and patients that many Mansfielders, especially women, do unlicensed home care at rates below the minimum wage. These freelance jobs are often established between family members (for example, a niece caring for a widowed aunt) or among neighbors (a stay-at-home mom may assist her elderly neighbors with light housecleaning and changing bandages three times a week).

Medical technology and assistant jobs, and much of the primary and secondary schooling administered in the city, do not prepare Mansfielders to prescribe treatment in an emergency room or perform surgery in the local cardiac clinic. Nor do the associate and bachelor degree programs, and pre-professional high school curricula adequately train Mansfield's youth and young workers for the white-collared administrative jobs that are also being generated in the rust belt. Instead of functioning as college preparatory institutions, the high school and local technical college have become service schools. Donald Castle, a researcher of Mansfield City Schools, traced how the high quality of public education declined during the 1980s because sharply reduced school funding limited course work opportunities and did not replace aging equipment or keep up with new technologies.[52] In his dissertation, Castle delineated how factory closures led to lower property tax revenues from companies and individual homeowners who were laid off and losing their homes. Those families who had the financial ability to pay property taxes often used their resources to move to nearby towns, thus moving into a new school district.

The lasting impact of losing high-paying jobs is evident on the current educational opportunities for students today: only 30 percent of all residents paid their city income taxes in 2008, meaning that the most recent school levy actually generates only one-third of the promised revenues.[53] The same shortfall applies to a 2008 library levy, and recent county nursing home and elderly services levies. Many residents remaining in Mansfield simply cannot afford to pay property taxes, or in the case of some landlords (especially out of town landlords), choose not to. With high numbers of renters (who do not pay property taxes), as well as so many people with burdensome mortgages and constricted incomes, it is no wonder that Mansfield has had a difficult time finding the necessary monies to run basic social services and educational programs. The lack of funds, except in rare cases, also prevents the city from building investigative cases and suing individuals and companies for back taxes.

Additionally, with "School Choice" programs established by No Child Left Behind legislation, city residents can take the money the state and local school district allocate to their school-aged children and use it to pay for private school tuition or out-of-district fees. This federally sanctioned option further exacerbates the public schools' financial deficit and favors bureaucratically savvy parents and guardians. Many of the medical elites and white-collared professionals in Mansfield use "EdChoice" (as it is called in Ohio) to subsidize their children's tuition for Mansfield's private elementary school, one of its two private Christian schools, or stronger school districts nearby. Often, fundamentalist Christain families use EdChoice to recoup homeschooling costs. Like most programs associated with No Child Left Behind, EdChoice uses public monies to pay for-profit, private contractors.

To finance the last months of fieldwork in 2008, I worked as a tutor for a private tutoring company which contracted exclusively with state education departments. My employer received $40 per tutored hour from the state of Ohio; I was classified as a third-party contractor and received half the tutored hour (i.e. $20) in untaxed wages. The students I worked with were each eligible for up to 28.5 hours of tutoring or $1,140 worth of private tutoring, funded through state dollars. Through the neoliberalization of education, the divide between the financially secure and the insecure continues to widen.

Making New Hierarchies

The expansion of the health care industry has reenergized long-standing class and racial divisions in Mansfield while also creating new fissures in the social terrain. Mansfield has become more multiracial and class stratified in the last two decades because, as many residents have pointed out to me, there were very few homegrown professionals during the 1990s. As a result, there has been a small, but steady, in-migration of medical elite who staff specialty departments and clinics, and white-collared professionals with advanced degrees who administer the government agencies, educational programs, and human service nonprofits that expanded in response to corporate withdrawal. While a few "locals" fill these jobs, many of the doctors are "foreigners" and most of the human services positions are held by "imports." In the last twenty years fewer people have moved to Mansfield and the kinds of people moving to Mansfield have tended to be middle class, not working class as before in the interwar and postwar period. The slow down of in-migration rates, as well as the changing face of migrants has brought the backgrounds and attributes of current "imports" to the fore in ways that were not as emphasized previously.

Those born, raised, and still living in Mansfield as adults usually call themselves and are called "locals," "natives," or "real Mansfielders." This category applies to white Mansfielders and Mansfielders of color, no matter their occupation, class position, or ancestral geocultural origin. When discussing the city's social categories, residents most often emphasize commitment to community and pride in the city as the defining criteria of localness. Localness comes from one's embeddedness in social and familial networks that stretch throughout the city and over generations.

Locals often call the recently arrived medical elite "foreigners" as they tend to be South Asian, South Asian American, East Asian, East Asian American, and sometimes Eastern European. Local Mansfielders often do not make a distinction between internationally born and U.S.-born physicians, surgeons, and specialists. These nonwhite elites frequently are not part of white and black local Mansfielders' images of their city, although their presence, especially in health care settings, is often hypermarked and a source of tension and frustration for native Mansfielders. In doing research, I met three medical professionals (and suspect there are many more) who moved to the area for the fabulous packages offered by firms contracted by the nonprofit hospital, and for job opportunities in Mansfield that are much more difficult to attain in larger urban settings. Some moved to Mansfield on four to five year contracts (this is how emergency room work is contracted throughout the nation), others had moved permanently.

In general, the medical elite keep a very low profile in Mansfield because they are treated as "foreign" to small city life and because many have interests that lie beyond the city limits. Moreover, four- and five-year contracts often inhibit medical professionals from establishing local roots. In spite of their low public visibility, Mansfield's racial terrain is becoming increasingly variegated as more and more foreign born medical professionals arrive in Mansfield to staff the growing health care industrial complex. For example, according to one South Asian American informant, 90 percent of Indians and Indian Americans in the Mansfield area are affiliated with the health care industry. I would estimate there are about two hundred South Asians and South Asian Americans in the city. Because Mansfield is so small, to maintain the anonymity of residents, the 2006–2008 American Community Survey does not reveal the breakdown of countries of origin of foreign born inhabitants. In 2008, the Census estimated that less than 1,000 Mansfielders were foreign born, the majority of whom were naturalized citizens.[54]

In contrast to the "local" category and racialized medical elite category, U.S.-born African-American and white professionals who moved to Mansfield as adults are called and call themselves "imports." Nonblack domestic professionals of color, like internationally born medical elites, are often considered "foreign" or are racially indeterminate in Mansfield's biracial imaginary. They, like the medical elites, usually call themselves imports or "transplants." Working class people who move to Mansfield as adults may be called imports, but the term is usually reserved for middle-class, highly educated, white-collared arrivals. Imports tend to socialize with each other and a few locals. In this way, categories of local, foreign, and import index intersecting vectors of social insider/outsider, place of origin, race, occupation, and class.

One self-identified transplant explained she had come to Mansfield because:

> the rich [local] people felt it was below them to allow their children to work these kinds of "in the trenches" jobs so they didn't learn these skills or come back here to use them. The rest of the city, the majority of the city, was never adequately prepared to go to college. People thought the factories would be here forever. So there was a real vacuum. We all arrived here fifteen, twenty years ago when there was another recession going on. We were desperate for work and willing to take it anywhere, even if it wasn't our dream destination.

This interview occurred before the 2008–2009 economic crisis became apparent nationwide; the recession my informant is referring to is the early 1990s period of deindustrialization. Mansfielders of all stripes were, on the whole, rather blasé about the 2008 economic meltdown, telling me "we've been in a recession for at least the last eighteen months. Finally the rest of the country is seeing it too."

Some adult local women went back to college in the 1990s and took jobs in the expanding health and human services fields with their newly-obtained masters of social work and bachelor's of nursing degrees. Recently, more and more local college graduates have decided to remain in or return to Mansfield after obtaining liberal arts degrees. One local young man with a B.A. degree told me, "I love my job [as a middle manager]. I feel like it's a personal contribution. I'm doing my part to bring 500 new jobs to my city. . . . Mansfield is poverty-stricken. This [business] is going to make a difference." Many young, highly educated locals, expressed similar sentiments when I asked them in interviews why they returned to the city after college.

However, Census datum corroborates the common narrative among imports: 14 percent of Mansfielders hold a bachelor's degree or higher. Nationally, 27.4 percent of the population has a higher education degree.[55] While there are plenty of locals who hold professional white-collared jobs and may not have a degree, overall, the low numbers of college graduates in the city is indicative of constrained education opportunities and the region's "brain drain." As a result, the city has had, and continues to have, a reduced pool of locals who fulfill the ongoing and increasing need for adult literacy teachers, child development physical therapists, school psychologists, case managers, social workers, workplace retraining coaches, reference librarians, directors and administrators for the free mental health and medical clinics, the homeless shelter, and the women's shelter. Disparities between working-class and poor residents, and middle- and upper-class residents are reinforced by the arrival of professionals and medical elites.

Plenty of members from elite black and white families have remained in Mansfield, although many generation Xers and Yers never returned after leaving for college on the economic and educational privileges provided by their parents. Those who have come back to Mansfield tend to run family businesses still in existence. Most feel that they are fulfilling a civic and neighborly duty by returning to their city and keeping open long-running businesses. In many ways, they are positively influencing their hometown. However, often times their community service occurs from a distance. For example, although many white elites sit on boards of directors for nonprofits, few work the "in the trenches" jobs that the city needs from these nonprofits in the deindustrializing era. In contrast, most black elite families are elite precisely because they were and are school teachers, ministers, union officials, city government officials, civil rights leaders, and other "in the trenches" workers.

Imports are dedicated to the city in a broad philosophical sense—their jobs by their very nature are "do-gooder" positions. But few medical elites or white collared professionals feel welcomed in the local community and hardly any formally participate in community politics, the public school board, or local nonprofit institutions. For example, during my fieldwork years, no imports sat on the city council; a young professional who has moved to Mansfield from another state was added to the school board mid-term to fill a seat that had opened on account of a death. He was voted out in the next election. The composition of community politics is slowly changing with the arrival of new nonlocals on the school board and in administrative positions in key cultural institutions and nonprofit organizations. However, in many cases, one is invited to join the local chamber of commerce or to participate on the boards of local nonprofits (all these institutions are overwhelmingly run by "locals"). The one exception to the scarcity of imports and medical elites in civic life is committee work at the local private schools where many of their children attend.

Although white-collared professionals are financially secure, many imports do not participate in the (usually expensive and time-consuming) activities that cement one's place in Mansfield's sociopolitical scene. For one,
most white-collared professionals do not bring in the kind of paychecks that
allows them to bid at high-priced charity auctions, attend expensive dinners,
or join private athletic clubs where alliances and power relationships are bro-
kered and cemented. Additionally, many are busy raising children who will,
without question, attend college. Moreover, all imports emphasize the tem-
porariness of their stay in Mansfield. Even though they might have lived in
the city for fifteen years already, they regularly made clear in interviews that
they do not intend to stay in the city after they retire. Instead of becoming
members in organizations that might garner them local status, many imports
prioritize saving money for college funds, dedicating energy and time to family and children's extracurricular activities, and traveling out of Mansfield
on a regular basis. Like the human services professionals, few medical elite
participate in community activities writ large, though they create their own
communities through religious institutions and through culture schools.[56]

At times, nonnatives are asked to participate on a board or to run for local elected positions. But overall, power in the city tends to be held by local
elites. According to many nonelite locals, those (usually white) local elites
who sold family businesses in the 1970s or 1980s still hold fantastic sums
of wealth in the form of stock and property investments. While this claim
seems likely (though unverifiable by an outsider anthropologist), those elite
families and individuals who have stayed in Mansfield do access enormous
funds of historically constituted social and political power. As a result, they
continue to reap the benefits of being, as one import cynically characterized
it, "very big fish in a very little pond." While these positions of influence are
occasionally abused, they are often utilized for the community good.

On the whole, there are marked divisions between imports and local
elites, based on generation, educational background, life philosophies, and
often political persuasions and cultural interests. These differences are not
idle, but are at the heart of the city's struggle to redefine and understand
itself in the new millennium. A struggle over visions for the city's future creates ongoing tensions between locals and imports. As a result, very different
worldviews and methods of accomplishing these projects are simultaneously
shaping the city. While there is sometimes convergence between differing
visions, just as often imports and elites work at odds with one another. Imports are eager to use their cultural and human service institutions for broad
goals of equality and inclusion; bettering the city is a corollary benefit. Some
locals approve of these new visions of the city but many are slow to embrace

the accompanying changes. Most locals are more focused on improving the city—reclaiming the financial security and regional prominence it once had—equality and inclusion are by-products, not the primary aim, of most locals' projects. These similar objectives, but very different approaches, to the city's future mean that energies, resources, and goals diverge in significant and conflicting ways.

Imports who are involved in formal politics, and the many more who administer nonprofit and government assistance and human service agencies, often raise the hackles of old timer power players. Trained in universities and business schools, imports tend to institutionalize protocols and formalize agreements and partnerships. They prefer e-mails and their Blackberries or iPhones to in-person meetings or phone calls. New visions and new ways of "doing business" collide with old-school machine politics, old boys' networks, politicking, and the reliance on well-placed friends.[57] Certainly imports massage the system and participate in nepotism, but they don't have access to important networks or the social capital or trust needed to proficiently and effectively manipulate power in long lasting, expansive kinds of way.

As a small city, Mansfield is a place that remembers generations of genealogical information, neighborly histories, and the associated scandals with each. This familiar, if at times impersonal, knowledge of one's neighbors defines small city social life as much as its geographical boundaries and built environment. Thus, the composition of Mansfield's small city life is changing as power shifts to people whose familial histories are not tied up in extended local families or in decades of exchanged favors. The lack of "references" for newcomers concerns locals and makes them wary of proposed projects and protective of small city life. Because so many imported professionals appear to not feel a significant commitment or connection to the city *itself*, many of the old guard lament the lack of engagement with civic responsibility. When imports attempt to implement or enforce their visions for the city, locals question their right and ability to make claims on the community.

Despite the tensions between old and new ways of doing business, Mansfield creatively copes with community and government cash shortages in ways that speak to the specificity of small city political and social dynamics and the accommodation of disparate world views. Several decades ago, major philanthropic foundations in Mansfield, which are primarily holdovers from family-owned companies, organized themselves into a consortium. The local charitable foundations give their budgeted philanthropic monies to a scheduled pool which then annually allocates the majority of the monies to one receiving charity or organization. In this way, United Way, the art museum, the performing arts theater, the drug and alcohol counseling facility, and other nonprofits do not compete against each other, but receive a sizable donation every several years. This method equitably shares local financial resources and reduces competition. Certainly this arrangement is a gatekeeping mechanism—funding only goes to those organizations recognized by the consortium and which the group feels are doing good work—but it is also in line with older notions of social responsibility and community commitment. The existence of such an agreement points to the advantages of small city social life, highlighting both the strength of gentlemen's agreements among movers and shakers and the formalization of business management by imports.

Conclusion

The social, economic, and political changes found in Mansfield are happening in hundreds of small rust-belt cities. In examining deindustrialization more closely, it is clear that factory closures withdrew massive amounts of community wealth from small cities around the country, but capital did, and continues to, trickle into cities like Mansfield via health care and human services. Yet the expansion of the heath care industry and human services programs has not replaced and enriched the region as boosters and planners might have hoped. Instead, these new industries have provided high-paying jobs to "outsiders" at the expense of local working-class, working-poor, and poor residents. In fact, nonelite locals are increasingly held hostage to the whims and financial decisions of local elites and imported white-collared professionals. As a result, the disparities between the rich and the poor continue to widen with those with professional degrees and college educations almost completely removed from the rust belt's continued economic hardships. In the seams of neoliberal economic programs and social practices, class disparities are being reconstituted, even as cities become more racially, culturally, and socially diverse.

While reproducing longstanding class hierarchies, recent economic programs and developments have brought in a more heterogeneous mix of highly-skilled professionals which has reconfigured the sociocultural landscape of Mansfield and other small cities like it. Residents have struggled to reconcile the multiracial, class stratified reality of their city with their former image of it as being biracial and blue collared middle class. The introduction of new ways of doing business has also importantly impacted the social fabric and sense of what Mansfield is. Struggles over visions for the city's future and who has the sociopolitical weight to make changes continues to plague local elites and white-collared professionals.

Small cities around the nation (and beyond) are experiencing economic and social changes, similar to Mansfield. There is clearly need for more research on the question of race and class within small cities, especially as more and more middle class people in these small cities are people of color. As an initial study, Mansfield's case demonstrates, on a small scale, the shortcoming and limitations of current neoliberal economic policies and cultural practices that claim to uplift all sectors of society.

Notes

My sincere and appreciative gratitude goes to all of Mansfield's residents. Without their generous hospitality and candor, this research would not have been possible. Thanks to participants of the 2009 Ball State University Small Cities Conference for their comments on an earlier draft of this paper; mega props to Jim Connolly for his excellent feedback and abundant patience. This chapter was greatly improved by conversations with my advisor, Professor Alejandro Lugo, and fellow members of his advisee writing group: Aidé Acosta, Korinta Maldonado Goti, and Cristóbal Valencia Ramírez. Thanks to Joe VanCamp for suggestions, math help, and support at every writing stage. This research was funded by a National Science Foundation Dissertation Doctoral Improvement Grant in cultural anthropology and a dissertation fieldwork grant from the Wenner-Gren Foundation.

1. United Telephone Company of Ohio. *Mansfield City Directory* (Mansfield, Ohio: United Telephone Company of Ohio, 1966), blue page 6.
2. Of Mansfield's 55,500 residents, 21,570 were employed during the 1970 Census. Unemployment was 4.4 percent. 15,664 Mansfielders, or 28.5 percent of the city, were fifteen or younger. The remaining 17,766 residents were over the age of sixty-five, inmates, or students not in the labor force. U.S. Census Bureau, *1970 Census: Age by Race and Sex, for Areas and Places, Ohio* (Washington, D.C.: Government Printing Office, 1971), Table 24; U.S. Census Bureau, *1970 Census of General Social and Economic Characteristics Tables: Industry of Employed Persons for Areas and Places, Ohio* (Washington, D.C.: Government Printing Office, 1971), Table 87; U.S. Census Bureau, *1970 Census: Employment Status by Sex, for Areas and Places, Ohio* (Washington, D.C.: Government Printing Office, 1971), Table 85.
3. U.S. Census Bureau, *2006–2008 American Community Survey: Population and Housing Narrative Profile: Mansfield City, Ohio* (Washington, D.C.: Government Printing Office, 2008), factfinder.census.gov/servlet/NPTable?_bm=y&-geo_id=16000US3947138&-qrname=ACS_2008_3YR_G00_NP01&-ds_name=&-redoLog=false (accessed February 23, 2010).
4. Like other scholars, I use rust belt to name the "re-imagined community" that insiders and outsiders construct of the former industrial midwest and northeast. Benedict Anderson, *Imagined Communities: Reflections on the Origin and Spread of*

Nationalism (New York: Verso, 1991); Alejandro Lugo, *Fragmented Lives, Assembled Parts: Culture, Capitalism, and Conquest at the U.S.-Mexico Border* (Austin: University of Texas Press, 2008). Rust belt is not city- or size-specific, but instead indexes the lost dreams that so many people and places have experienced. Steven High, *Industrial Sunset: The Making of North America's Rust Belt, 1969–1984* (Toronto: University of Toronto Press, 2003); Jefferson Cowie and Joseph Heathcott, eds. *Beyond the Ruins: The Meanings of Deindustrialization* (Ithaca: ILR Press, 2003).

　　5. U.S. Census Bureau, *1970 Census: Age by Race and Sex, for Areas and Places, Ohio* (Washington, D.C.: Government Printing Office, 1971), Table 24; U.S. Census Bureau, *2006–2008 American Community Survey: Fact Sheet: Mansfield city, Ohio* (Washington, D.C.: Government Printing Office, 2008) factfinder. census.gov/servlet/ACSSAFFFacts?_event=Search&geo_id=&_geoContext=&_ street=&_county=mansfield&_cityTown=mansfield&_state=04000US39&_ zip=&_lang=en&_sse=on&pctxt=fph&pgsl=010 (accessed February 23, 2010).

　　6. U.S. Census Bureau, *2006–2008 American Community Survey: Table B05002, Place of Birth By Citizenship Status, Mansfield City* (Washington, D.C.: Government Printing Office, 2008), factfinder.census.gov/servlet/DTTable?_bm=y&-context=dt&-ds_ name=ACS_2008_3YR_G00_&-CONTEXT=dt&-mt_name=ACS_2008_3YR_ G2000_B05002&-mt_name=ACS_2008_3YR_G2000_C05002&-mt_ name=ACS_2008_3YR_G2000_B05006&-mt_name=ACS_2008_3YR_ G2000_C05006&-mt_name=ACS_2008_3YR_G2000_B05007&-mt_ name=ACS_2008_3YR_G2000_C05007&-mt_name=ACS_2008_3YR_G2000_ B05008&-mt_name=ACS_2008_3YR_G2000_C05008&-tree_id=403&- redoLog=true&-all_geo_types=N&-currentselections=DEC_2000_SF3_U_ P022&-geo_id=01000US&-geo_id=16000US3947138&-geo_id=NBSP&-search_ results=16000US3947138&-format=&-_lang=en (accessed February 24, 2010).

　　7. For a similar case study, see S. Paul O'Hara, "Envisioning the Steel City: The Legend and Legacy of Gary, Indiana" in eds. Jefferson Cowie and Joseph Heathcott, *Beyond the Ruins: The Meanings of Deindustrialization* (Ithaca: Cornell University Press, 2003), 219–36.

　　8. Robert M. Emerson, Rachel I. Fretz, Linda L. Shaw, *Writing Ethnographic Fieldnotes* (Chicago: University of Chicago Press, 1995); David M. Fetterman, *Ethnography: Step by Step*, second edition (Thousand Oaks, CA: Sage Publications, 1998); Danny L. Jorgensen, *Participant Observation: A Methodology for Human Studies* (Thousand Oaks, CA: Sage Publishing, 1989).

　　9. Except for Mansfield, all other place and contemporary corporate names are pseudonyms, per usual anthropological practice.

　　10. The Department of Housing and Urban Development's two primary redevelopment programs—Community Development Block Grants and HOME grants—provide monies and tax credits to create affordable housing and to redevelop economically depressed neighborhoods. Mansfield competes for HUD funds as an "entitlement community," a designation that applies to participating jurisdictions (usually cities) with 50,000 people or more and gives the community direct control

over HUD funds. Locales with less than 50,000 residents are grouped together and their funds are collectively administered by their state's government. My thanks to Mansfield's Community Development Officer for explaining to me HUD classifications and their implications for Mansfield. Also, Department of Housing and Urban Development, *Community Development Block Grant Program-CDBG* (Washington, D.C.: Government Printing Office, 2009), www.hud.gov/offices/cpd/community development/programs/ (accessed February 21, 2010).

11. U.S. Census Bureau, *2006–2008 American Community Survey: Selected Economic Characteristics: Mansfield City, Ohio* (Washington, D.C.: Government Printing Office, 2008), factfinder.census.gov /servlet/ADPTable?_bm=y&-geo_ id=16000US3947138&-qr_name=ACS_2008_3YR_ G00_DP3YR3&ds_name= ACS_2008_3YR_G00_&-_lang=en&-_sse=on (accessed February 23, 2010).

12. The major factories in Mansfield to close included Westinghouse, Tappan, Humphreys, Ideal Electric, and Barnes Electric (all appliance manufacturers or appliance parts suppliers), Ohio Brass, and Mansfield Tire.

13. Barry T. Hirsch and David A. Macpherson, *Union Membership, Coverage, Density and Employment by CMSA, MSA &PMSA, 1986* (2002), unionstats.gsu.edu/ Met%2086_.htm (accessed April 27, 2010); Barry T. Hirsch and David A. Macpherson, *Union Membership, Coverage, Density and Employment by State, 1986* (2002), unionstats.gsu.edu/State%20U_1986.htm (accessed April 27, 2010); Barry T. Hirsch and David A. Macpherson, *Union Membership, Coverage, Density and Employment by Combined Statistical Area (CSA) and MSA, 2009*, unionstats.gsu.edu/Met_109b. htm (accessed April 27, 2010); Barry T. Hirsch and David A. Macpherson, *Union Membership, Coverage, Density and Employment by State, 2009*, unionstats.gsu.edu/ State_U_2009.htm (accessed April 27, 2010).

14. Leon Fink and Brian Greenberg *Upheaval in the Quiet Zone: 1199SEIU and the Politics of Health Care Unionism*, Second Edition (Urbana: University of Illinois Press, 2009 [1989]).

15. Jean Comaroff and John L. Comaroff, *Millennial Capitalism and the Cultural of Neoliberalism* (Durham: Duke University Press, 2001); David Harvey, *2005 Brief History of Neoliberalism* (Oxford: Oxford University Press, 2005); Justin B. Richland, "On Neoliberalism and Other Social Diseases: The 2008 Sociocultural Anthropology Year in Review," *American Anthropologist* 111:2 (June 2009): 170–76.

16. Biju Mathew, *Taxi!: Cabs and Capitalism in New York City* (New York: New Press, 2005).

17. Neil Brenner and Nik Theodore, eds. *Spaces of Neoliberalism: Urban Restructuring in North America and Western Europe* (Hoboken, N.J.: Wiley Publishing, 2003); Naomi Klein, *The Shock Doctrine: The Rise of Disaster Capitalism* (New York: Metropolitan Books, 2007); Aihwa Ong *Neoliberalism as Exception: Mutations in Citizenship and Sovereignty* (Durham: Duke University Press, 2007); James Ferguson, *Global Shadows: Africa in the Neoliberal World Order* (Durham: Duke University Press, 2006); Jane Juffer "Introduction." Special Issue: The Last Frontier?: Contemporary Configurations of the U.S.-Mexico Border. *South Atlantic Quarterly* 105, no. 4 (Fall 2006): 663–80.

18. Carol J. Greenhouse, ed., *Ethnographies of Neoliberalism* (Philadelphia: University of Pennsylvania Press, 2009).

19. Michel Foucault, *Technologies of the Self: A Seminar with Michel Foucault*, ed. M. Luther, H. Gutman, and P. Hutton (Amherst: University of Massachusetts Press, 1988).

20. Arlene M. Dávila, *Barrio Dreams: Puerto Ricans, Latinos and the Neoliberal City* (Berkeley: University of California Press, 2004).

21. This paper, while about the health care and human services, just as easily could have been about the prison industrial complex and its attendant security industries. In February 2010, incarcerated persons accounted for 9.1 percent of the city's population. Six percent of Mansfielders work as prison employees or in the city's private security sector. Ohio Department of Rehabilitation and Corrections, *Bromfield Correctional Institution* (Columbus: Department of Rehabilitation and Corrections, 2010), www.drc.state.oh.us/Public/rici.htm (accessed February 21, 2010) and Ohio Department of Rehabilitation and Corrections, *Mansfield State Reformatory* (Columbus: Department of Rehabilitation and Corrections, 2010), www.drc.state.oh.us/Public/manci.htm (accessed February 21, 2010). See Staughton and Alice Lynd's work on Youngstown prisons for more on the prison industrial complex in the rust belt. Staughton and Alice Lynd, "Prison Advocacy in a Time of Capital Disaccumulation," *Monthly Review* 53, no. 3 (July–August 2001):128–46.

22. Arnold S. Relman, *A Second Opinion: Rescuing America's Health Care: A Plan for Universal Coverage Serving Patients Over Profit* (New York: PublicAffairs, 2007).

23. Arnold S. Relman. "The New Medical-Industrial Complex," *The New England Journal of Medicine* 303, no. 17 (October 23, 1980): 963–70. Arnold S. Relman, "Shattuck Lecture—The Health Care Industry: Where Is It Taking Us?," *The New England Journal of Medicine* 325, no. 12 (September 19, 1991): 854–59.

24. Since 2000, Ohio has been among the top five states for biotechnology start-up firms. These companies are clustered in Cleveland, Columbus, Cincinnati, and Akron. Proctor and Gamble is headquartered in Cincinnati; Cleveland is home to a Mayo Clinic; Akron a world-renowned children's hospital that specializes in cancer and burns. Despite these industries being located a distance from Mansfield, they, like the health care industry writ large, contribute to the health care industrial complex in the rust belt. Mary Vanac, "Ohio Takes the Lead in Health Ventures," *Cleveland Plain Dealer* May 18, 2008, www.bioenterprise.com/images/company_assets/512F1C7F-0D64-4A5E-9D91-785DC064755F/pdohiotakesthelead may2008_a96a.PDF (accessed February 23, 2010).

25. Sue McGregor, "Neoliberalism and Health Care," *International Journal of Consumer Studies* 25, no. 2 (June 2001): 82–89; Katherine Teghtsoonian, "Depression and Mental Health in Neoliberal Times: A Critical Analysis of Policy and Discourse," *Social Science & Medicine* 69, no. 1 (March 2009):28–35.

26. Chelation therapy removes heavy metals from the body. The FDA approves only a few of the processes and for very specific situations of metal poisoning. Chelation therapy is controversially used for non-FDA approved conditions, like autism and heart disease. *American Heart Association*, "Questions and Answers about

Chelation Therapy," www.americanheart.org/presenter.jhtml?identifier=3000843 (accessed March 3, 2010).

27. Conor Dougherty, "Factories Fading, Hospitals Step In," *Wall Street Journal*, April 15, 2008, online.wsj.com/article/SB120820362569213693.html (accessed September 23, 2009).

28. *Sunshine Health System*, "Cardiac Surgery Ranked #1 in Ohio Two Years in a Row," www.medcentral.org/ body.cfm?id=272> (accessed October 25, 2009); *Sunshine Health System*, "North Central Ohio's Cancer Care Specialists," www .medcentral.org/body.cfm?id=19 (accessed October 25, 2009).

29. *Reid Hospital & Health Care Services*, "Medical Services:Heart Care," www.reid hospital.org/index.cfm?pageID=29 (accessed October 25, 2009); *Decatur Memorial Hospital*, "DMH Nationally Certified as a Joint Commission Primary Stroke Center," www.dmhcares.org/news/StrokeCert4-1-08.asp (accessed October 25, 2009).

30. The census classifies retirement income as: "(1) retirement pensions and survivor benefits from a former employer; labor union; or federal, state, or local government; and the U.S. military; (2) income from workers' compensation; disability income from companies or unions; federal, state, or local government; and the U.S. military; (3) periodic receipts from annuities and insurance; and (4) regular income from IRA and KEOGH plans. This does not include social security income." U.S. Census Bureau, *2000 Census: Census Data Information* "Income in 1999," (Washington, D.C.: Government Printing Office, 2008), factfinder.census.gov/servlet/MetadataBrowserServ let?type=subject&id=INCOMESF3&dsspName=DEC_2000_SF3&back=update&_ lang=en (accessed February 20, 2010); U.S. Census Bureau, *2006–2008 American Community Survey: Table B19059, Retirement Income in the Past 12 Months for Households* (Washington, D.C.: Government Printing Office, 2008), factfinder.census. gov/servlet/DTTable?_bm=y&-context=dt&-ds_name=ACS_2008_3YR_G00_&- CONTEXT=dt&-mt_name=ACS_2008_3YR_G2000_B19059&-tree_id=3308&- geo_id=01000US&-geo_id=16000US3947138&-search_results=01000US&-for- mat=&-_lang=en (accessed February 23, 2010).

31. I use spouse, instead of the more inclusive term "partner," to accurately reflect the heteronormative reality of union contracts and retirement packages in Mansfield.

32. GM announced the closure of the Mansfield plant in June 2009. As of June 2009, AK Steel had been on complete shut down five of the previous six months. Still, prior to the 2008 economic downturn, these factories were running at least one, if not two or three, shifts a day. The prisons are beyond capacity and, despite state budget cuts, require more staff to handle the crowded conditions.

33. U.S. Census Bureau, *2006–2008 American Community Survey: Table B19059, Retirement Income in the Past 12 Months for Households* (Washington, D.C.: Government Printing Office, 2008), factfinder.census.gov/servlet/DTTable?_bm=y&-context=dt&- ds_name=ACS_2008_3YR_G00_&-CONTEXT=dt&-mt_name=ACS_2008_3YR_ G2000_B19059&-tree_id=3308&-geo_id=01000US&-geo_id=16000US3947138&- search_results=01000US&-format=&-_lang=en (accessed February 23, 2010).

34. U.S. Census Bureau, *2006–2008 American Community Survey: Table B19055, Social Security Income in the Past 12 Months for Households* (Washington,

D.C.: Government Printing Office, 2008), factfinder.census.gov/servlet/DTTable?_bm=y&-context=dt&-ds_name=ACS_2008_3YR_G00_&-CONTEXT=dt&-mt_name=ACS_2008_3YR_G2000_B19055&-tree_id=3308&-redoLog=true&-geo_id=01000US&-geo_id=16000US3947138&-search_results=01000US&-format=&-_lang=en (accessed February 20, 2010).

35. U.S. Census Bureau, *2006–2008 American Community Survey: Population and Housing Narrative Profile: Mansfield city, Ohio* (Washington, D.C.: Government Printing Office, 2008), factfinder.census.gov/servlet/NPTable?_bm=y&-geo_id=16000US3947138&-qr_name=ACS_2008_3YR_G00_NP01&-ds_name=&-redoLog=false> (accessed February 23, 2010).

36. U.S. Census Bureau, *2000 Census: Summary File 3: Table P61, Interest, Dividends, or Net Rental Income in 1999 for Households* (Washington, D.C.: Government Printing Office, 2000), factfinder.census.gov/servlet/DTTable?_bm=y&-state=dt&-context=dt&-ds_name=DEC_2000_SF3_U&-CONTEXT=dt&-mt_name=DEC_2000_SF3_U_P061&-tree_id=403&=-redoLog=true&-all_geo_types=N&-_caller=geoselect&-geo_id=01000US&-geo_id=16000US3947138&-search_results=16000US3947138&-format=&-_lang=en (February 20, 2010); U.S. Census Bureau, *2006-2008 American Community Survey: Table B19053, Interest, Dividends, or Net Rental Income in the Past 12 Months for Households* (Washington, D.C.: Government Printing Office, 2008), factfinder.census.gov/servlet/DTTable?_bm=y&-context=dt&-ds_name=ACS_2008_3YR_G00_&-CONTEXT=dt&-mt_name=ACS_2008_3YR_G2000_B19054&-tree_id=3308&-redoLog=true&-geo_id=01000US&-geo_id=16000US3947138&-search_results=01000US&-format=&-_lang=en (accessed February 20, 2010).

37. According to the *Mansfield News Journal*, 15.1 percent of the county's population under the age of 65 was uninsured in 2008. This is up from 11.7 percent uninsured in 2006. 13.4 percent of Ohioans were uninsured in 2008. The newspaper article is pulling from *2006–2008 American Community Survey* results. Russ Zimmer, "More in [Bromfield] Co. Doing Without," *Mansfield News Journal*, September 28, 2009, A6.

38. See Carol Stack, *All Our Kin: Strategies for Survival in a Black Community*, (New York: Harper Torchbook, 1974) for more on this point and for another example of a small city struggling with economic change.

39. Sharon Popp and Maria Swora, "An Ethnographic Study of Occupationally-Related Drinking in the Skilled Building Trades," *Anthropology of Work Review* 12, no. 4 (December 2004): 7–20.

40. Thomas Dunk, "Remaking the Working Class: Experience, Class Consciousness, and the Industrial Adjustment Process" *American Ethnologist* 29, no. 4 (December 2002): 878–90.

41. Dani Filc, "The Health Business under Neo-liberalism: The Israeli Case," *Critical Social Policy* 25, no. 2 (2005): 190.

42. João Biehl and Amy Moran-Thomas, "Symptom: Subjectivities, Social Ills, Technologies," *Annual Review of Anthropology* 38 (October 2009): 267–88;

Katherine Teghtsoonian, "Depression and Mental Health in Neoliberal Times: A Critical Analysis of Policy and Discourse. *Social Science & Medicine* 69, no. 1 (July 2009): 28–35.

43. It is important to note that the shift in the welfare system to a neoliberal one occurred under Clinton, as did many other legislative acts that helped to usher in the current neoliberal turn. For more, see Lisa Duggan, *Twilight of Equality?: Neoliberalism, Cultural Politics, and the Attack on Democracy* (Cambridge: Beacon Press, 2003).

44. The twelve health and human services associate degrees include majors like bioscience, criminal justice, radiology sciences, respiratory care. Eight other associate degrees are in the engineering, computer, and digital arts fields, an indicator of the continued presence of manufacturing and heavy industry in north central Ohio. The final seven degrees are in business, finance, and professional services management. Of the eighteen offered certificate programs, ten are in finance and professional services (e.g., office skills, PC repair, networking-Microsoft, etc) and eight are in health and human services (e.g. early childhood education, educational assisting, community health worker, practical nursing, etc.). Mansfield Community College, "Associate Degrees," www.ncstatecollege.edu/cms/academics/degrees/associate-degrees.html (accessed February 23, 2010).

45. Of the five on-campus bachelor degree programs, three are in education and health services, one in electrical engineering and one in business administration. Of the seventeen online programs, ten are in technology fields, five in health care and human services, and three in business programs. *Mansfield Community College*, "Bachelor's Degrees," www.ncstatecollege.edu/cms/academics/degrees/bachelors-degrees (accessed October 15, 2009).

46. Prior to the incorporation of Sunshine Health System, Mansfield General Hospital had had a school of nursing and offered a hospital-based diploma program which was similar to an on-the-job training and certificate program. The Sunshine College of Nursing is the new millennium's version of that school and now solely offers bachelor of science in nursing degrees at $14,000/year for tuition. *Sunshine College of Nursing*, "Traditional BSN Program," www.medcentral.edu/academics/tradprogrambrochure.pdf (accessed October 15, 2009).

47. *Mansfield City Schools*, "Career Tech," www.tygerpride.com/page.cfm?p=2026 (February 23, 2010).

48. *School Matters*, "Mansfield High School," www.schoolmatters.com/schools .aspx/q/page=sp/sid=60025(February 23, 2010).

49. Bureau of Labor Statistics, *Occupational Employment Statistics: May 2008 National Occupational Employment and Wage Estimates in United States*, (Washington, D.C.: Government Printing Office, 2008), www.bls.gov/oes/2008/may/oes_nat .htm#b29-0000 (accessed February 19, 2010).

50. Bureau of Labor Statistics, *Occupational Employment Statistics: May 2008 National Occupational Employment and Wage Estimates in United States*, "Healthcare Support Occupations," (Washington, D.C.: Government Printing Office, 2008), www.bls .gov/oes/2008/may/oes_31900.htm#b31-0000 (accessed February 19, 2010).

51. *Sunshine Health System*, "Job Opportunities," www.medcentral.org/wide_body .cfm?xyzpdqabc=0&id=120> (February 19, 2010).

52. The city opened a new high school in 2004 which is completely teched out and is every educator's dream facility. Improvements to the elementary and middle schools are slowly occurring. Donald R. Castle, "The Response of the Mansfield City School District to Local Deindustrialization" (PhD dissertation, University of Akron, 1990).

53. My thanks to the superintendent of the Mansfield City Schools, and the president of Mansfield's NAACP branch for alerting me, in 2009, to this circumstance and its ramifications.

54. U.S. Census Bureau, *2006–2008 American Community Survey: Table B05002, Place of Birth By Citizenship Status, Mansfield City* (Washington, D.C.: Government Printing Office, 2008), factfinder.census.gov/servlet/DTTable?_bm=y&-context=dt&-ds_name=ACS_2008_3YR_G00_&-CONTEXT=dt&-mt_name=ACS_2008_3YR_G2000_B05002&-mt_name=ACS_2008_3YR_G2000_C05002&-mt_name=ACS_2008_3YR_G2000_B05006&-mt_name=ACS_2008_3YR_G2000_C05006&-mt_name=ACS_2008_3YR_G2000_B05007&-mt_name=ACS_2008_3YR_G2000_C05007&-mt_name=ACS_2008_3YR_G2000_B05008&-mt_name=ACS_2008_3YR_G2000_C05008&-tree_id=403&-redoLog=true&-all_geo_types=N&-currentselections=DEC_2000_SF3_U_P022&-geo_id=01000US&-geo_id=16000US3947138&-geo_id=NBSP&-search_results=16000US3947138&-format=&-_lang=en (February 24, 2010).

55. U.S. Census Bureau, *2006-2008 American Community Survey: Selected Social Characteristics, Mansfield City* (Washington, D.C.: Government Printing Office, 2008), factfinder.census.gov/servlet/ADPTable?_bm=y&-context=adp&-qr_name=ACS_2008_3YR_G00_DP3YR2&-ds_name=ACS_2008_3YR_G00_&-tree_id=3308&-redoLog=true&-geo_id=16000US3947138&-_sse=on&-for mat=&-_lang=en (Feb. 2010); U.S. Census Bureau, *2006-2008 American Community Survey: Selected Social Characteristics, United States*, factfinder.census. gov/servlet/ADPTable?_bm=y&-context=adp&-qr_name=ACS_2008_3YR_G00_DP3YR2&-ds_name=ACS_2008_3YR_G00_&-tree_id=3308&-redoLog=false&-_caller=geoselect&-geo_id=01000US&-format=&-_lang=en (accessed February 26, 2010).

56. The Islamic Society of Mansfield Area serves mostly South Asian, some Arab, and a few Nation of Islam Muslims. Their congregation is about 130 people. There is a Korean Methodist Church in Linden that ministers about 150 people. There is an Indian Dance Academy for children. The Jewish synagogue has sporadically held Yiddish and Hebrew language classes. Many more informal in-home get-togethers occur among families.

57. Without question, I relied on, and occasionally contributed to these extensive and informal networks. While I sound critical of them, I am completely and forever indebted to informants, colleagues, and friends who "knew someone" for my research.

~

CHAPTER SEVEN

Do Economic Growth Models Explain Midwest City Growth Differences?

Michael J. Hicks

Introduction

A lingering question among economists is whether regional differences in economic growth will tend to cause regions to converge towards similar levels of income. Economists have long been interested in both these dynamics of inter-regional growth and factors which might potentially contribute to differences in both growth and levels of income and other measures of economic activity. Concern about growth is motivated by basic concerns for the welfare of residents. Growth boosts incomes, reduces morbidity, increases life expectancy and in the United States increases income mobility. The presence of convergence is a more subtle issue. Larger regional differences in income have historically led to greater levels of state and federal fiscal involvement in local matters. It also tends to increase intra-national migration, and concentrates transfer payments regionally. The U.S. experience with regional convergence at the sub-state level has involved unequal, but robust growth. In the American rust belt, it may be caused by decline in some areas, and growth in others. For these reasons it is worthy of study.

The basis for most of these types of questions begins with the well-known neoclassical growth model. The foundation of this model considers growth that leads to regional convergence of two types; σ (sigma) and β (beta) convergence. Sigma convergence is measured as the reduction in the dispersal of income around a mean, or convergence in similarity of income.

Sigma convergence would mean that regions are becoming more similar in their economic outcomes. Beta convergence describes a circumstance where poorer regions grow faster than richer regions, and hence "converge" in terms of income or gross regional product on their richer neighbors. The basic neo-classical growth models, and their extensions, predict a form of convergence conditioned on the underlying growth rates of factors of production (most commonly population). However, there is considerable empirical disagreement as to the speed of this convergence.

This chapter seeks to measure both sigma and beta convergence on a panel of carefully selected American cities from 1950 through 2000 in the Great Lakes region. This panel model consists of decennial data for each city, or a time series, cross sectional data set. Modeling this data set permits us to estimate the incremental effect basic growth elements have on income growth in these cities. That is followed by the estimate of a traditional neo-classical growth model (the basis of the Solow-Swan growth model) and its best known extension a simple cross sectional endogenous growth model. I begin with a review of the literature.

Recent Findings

The neoclassical growth function—a regional extension of the Cobb-Douglas production function offered by Solow and Swan independently a half-century ago provide a convenient point of departure for any analysis of regional growth.[1] The model itself posits that growth is a function of labor (N) and capital (K).[2] Following from the Cobb-Douglas model, the relationship includes an exogenous technology parameter, and permits the estimate of returns to scale in the region. The model begins with $Y = f(A, N, K)$ where it is commonly written as $Y = AN^\alpha K^\beta$. A logarithmic transformation of the equation gives it the usual form $\log(Y) = \log(A) + \alpha \log(N) + \beta \log(K)$ which allows us to estimate the equation. Of interest are the values of α and β. When estimated, these coefficients α and β provide a test of returns to scale. Estimates of these values provides some inference as to whether a region enjoys agglomeration economies (increasing returns to scale) or has constant or declining returns to scale (no agglomerations). This is expressed such that:[3]

$$(\alpha + \beta) > 1 \text{ increasing returns to scale}$$
$$(\alpha + \beta) = 1 \text{ constant returns to scale}$$
$$(\alpha + \beta) < 1 \text{ decreasing returns to scale}$$

These relationships are derived from empirical analysis, and typically subject to a signal to noise test (typically the Wald test). Almost all published research on economic development and growth follows from this basis.

The Solow-Swan begins with this model, and focuses on what has been referred to as economic development; since it focuses on the less developed regions (economic growth is more often used in economic literature to describe this phenomenon in developed regions). In the model of growth, Solow in particular focused on the rate of return to capital. In his model, labor was immobile, and there were no other markets than labor, capital, and outputs. Regional differences in growth were attributable to different levels of capital accumulation. Due to diminishing returns, the rate of return on capital in richer regions was beneath that in poorer regions (where it was relatively scarce). As a consequence of capital mobility, investors would seek the higher rate of return. New capital flows would tend to accrue to poorer, not richer regions until the rate of return in regions equalized. This would only occur when regions then experienced identical measures of output (and hence incomes).

In Solow's model, the process by which owners of capital sought out higher rates of return led to a convergence in income. We refer to this as β convergence.[4] The past half-century has seen significant improvements in Solow's model. By relaxing his assumptions a number of useful extensions emerge. Regions with lower savings rates will not enjoy the same rate of capital accumulation if there is any imperfection in capital markets. Thus, the notion of convergence 'conditioned' upon individual regional savings rates provides an important explanation of inter-regional growth differentials. This conditional convergence allows for different steady state growth paths for economies. The factors which are most commonly attributed to conditional convergence are imperfect markets (or monopolization), rigidity in labor markets, failures in government or restrictive trade policies.

The most significant improvement in the model is with the inclusion of human capital into the explanation for growth. Human capital defines a set of attributes: education, health, skills, culture, which contributes to economic growth through labor or entrepreneurial and managerial activity. The human capital augmented, Solow growth model has become standard fare for development economics.[5] Models which account for human capital do so either by directly including measures of human capital differences across regions, or by treating these human capital differences as endogenous to growth. Endogeneity in this context refers to the simultaneity of the relationship or the ambiguity of the direction of causation. The corrections for this lies either in separate modeling of a system of simultaneous equations, or in an identification strategy for a traditional growth model which corrects for inter-regional differences in human capital.[6]

Recent studies of the United States employ one or more of these approaches. Barro, Sala-I-Martin, Blanchard and Hall (1991, hereafter Barro et al.) use a traditional convergence model in the United States, examining states and larger U.S. census regions.[7] Higgins, Levy, and Young (2005, hereafter Higgins et al.) test the convergence model on U.S. counties and extend this analysis in a subsequent paper (2007).[8] Rey and Montouri (1998) estimate convergence in U.S. states, reporting almost identical results to Barro et al. and Higgins et al.[9] Studies of factor contributions to growth have been performed by Glaeser, Scheinkman and Shleifer (1995) and by Bhatta and Lobo in (2000).[10]

The four convergence studies largely confirm the usefulness of the Solow-Swan growth models and their extensions. The remaining studies provide evidence of individual regional contributions to growth, with a main focus on human capital. Stiroh (2000) outlines the differences between the sets of models. He offers the conclusion that the family of neoclassical (Solow-Swan) models and those which treat human capital as endogenous are both important in a full understanding of regional growth.[11] The remainder of the chapter offers tests of each of these models.

Data and the Motivation for this Sample

The data employed in this chapter are derived from a sample of seventy-nine U.S. cities located in the Great Lakes states of Wisconsin, Michigan, Illinois, Indiana, Ohio, and Pennsylvania. These cities were selected as part of a quasi-experimental design for a larger project on traditional Great Lakes cities conducted at Ball State University. All cities were chosen upon their county level population in 1950 (with 50,000 to 125,000 residents). Cities that were later absorbed into a larger multi-county metropolitan statistical area (MSA) were excluded from the sample. The data include both cross-sectional data for each decade prior to 1970, and annual data from 1969 to the present. From these data we construct both panel and cross sectional data sets for testing. Summary statistics appear in table 7.1.

These data, unless otherwise noted, are from 2000. They include count variables of colleges and school districts collected by CBER staff. The GINI Index was obtained from Nielsen (2002), nonprofit income from the Regional Economic Information Systems, and HHI Religion from the Association of Religion Data Archives, with author's computations.[12] Information concern-

Table 7.1. Summary Statistics

Variable	Mean	Std. Dev.	Source
Associates Degree Institution	0.037975	0.192356	Census
Bachelor's Degree Institution	0.151899	0.361216	Census
BA/MA Institution	0.177215	0.384291	Carnegie Foundation
Technical University	0.012658	0.112509	Carnegie Foundation
Theological College	0.075949	0.26661	Carnegie Foundation
Comprehensive University	1.265823	0.857977	Carnegie Foundation
Doctoral Research Institution	0.063291	0.245042	Carnegie Foundation
School Districts (Public)	9.962025	4.836939	National Center for Educational Statistics
GINI Index	31.99101	1.69625	Nielsen, 2002
Nonprofit Income	24271.14	11925.36	Bureau of Economic Analysis
HHI Religion, 2000	4315.225	531.5332	Association of Religion Data Archives
HHI Religion, 1950	2120.053	800.0084	Association of Religion Data Archives
Rail lines	2.658228	1.072812	Bureau of Transportation Statistics
US Highway	0.949367	0.220648	Bureau of Transportation Statistics
Interstate	0.759494	0.430122	Bureau of Transportation Statistics
Miles to International Airport	109.4557	55.20981	Bureau of Transportation Statistics/author's calculations
Water Port	0.139241	0.348409	Bureau of Transportation Statistics
Census Rural Urban Code	2.974684	1.349023	Census

ing the presence of rail lines and U.S. highways (both are count data) was obtained from the National Center for Transportation Statistics. The presence of an interstate was obtained from commonly available roadway maps and the presence of a water port by Ball State Center for Business and Economic Research (CBER) staff using maps (water areas include the Mississippi and Ohio Rivers and Lake Michigan). The distance in miles to an international airport was obtained using MapQuest driving distance estimates and the Census Rural-Urban Code from the U.S. Census (1994 version of estimates).

The sample outlined here (as part of the larger study) is important because it offers a very homogenous sample from which to derive conclusions about growth in what is colloquially referred to as the rust belt. The purpose is to isolate this region and analyze factors related to growth in a setting that is comprehensive and regionally focused. This essay is part of that effort. The next steps are to test growth, convergence, and models of endogenous growth.

The Neoclassical (Solow-Swan) Growth Model

We next turn attention to an analysis of individual factors which may affect growth. For this we turn to a cross-sectional analysis of our sample, which is needed to supply the richness of variables for the analysis. The first model of interest is a basic restatement of traditional neoclassical growth model. This growth model has been used since the 1950s to aggregate regional characteristics which affect growth. The model typically relies upon broader measures of available labor force, physical capital, and human capital for two reasons. First, in many instances, detailed data is unavailable across regions. A more compelling reason is that there is such strong collinearity across different measures that any single variable serves as a proxy for the others. For example, we could use dozens of measures of educational attainment to rank each of our cities. With almost no exception would any of the cities change relative rankings based upon these choices. As a consequence, variable choice is based on data availability or judgment regarding those variables most reflective of the item to be measured. The model takes the form:

$$Y = AN^\alpha K^\beta H^\theta$$

where output is a function of an exogenous technology function, A, the available labor force N, physical capital K and human capital H. I proxy output with personal income, labor force with employment, physical capital the number of U.S. highways, rail lines and interstates, and for human capital I use the share, $\in 1,100$, of adults with high school diplomas. Recalling the logarithmic transformation from earlier permits us to isolate the coefficients α, β, and θ which reflect the percent change in Y when there is a 1 percent change in N, K, and H respectively. The estimated value of A is the technology parameter accounting for fixed changes to growth. The results appear in table 7.2.

These results are a textbook result for a neoclassical growth model in a region with highly homogeneous physical capital. In this estimate the technology value is high, as are measures of labor force, and labor force quality. For example, the 0.89 on the labor force estimate suggests that a 1 percent increase in labor, holding all else constant, will increase income by 0.89 percent. From these estimates we can reject linear returns to scale, so $\alpha + \beta + \theta > 1$. This implies that increases in the aggregate inputs lead to increasing growth.[13] Importantly, human capital and the size of the labor force play a strong role in growth in this sample, while capital did not. The latter failure to experience statistical significance is likely due to very common physical

Table 7.2. Regional Growth Function Estimation Results

	Coefficient (t-statistic)
A – technology	7.415844 (4.20)
N – labor force	0.890552 (26.07)
K – physical capital	0.060249 (0.47)
H – human capital	1.002170 (2.49)
Adjusted R-squared	0.65
Standard error of regression	0.311680
F-statistic	51.36
Durbin-Watson stat	1.96

Source: See Table 7.1

capital levels in these cities. The t-statistics on capital did not rise to any level of meaning, while those for technology, labor and human capital were strongly significant. The technology coefficient is more difficult to interpret, as it is a common level of unobserved growth factors across cities.

As an exercise, I estimated a similar growth model for both 2000 and 1950 (substituting population for employment). The technology coefficient in 1950 was less than one third of the 2000 level. This suggests that technology led growth plays a much stronger role in regional growth today than in 1950—again a fairly straightforward conclusion. Likewise, the labor force effect on output was much larger by more than double, than in 2000. In 1950, growth was more influenced by population levels than it is today. This is an unsurprising finding given the typical production processes that were apparent in 1950. These results are strong support for the traditional neoclassical growth model for this region. This allows us to now turn our attention to convergence of regional economies.

The Modeling Approach—Beta Convergence

Growth over time in a region would potentially lead to both beta and sigma convergence among regions.[14] The formal steady state expression is then denoted as:

$$\text{growth} = \frac{1}{T}(y(T) - y(t)) = \sigma + \left[\frac{1 - e^{-\beta T}}{T}\right](\hat{y} - y(t))$$

where σ is the technological rate of progress (sigma convergence parameter) and β is the beta converge coefficient to be estimated.

Estimating beta convergence in this context provides a measure of the predicted effect of poorer regions "catching up" to richer regions. The notion of conditional convergence discussed earlier is directly applicable to beta convergence because it is in effect, an empirical accounting for cross sectional differences in labor mobility and capital acquisition. This is motivated by the assumption in the basic Solow-Swan growth models of perfectly mobile capital, and immobile labor. The empirical reality is that capital is neither perfectly mobile, nor is labor immobile. "The level of these differences form the modeling assumptions, which may affect the rates of beta and sigma convergence."

A third feature of relevance is in inter-regional differences in savings rate, which when combined with deviations from the assumption of perfectly mobile capital and immobile labor offers capital accumulation differences which will empirically present themselves when estimating the rate of convergence. From this the literature has argued that convergence, as predicted in the base model, will be conditioned on cross sectional differences in savings. In practice the observed differences in capital mobility and labor immobility tend to reinforce the (nonstatistical) bias introduced by differences in savings rates. The rate of convergence is then an empirical question.

To estimate the steady-state equation above, with an eye toward measuring the magnitude of beta convergence, we employ our panel of seventy-nine cities, using county-wide data on income and employment (the most refined data we have for the cities in question). These series are from 1950 through 2000, from the decennial census. We estimate the model to account for conditional convergence and convergence employing cross sectional specific error terms to account for regional specific characteristics which do not vary with time. The rationale for this is that this error term will likely be highly correlated with local and state capital costs and human capital investments, one of the chief sources of heterogeneity in the sample. The econometric specification of the model permits estimation of β in these two settings of convergence and conditional convergence using ordinary least squares in the panel setting.

Another concern in this model is the previously mentioned endogeneity of human capital and growth. One obviously clear mechanism to account for this within the context of the theoretical growth model is to adopt an identification strategy which accounts for human capital. This results in an empirical specification where the dependent variable from the base convergence equation is substituted for the predicted value of the dependent variable in the identifying equation. In the identifying equation I employ lagged percentages of bachelor degree graduates and high school graduates.[15] This will be estimated using ordinary least squares, the generalized method of moments and two stage least squares. The results along with comparisons from Barro et al. appear in table 7.3.[16]

Estimates of β convergence in the standard OLS setting offers annual convergence rates at roughly 2 percent. This is virtually indistinguishable from the growth rates estimated over the same time period by Barro et al. and Rey and Montouri. The conditional convergence estimate is also not statistically or economically different from the Barro et al. results of U.S. states or the pure convergence estimate (without cross section error terms).

The estimates which account for human capital endogeneity yield a larger convergence rate of roughly 3 percent (in both the GMM estimate and 2SLS estimates). This higher level of convergence when performing the adjustment for endogeneity was noted by Higgins et al.[17] These authors found that the OLS estimates were similar to those reported here (and in Barro et al.) while the endogeneity corrections were far higher than estimates from this paper (at roughly 6 to 8 percent versus the 3.1 percent reported here).

The similarities between the basic estimates reported here, Barro et. al., Rey and Montouri, and Higgins et al. are remarkable. The only meaningful differences occur with respect to the endogeneity question posed here. Barro et al. do not treat the problem. Their model, like mine is calibrated on a long panel model with few attractive instrument choices. Higgins et al. rely

Table 7.3. Estimates of Beta Convergence

	β	$\bar{R}^2$
OLS—Convergence (1950–2000)	0.019	0.41
OLS—Conditional Convergence (1950–2000)	0.020	0.41
GMM—Conditional Convergence (1950–2000)	0.031	0.27
2SLS Conditional Convergence (1950–2000)	0.031	0.27
Barro et al. (1992)	β	$\bar{R}^2$
OLS—Convergence (1950–1960)	0.019	0.42
OLS—Convergence (1960–1970)	0.025	0.51
OLS—Convergence (1970–1980)	0.019	0.21
OLS—Convergence (1880–1988)	0.018	
Rey and Montouri (1998)		
OLS—(1929–1994)	0.018	
OLS—1929–1945	0.032	
OLS—1946–1994	0.014	

Note: Estimates have been annualized for ease of comparison.

Source: See table 7.1.

upon a large set of instruments since they depend only on three recent observations (decennial census) for which detailed local data is available. The continued difficulty in justifying identification strategies continues to argue for caution in their interpretation.

The weight of recent evidence suggests that within the United States, at the county and state level, β convergence is occurring at an annual rate of roughly 2 percent over the second half of the last century. This is fairly strong evidence that the neoclassical growth model offers a robust explanation of growth in the United States. But, as we have only dealt with β convergence, a closer examination of σ convergence is called for.

The Modeling Approach—Sigma Convergence

The evidence reported above offers strong evidence of β convergence, and hence robust support for the family of Solow-Swan growth models. However, deriving solid σ convergence estimates requires some alternative modeling approaches in addition to a stronger understanding of the relationship between β and σ convergence.

Barro et al. and Higgins et al. offer detailed explanation of this relationship.[18] It is also intuitive, and so I will adopt that approach in explaining the phenomenon.

Suppose there are two cities, A and B. Each possesses a different steady state growth path conditioned on their initial conditions (human capital, industry structure, etc.). Suppose that both cities start growth at the same level of income, implying that one is far beneath its steady state growth, while the other is closer. During the early period of growth σ convergence (the variance between cities) will be low. However, as each city converges on its steady state growth path (due to the aforementioned β convergence) the variance between their incomes rise from its initial level of zero. In this case, the presence of β convergence leads to σ nonconvergence, or increasing variance between the incomes of the two cities.

So, if cities posses different endowments of human capital or industry structures, and so experience different steady state growth paths, the presence of β convergence requires an increasing (or at least steady) variation between incomes. Only in the very rare circumstance of common initial endowments, and the absence of random shocks would both β and σ convergence occur simultaneously.

The sample with which we test this model is nearly as close to a homogeneous steady state growth set as has yet been offered in published research. The cities were carefully chosen in the industrialized midwest based upon

1950 population similarities. Even today, this area is the manufacturing belt of the United States—albeit a bit rusty. In this sample the presence of both β and σ convergence would on the face appear the most probable. However, this region has also been subject to considerable shocks. Even in this homogenous sample, finding σ convergence may prove elusive. Indeed, estimates of σ convergence from above strongly reject σ convergence. Under an alternative hypothesis, divergence cannot be rejected. So, if random shocks are the culprit, then we may still expect higher income variance between cities in this highly homogeneous sample. So, as these initial estimates portend, even in a very homogenous sample, σ convergence may not occur.

To test for σ convergence in a situation with random shocks we would prefer a long time series with high frequency data. This is not available, and so an attractive alternative is simply to model variability of growth around a cross section mean (in lieu of a variance estimate—or σ, which would not have much meaning in a six-decade census observation time series). Hence, we propose to measure σ as the deviation of output in an individual county from the mean of the sample or $|y - \bar{y}|$ for each cross section. This is the absolute value of the deviation from the mean level of income of each observed cross section, in each time period. With this definition we are interested in measuring both the σ convergence as well as the symmetry of convergence around the mean income levels.[19]

From this format we can structure the symmetry test by separating the sample into cities with per capita incomes above, and below the mean. This provides us relatively poorer and richer regions, but not necessarily different steady state growth levels. The results appear in table 7.4.

These results suggest asymmetry in σ convergence with respect to income levels relative to the sample mean. Regions with per capita incomes beneath the mean are experiencing divergence, while in the full sample and in the estimate with the higher income group the results are inconclusive. The effects are not, in aggregate large. The total increase in the difference between the mean and observed level of per capita income over the entire period was 0.6 percent. However, this masks rather large individual differences.

Table 7.4. Sigma Convergence Estimation Results

	$y < \bar{y}$	Full sample	$y > \bar{y}$
Cumulative effect	−2.12	−0.41	−0.01
(t-statistic)	(−4.18)	(−0.74)	(−0.31)
$\bar{R}^2$	0.93	0.22	0.34
N	86	158	72

Source: See table 7.1.

The asymmetry observed in this sample is most likely attributable to random shocks, very plausibly to individual industry sectors. The changes to income variation explained by these data are modest. However, σ convergence is a critical policy issue. Relative changes in income mask overall growth, and there is considerable public sector intervention aimed at mitigating the effects of nonconvergence. This is colloquially known as economic development efforts.

The results presented here find strong evidence of β convergence in our sample of Great Lakes region cities from 1950 through 2000. This is strong support for traditional economic growth models. We find evidence of σ divergence in the poorer cities. This is consistent with other reported findings of σ convergence.

Human Capital and Endogenous Growth

The leading competitor to the traditional Solow-Swan growth model is a family of models that treat human capital or other aspects playing a special role in the growth of regions. So, interest into the factors which may lead to growth—beyond labor force and capital accumulation plays a role in these models. For our purpose, we model this issue cross-sectionally we construct the basic empirical relationship where growth in real personal income from 1950 to 2000 is a function of initial per capital income and several different explanatory variables.[20]

We estimate this relationship using data on local amenities, physical capital attributes, and economic structural variables for each region. However, since human capital is likely endogenous we identify the equation on the change in human capital from 1950 to 2000 employing data on the share of residents with bachelor's degrees and high school degrees as a human capital proxy. This identification process then adjusts the growth variable upon the initial level of human capital (bachelor's degree).

Selecting the variables with which to explain growth is an important step. I begin by collecting the random error term from the initial equation and sum them for each cross-section over the observed time period. This serves two purposes. First, since most random shocks appear to be correlated with changes in industrial structure, this eliminates the need to include sets of explanatory variables on industrial composition. This is, in essence, a method for testing whether or not exogenous shocks to specific industries may account for differences in growth in the combined regression.[21]

As discussed before, the extensions of the traditional Solow-Swan model posit that growth would be a function of human and physical capital, along with measures of amenities and social capital. Theory is largely silent on the functional form of estimation, and largely on the choice of proxies for each. Since I have already accounted for human capital in the first stage, or identification of the equation, I need only find physical capital proxies and amenities and social capital proxies.

For amenities I use counts of different types of colleges (associates, BA degree-granting and research universities), and number of school districts within a city. Weather-related amenity bundles are captured within the dummy variables. For social capital I employ the GINI index, nonprofit income and the change in the concentration of churches. This is the difference in the Herfindahl-Hirschman Index from 1950 to 2000. For physical capital I use counts of rail lines and U.S. highways in each county, and presence dummies for interstates, water ports, and modified Euclidean distance to the nearest FAA-rated airport. I also use interaction terms for water and distance to airports, water and interstate, and distance to airport and interstate. I include in the regression the Census rural/urban index and the initial levels of population.

This basic regression is performed on population growth and per capita income growth in two separate regressions. Population is often considered an important variable of interest in these models. The standard errors are estimated with White's (1980) heteroscedasticity invariant variance-covariance matrix.[22] The results appear in table 7.5.

The population estimate and the per capita income estimate both reveal that initial income and population levels are positively correlated with growth rates. In the population regression, the random shock variable from the initial regression is very statistically significant, though its magnitude is difficult to interpret in the context of this estimation. It does imply that population changes are strongly associated with the unexplained variation in growth obtained from the 1950 through 2000 convergence model. This offers a clue that it is industry shocks which comprise a significant part of a region's population changes. The effect was not observed in the per capita income estimate.

Turning our attention to the social capital measures, neither model showed an affect of the region's population of per capita income because of the presence of colleges or universities. Likewise income inequality, as measured by the GINI index, played no role in regional differences in income or population. However, income from nonprofit groups was positively correlated with population changes. The magnitude is however, quite small, but from a purely correlative standpoint this is a clue that social service organizations do play a role in population changes in a region.

Table 7.5.   Estimation Results of Endogenous Growth Models

	Population		Per Capita Incomes	
	Coefficient	(t-statistic)	Coefficient	(t-statistic)
Intercept	10.28118	30.09	10.06213	79.30
1950 Population	1.22E-05	12.62	2.77E-05	11.03
Random Shock Variable	0.583	2.12	-0.00618	-0.08
AA Colleges	-0.14084	-1.30	0.003614	0.18
BA & MA Universities	-0.018317	-0.73	0.001028	0.15
Comprehensive & Research Universities	0.004925	0.14	-0.00263	-0.30
School Districts (Public)	0.003381	1.15	0.001044	0.92
GINI Index	0.011207	1.11	-0.00035	-0.08
Nonprofit Income	8.17E-06	4.38	1.94E-07	0.49
HHI-HHI1950	-7.30E-05	-4.00	-1.00E-05	-3.21
Number of Rail Lines	-0.005357	-0.36	-0.00581	-1.07
Number of US Highways	0.018795	0.42	0.010835	0.86
Number of Interstates	-0.005317	-0.05	-0.02311	-1.05
Miles to Int'l Airport	-0.000128	-0.16	1.79E-05	0.12
Water Port	-0.196357	-2.58	-0.02147	-1.28
Interaction (Water & Interstate)	0.136038	1.30	0.04012	2.32
Interaction (Water & Airport Distance)	0.000935	1.33	-3.33E-05	-0.19
Interaction (Interstate & Airport Distance)	-0.000498	-0.57	9.48E-05	0.49
Rural Urban Code	0.000539	0.02	0.004848	1.06
IL Dummy	0.063374	1.11	0.021228	1.17
IN Dummy	-0.047998	-0.81	-0.0018	-0.09
MI Dummy	-0.002455	-0.03	0.005412	0.26
OH Dummy	-0.024288	-0.52	0.013317	0.80
Adjusted R-squared	0.80		0.56	
S.E. of regression	0.132801		0.032975	
F-statistic	15.78648		5.640899	

Source: See table 7.1.

The single most interesting result is the impact the level of concentration in religion plays on growth. In both estimates the smaller the concentration church membership in a particular denomination the higher the level of population or per capita income. As with social service organizations, this impact is quite small, but suggests a role of social capital in growth.

Of the remaining variables, on the presence of a water port (negatively) affected population while the interaction of a water port and the distance to an airport interacted to affect per capita income (negatively). There's no notable regional differences (I alternated state dummies, and found no statistically meaningful combinations).

Conclusions

This chapter offers evidence that the traditional neoclassical growth model performs well in predicting both regional β convergence and the overall structure of regional growth. The estimates of β convergence reported here are consistent with estimates offered by Barro et al., Rey and Montouri, and Higgins et al. So, β convergence of roughly 2 percent a year marks the cities in this sample—a finding repeatedly echoed by studies of U.S. states and counties which estimate convergence from the Solow-Swan models.

We find no evidence of σ convergence. Indeed, there is evidence of divergence, and that the variation in incomes is increasing over time across this sample. Economic theory largely argues that this type of divergence is likely caused by random shocks, most probably relating to changes in demand for traded goods. Casually, this looks like the deindustrialization that has plagued the rust belt. However, it is important to understand that the loss of manufacturing jobs is partly an endogenous phenomenon, and not merely a random shock. This is why, though enjoying economic growth and β convergence, the cities in this sample are colloquially referred to as the rust belt.

When including endogenous factors such as human and social capital and amenities we find only a hint at growth strategies and policies. There is no silver bullet. Regions can do little about random shocks to their economy due to demand fluctuations for their dominant industries. They can influence the factors which contribute to endogenous growth. That is fortunate, since the regression results reported in this paper argue that human capital—broadly defined, local amenities and social capital are more likely to lead to higher levels of per capita income and population.

The policy prescriptions then argue that a focus on large scale infrastructure improvements is unlikely to foster the type of economic change sought by citizens of these communities. Instead local efforts to improve and enhance amenities, nurture social capital and most importantly improve educational outcomes are the source of future growth.

Notes

1. See Robert M. Solow, "A Contribution to the Theory of Economic Growth," *The Quarterly Journal of Economics* 70, no. 1 (1956): 65–94, and T. W. Swan, "Economic Growth and Capital Accumulation," *The Economic Record* 32, no. 2 (November 1956): 334–61.

2. The use of the notation N for employment is a nod to John Maynard Keynes' use of the notation, and the use of K an homage to Karl Marx's third volume of *Das Kapital*.

3. The algebra for this is straightforward. Dividing both sides of the expression by the number of workers gives the per-worker output on the left side, and a numeraire on the right side. The first order conditions of this expression yield the marginal product of capital, which is the rate of return on capital.

4. Karl Marx called this process capitalism, but was dismissive of the law of diminishing returns in this context. This was most probably because Europe in the middle part of the nineteenth century was experiencing significant increasing returns to industrialization. This omission plagues his work.

5. See N. Gregory Mankiw, David Romer and David N. Weil, "A Contribution to the Empirics of Economics of Growth," *Quarterly Journal of Economics* 107, no. 2 (May, 1992): 407–37.

6. Human capital is not a measured variable. Suitable proxies in international settings typically include health measures, morbidity, and mortality. In developed nations, where health outcome differences are modest, educational achievement is nearly the only proxy employed.

7. Robert J. Barro, Xavier Sala-I-Martin, Olivier Jean Blanchard and Robert E. Hall, "Convergence Across States and Regions," *Brookings Papers on Economic Activity 1991*, no. 1 (1991): 107–82.

8. Matthew J. Higgins, Daniel Levy and Andrew T. Young, "Growth and Convergence across the U.S.: Evidence from County-Level Data," *Review of Economics and Statistics*, 88 (2006): 671–81. Andrew T. Young, Matthew J. Higgins and Daniel Levy, "Sigma Convergence versus Beta Convergence: Evidence from U.S. County-Level Data," *Journal of Money, Credit and Banking* 40, no. 5 (Aug., 2008): 1083–93.

9. Sergio J. Rey and Brett D. Montouri, "US Regional Income Convergence: A Spatial Econometric Perspective," *Regional Studies* 33, no. 2 (1998): 143–56.

10. See Edward L. Glaeser, Jose A. Scheinkman, and Andrei Schleifer, "Economic Growth in a Cross-Section of Cities," *Journal of Monetary Economics* 36 (1995): 117–43, and Saurav Dev Bhatta and Jose Lobo, "Human Capital and Per Capita Product: A Comparison of US States," *Papers in Regional Science* 79 (2000): 393–411.

11. Kevin J. Stiroh, "What Drives Productivity Growth," *Economic Policy Review, Federal Reserve Bank of New York* (2000).

12. Francois Nielsen, "Income Inequality in U.S. Counties: GINI Coefficients," 2002, www.unc.edu/nielsen/data/data.htm (accessed May 24, 2010); Association of Religion Data Archives, U.S. Church Membership Data, www.thearda.com/Archive/ChCounty.asp (accessed May 24, 2010).

13. A Wald test reject $\alpha + \beta + \theta = 1$.

14. The growth rate for a region from time $t \to T$ is expressed as:

$$\frac{1}{T}(y(T) - y(t))$$

which is a function of the rate of technological progress and a speed of adjustment factor expressed as $1 - e^{-\beta T}$, which dictates the convergence to the steady state growth level of $\hat{y} - y(t)$ where $\hat{y}$ is the steady state growth rate to which each region would converge.

15. I propose the following first stage estimation:

$$\frac{1}{T}(y(T) - y(t)) = Z\gamma + e$$

where $Z\gamma$ represents a matrix of human capital variables and their coefficients to be estimated.

16. Barro, Sala-I-Martin, Blanchard, and Hall, "Convergence Across States and Regions," 107–82.

17. Higgins, Levy, and Young, "Growth and Convergence across the U.S.: Evidence from County-Level Data."

18. See Barro, Sala-I-Martin, Blanchard, and Hall, "Convergence Across States and Regions," 107–82, and Higgins, Levy and Young, "Growth and Convergence across the U.S.: Evidence from County-Level Data."

19. This model takes the form of a polynomial distributed lag where: $|y - \bar{y}| = \theta(L) + e$ where $\theta(L) = L_1 y + L_2 y + L_{13} y + L_4 y + L_1 y^2 + L_2 y^2 + L_3 y^2 + L_4 y^2$. The lag operator L then represents the first and second order income variable (in levels) lagged four periods. Hence the sum of the coefficients of L represents the cumulative effects of income on income variation.

20. Formally this is $\log(Y_i^{2000} - Y_i^{1950}) = \alpha_0 + \alpha_1 \log(\Gamma) + \phi_n X_n + D_s + e_i$. Where the log of the growth variable (per capita income ratio from 1950 and 2000, is a function of an intercept and measurement of initial conditions, Э, per capita income in 1950, and explanatory variables of economic and social conditions X, state dummy variables and a white noise error term.

21. The random shock variable is formally $\Sigma_{1=1}^{n} e_i$.

22. Halbert White, "A Heteroskedastic-Consistent Covariance Matrix Estimator and a Direct Test of Heteroskedasticity." *Econometrica* 48, no. 4 (May, 1980): 817–38.

CHAPTER EIGHT

~

Explaining Household Income Patterns in Rural Midwestern Counties

The Importance of Being Urban

THOMAS E. LEHMAN

Introduction

What variables explain household income levels in rural and micropolitan areas in the Midwest? This study seeks to identify these indicators. And, although this study is not exhaustive and investigates correlations more than causal explanations, it does begin a preliminary discussion on the questions about the factors associated with local economic development in rural and nonmetropolitan economies across the Midwestern United States; factors that may be sought after by businesses considering site selection and location decisions. In particular, a key hypothesis of this research is that rural Midwestern counties that can mimic, emulate, or connect in some way with neighboring larger urban economies will have the best chance of experiencing economic development and growth. Those rural economies that can "be urban" or exhibit "urbanness" by increasing population density, raising education and human capital levels, and gaining access to more specialized markets through transportation networks, are expected to demonstrate greater levels of economic development and higher income.

This chapter is structured as follows: the first section provides a brief overview of the sparse literature on economic development in rural and/ or Midwestern communities. The second section of this study summarizes the data sources used, methodology employed, and univariate analysis of the data. It explains the estimation techniques employed in the study, lists the factors believed to influence local economic development, and gives a brief explanation as to why these variables were selected. The third section discloses the findings of the study followed by a discussion of important observed associations, and the final section concludes with a summary of those findings accompanied by brief policy implications and recommendations for future research.

Literature Review

A topic so narrowly defined as the one explored in this study can expect to have some difficulty in building on or linking with prior research. Indeed, there are only limited studies investigating economic planning and development in rural areas in the United States, and virtually none that explain household income patterns exclusively in the Midwest. The following is a brief discussion of the studies that do investigate rural economic development in the United States and which, in part, form the theoretical foundation for the investigation undertaken in this study. The remaining theoretical basis for this study is grounded in prior research investigating urban (as opposed to rural) areas, and borrows more heavily from the techniques used in that literature.

Lapping, Daniels, and Keller provide one of the earliest and most thorough analyses of modern rural economic development in the United States.[1] According to these authors, rural economic development is threatened by the decline in agricultural employment (the "farm exodus") which historically formed the largest part of its economic base. According to these authors, the rise of urban areas as the primary engines for economic development in a postindustrial economy has created a crisis for rural economies, leading to a social clash of rural and urban attitudes and a lack of political leadership and organization in rural communities. The conflict paradigm employed by these authors leads them to argue that rural America is in some sense trapped in an economic development war with urban places in a zero-sum game.

Frederic criticizes Lapping et al. for casting the debate in conflict terms, arguing, on the basis of Lewis, that rural economic development in a post-agrarian and postindustrial age must occur within an economy driven largely by urban places.[2] Rural economic development planners must recognize this and make efforts to exploit the connections with larger metropolitan areas, according to Frederic, if they hope to be successful. Frederic argues that regional economic development cannot hope to be successful utilizing an urban vs. rural approach. Instead, the two regions must develop a more symbiotic relationship to maximize the opportunities that each presents to the other.

If rural communities are experiencing an erosion of their economic base in a postindustrial economy, could the attraction of high-tech industry and educated workers reverse this trend? This is a question taken up by Glasmeier, and her tentative answer suggests that high tech is not usually a viable option for rural economies.[3] In spite of hope to the contrary, Glasmeier is not confident that high technology industries and firms can effectively utilize the human capital and infrastructural resources provided by rural communities. The greatest hope lies in rural economies' abilities to lure high tech firms to locate within their borders. Yet, according to Fik, most rural areas "remain at a disadvantage relative to urban areas, as they tend to be associated with less-productive and lower-skilled labor forces, infrastructurally poor and agglomerationless environments, and lower overall degrees of accessibility to markets, information, and innovation technology."[4] Both Glasmeier and Fik conclude that attracting high technology industries to rural economies is not a panacea for the challenges faced in these areas. Geography, human capital, and infrastructural needs may simply not be suitable.

It should be recognized, however, that Glasmeier's research was published several years before the Internet explosion of the mid-1990s. Many saw this digital revolution and the accompanying reduction in communication and transaction costs as an opportunity to reshape the economic landscape with tremendous hope for rural areas to attract high-tech industry for which place and proximity would no longer matter, at least in theory.[5] In addition, rising land and residential home values in many metropolitan areas may make rural communities a relatively more attractive (less costly) option for educated workers in technology industries where long-distance commutes would be unnecessary. The question remains whether these changing forces, occurring since Glasmeier's research, have made rural areas any more attractive for high-tech businesses.

The interrelationships between gender and rural economic development in the Midwest are explored by Gringeri.[6] This work investigates informal home-based industrial work by women as an economic development strategy, chronicling case studies of women in two rural Midwestern towns who accept home-based jobs to supplement declining spousal income from farming. Gringeri documents the pros and cons of home-based work by women serving as independent contractors for manufacturing firms, from the flexibility and additional income it brings, to the disruption of household duties and the challenges of managing the home economy alongside a home-based business. Although Gringeri's research may provide important insights into the gender- and class-based conflicts inherent in this type of economic development strategy for rural communities, unfortunately there is no mention of the potential relationship between, say, female labor force attachment or female occupational classifications and median household income.[7]

Richard Florida suggests that economic development is coalescing around "mega-regions:" large consolidated metropolitan statistical areas (CMSAs) that attract "creative class" workers in professional and artistic fields.[8] These large metropolitan agglomeration economies are generating increasingly larger proportions of both domestic and global output, according to Florida, implying that economic development, both domestically and globally, is becoming more and more concentrated in these high-growth cities, leaving smaller cities and especially rural communities behind. Florida predicts that the result of this transformation in a postindustrial information economy will be growing wage and income inequality, not only between "mega-regions" and their rural and/or non-mega counterparts, but also between "creative class" and "service class" workers within these mega-regions themselves. Although not directly addressed by Florida, the implication of his research and argument is that rural communities and small cities that do not border metropolitan areas will tend to do poorly in terms of economic development and will likewise exhibit relatively lower household incomes. Conversely, rural areas bordering metropolitan economies, and especially those bordering CMSAs, will tend to exhibit relatively higher levels of economic development and household income by virtue of their geographic proximity to these growing regional mega-economies. A further implication of Florida's argument is that the future of economic development and economic growth for smaller cities and rural economies is to find economic ties to, and to develop labor-force and transportation networks with, these growing mega-regions. Obviously, those rural economies that have the good fortune of bordering one of these growing regional economies could be expected to have relatively brighter economic prospects by virtue of geographic luck, whereas those counties isolated away from growing mega-regions could be expected to decline in economic importance.

Methodology

The county jurisdiction is the geographic unit of analysis for this study. The scope of the study consists of 680 rural counties across ten states: Illinois, Indiana, Iowa, Kentucky, Michigan, Minnesota, Missouri, Ohio, West Virginia, and Wisconsin. These ten states contain a total of 913 counties, including urbanized counties within Metropolitan Statistical Areas (MSA).[9] This study seeks to identify factors related to regional economic development in rural communities (counties) which lie outside an MSA. Accordingly, the analysis is narrowed to n = 680 non-MSA counties in these ten states. The 233 counties dropped from the analysis are those defined as part of a Metropolitan Statistical Area in the 2000 census. The study employs standard OLS multiple regression statistical techniques using US Census Department data from Census 2000 on all 680 non-MSA counties across the ten-state area.

Data limitations are always a challenge in any research attempting to quantify relationships among variables which may serve as mere proxies for broader concepts, and that challenge holds true here. For purposes of this research, it was determined that county median household income in 1999 (year prior to Census 2000) would be the best (or "least bad") measure of local economic development available in county-level census data.[10] The concept "local economic development" will be operationally defined in terms of the level of median household income per county across this ten-state region, and this measure will serve as the dependent variable in the regression models developed for this analysis.[11] The weakness in this variable is that it tells us little if anything about actual business development decisions at the county level (i.e., business attraction or retention efforts, number and size of firms and organizations, etc.). However, given data limitations, this variable may be the most useful proxy for local economic development and economic growth, since it is likely to correlate positively with efforts at business attraction and retention.[12]

The approach used here, which will be tested in the following sections, takes the theoretical form expressed in the following equation: $y_i = bx_i + E_i$, where y_i is the predicted value of median household income for county i; x_i is a vector of factors in county i theoretically correlated with y; b is a computed partial coefficient (slope) measuring the influence of x_i on y_i; and E_i is a standard regression error term anticipating omitted variable bias.

The primary source of data came from the *U.S. Census Bureau, Summary File 3* for Census 2000 (www.census.gov). Information on county median age levels in 2006 was obtained from *Stats Indiana* (www.stats.indiana.edu). Two dichotomous (dummy) variables were employed, one on the presence of an interstate highway within county borders, data for which were gleaned from the author's analysis of an atlas, and the other indicating if the rural county did or did not border an MSA county in 2000, obtained from Census Bureau maps (factfinder.census.gov). Data on the presence and frequency of accredited colleges and universities within a county was obtained from the NCA Higher Learning Commission website (www.ncahlc.org) and the Southern Association of Colleges and Schools website (www.sacs.org/).

The regression analysis led to the development of eight distinct regression models, all of which exhibit relatively high r^2 values from a low of .79

to a high of .90, suggesting that the independent variables in these models provide a fairly good fit. Eight separate regression models were necessary because a handful of the independent variables in the analysis exhibited high levels of multicollinearity when placed together in the same model, making an interpretation of their independent effects on median household income difficult. For example, the unemployment rate and other measures of labor force attachment are highly collinear, masking the effect each has on the dependent variable when placed concurrently in the same regression model. Proportionate measures on immigrant population and ethnic composition within counties also exhibited multicollinearity when placed in the same model. Separating these variables from one another by isolating them into distinct regression models, while retaining other control variables not plagued with multicollinearity problems, allows a full exploration of their impact on household income while satisfying the assumptions of OLS methods.

Table 8.1. lists the dependent variable and all of the independent variables used in the eight models, along with their means and standard deviations.

The selection of the independent variables to be included in the model follows from prior literature and/or basic economic theory.

Counties with direct access to interstate transportation networks are hypothesized to exhibit higher levels of household income because interstates may expand the possibilities for trade and the division of labor available to local economies. Adam Smith first recognized that as the "extent of the market" expands, greater trade is made possible as people narrow their scope of specialization and reap higher incomes through market exchange.[13] Additionally, access to large transportation networks reduces the transaction costs of trade, making products and services more readily available from and to more distant regional markets.[14] A dichotomous (dummy) variable on the presence of an interstate highway within the county is included, and it is tentatively expected that the correlation will be positive with household income.[15] One weakness in this variable is that it is unable to quantify total interstate highway miles within a county. All counties with at least one interstate highway are counted equally, ignoring the impact that multiple interstate highways or lengthier stretches of interstate may have on county income.

The land and water area of a county may have some relationship to income levels, although the effect is likely ambiguous. Counties with a larger land mass may idiosyncratically possess other natural resources that boost incomes based upon the comparative advantages these resources provide. The land mass of a county may also have some unidentified historical association with wealth accumulation and household income levels, although

Table 8.1. Summary Statistics

Variable	Mean	Standard Deviation
Median household income in 1999	$33,769.67	$6,181.847
Interstate highway runs through or crosses part of the county	.35	.478
County shares at least one border with an MSA county (geography defined in Census 2000)	.50	.500
Land area in square kilometers	1,478.364	779.427
Water area in square kilometers	194.885	926.521
Total population in 2000	25,247.12	18,826.746
Population density (persons per square kilometer of land area)	19.163	14.840
Percentage of population foreign born (immigrants)	1.2956	1.205
Percentage of workers 16+ working outside county	34.632	14.532
Percentage of population 25+ with bachelors degree or more	12.943	4.427
Percentage of population 25+ with less than a HS diploma	22.381	8.180
Unemployment rate	5.785	2.375
Labor force participation rate	60.620	6.993
Employment-to-population ratio	57.229	7.540
Female labor force participation rate	54.740	6.893
Percentage of all households unmarried partner same sex	.3576	.184
Percentage of households below poverty line	13.005	6.324
Percentage of population black or African-American	1.7274	3.376
Percentage of population Hispanic / Latino	1.439	1.737
Percentage of population Asian / oriental	.379	.455
Percentage of population female	50.476	1.539
Median age of county population in 2006	39.82	3.322
Total number of accredited universities in county (2008) – 298 out of 680 counties, or roughly 44 percent, contain at least one accredited university	.43	.711

n = 680

Source: See Methodology section (computations by the author).

this remains speculative due to the absence of prior research and any well-developed theories on this correlation. On the other hand, larger county size in a rural area may theoretically imply that a greater portion of the local economic base is found in agriculture (although this need not necessarily be the case). If so, this may serve to depress median household income in the county if small farming households exhibit declining incomes and yet make up a proportionately large number of households in the county.[16]

The water area of a county may have an effect on county incomes linked to marine employment or recreation industries. For example, counties with more water area may exploit lakes and rivers to attract tourists seeking water-based recreation activities such as boating, fishing, skiing, and other water sports, which may boost income to local residents directly or indirectly tied to these industries. Land and water area of the county (measured in square kilometers) are included only speculatively to test these assumptions, but no predictions are made as to the direction of the correlation since we have little or no prior research to inform our theory.

Larger-sized counties may also hold larger populations. And, population levels may have independent effects on household incomes.[17] To overcome some of the ambiguity or endogeneity in the potential relationship between land mass, population and household income, a density coefficient was computed revealing the county population per square kilometer. By creating more opportunities for specialization and trade, population density levels may impact household income in ways similar to expanded transportation networks: by enlarging Smith's "extent of the market."[18] A larger population density increases the scope for the division of labor within a county and thus expands the opportunities for specialization and exchange, theoretically boosting incomes as a result. As population density grows, the transaction costs of trade and specialized exchange diminish as well. Additionally, there may be some endogeneity between population density and household income if counties with higher incomes attract larger populations, increasing density. In either case, we would expect counties with relatively higher population density to exhibit higher median household income levels, all else constant.[19]

Based upon Richard Florida's research, as well as basic economic theory predicting productivity gains from specialization and agglomeration economies, it is expected that rural economies bordering metropolitan areas will tend to exhibit relatively higher levels of economic development and household income by virtue of their geographic proximity to these larger regional economies.[20] Conversely, rural communities and small cities that do not border metropolitan areas are expected to do poorly in terms of economic development and likewise exhibit relatively lower household incomes. To test this hypothesis, a dichotomous (dummy) variable was computed for rural counties that share at least one partial or full border with an MSA county in 2000.[21] It is expected that rural counties sharing a border (even if only minimally) with counties that are part of a larger MSA, will exhibit higher median household income due to the potentially higher wages and better job opportunities offered by proximity to urban agglomeration economies.

Immigrants may play a role in explaining household income patterns in rural areas.[22] Their effect on income is ambiguous. On the one hand, the presence of more immigrants could potentially boost household income if immigrants are more prone to entrepreneurship and business development in their counties of residence, producing greater output and increasing demand for local workers. Further, the presence of more educated immigrants could boost incomes as well, since immigrants with higher levels of education are likely to earn more. However, if immigrants are generally less educated and/or lack entrepreneurial initiative, their presence may be reflected in relatively lower household incomes. County immigrant levels are estimated as a percentage of the county population that was foreign born in 2000, and the relationship between immigrant levels and household income is estimated while controlling for educational attainment of the county population.

Commuting patterns, apart from geographic locations or the presence of an interstate highway system, could also potentially impact county household income levels. The percentage of county labor force employed outside the county is included to test for this relationship. The expected direction of correlation is ambiguous a priori, although it is assumed that the opportunity costs of longer commute distances by workers, perhaps to jobs outside their county of residence, must be compensated in the form of higher wages or higher nonwage income. If lower-skilled rural workers with fewer career options must commute longer distances for only modestly better paying jobs, this may reduce median household income in local economies where more of the workforce commute to jobs outside their county of residence. On the other hand, and more likely, if skilled local workers are commuting farther distances to take advantage of higher-paying jobs that lie outside their county of residence (say, in nearby metropolitan areas), and yet choose to live and raise a family in the rural county of residence (a "bedroom community" effect), then this may put upward pressure on county household incomes for rural counties with more workers employed outside their county of residence.

Literature on local economic development consistently concludes that educational attainment is one of the most important factors determining income levels.[23] Local economies with a more educated workforce are very likely to exhibit higher levels of income due to the higher demand for a skilled labor pool expressed by local businesses and employers.[24] To confirm this theory and the prior research on this relationship, two measures on educational attainment are included: percentage of local adult population (age twenty-five and over) with a bachelor's degree or more, and percentage of local adult population with less than a high school diploma. We would expect the first of these two measures to be positively correlated with our dependent variable, and the latter measure to be negatively correlated. Because these two measures were found to be highly collinear, they are isolated in separate regression models.

County household income levels must be linked to employment opportunities both inside and outside the local economy. Thus, county labor force attachment is an important factor explaining county household income levels.[25] We would expect that counties with a higher proportion of employed workers and/or a higher proportion of their population active in the labor force to exhibit higher household income levels, all else equal. To test this hypothesis, four measures of labor force attachment are included: county unemployment rate, overall employment-to-population ratio, overall labor force participation rate, and, to test for gender-specific effects, female labor-force participation rate.[26] County unemployment rate is expected to be negatively correlated with household incomes, while the remaining measures of labor forces attachment are expected to exhibit a positive correlation.

Research by Richard Florida suggests that cities and communities that are more open to diversity, creativity, and the arts, and that are more tolerant of change and innovation and the dynamism that change and innovation bring, are much more economically successful than closed communities that attempt to preserve the cultural and economic status quo. As a proxy for cultural tolerance and openness to diversity, Florida correlates measures of local economic development with the relative presence of same-sex partner households, a data point gathered for the first time in the 2000 U.S. Census. Florida finds a positive correlation between these measures in metropolitan areas across the United States. A similar measure is included here to test whether Florida's research can be supported for rural nonmetropolitan areas in the Midwest. If Florida's findings for metropolitan areas are consistent with rural areas, we would expect to find a positive correlation between percentage of same-sex households and county household income levels, all else equal.[27]

The presence of a college or university in a community has been found to boost metropolitan economic development and household income.[28] This could occur through a variety of channels. Institutions of higher learning may foster research that leads to entrepreneurial innovations and private for-profit business development in their local communities, boosting incomes as a result of this "town-and-gown" linkage. Assuming that a significant portion of college graduates remain in the community upon graduation, the presence of local colleges and universities may increase local educational attainment levels, in turn increasing the human capital and income levels of the labor force in the community. Further, colleges and universities may boost local household incomes through the relatively higher wages they pay to the skilled and educated employees they hire, especially faculty members and academic administrators. If the same dynamic holds true for rural and micropolitan areas in the Midwest, then for all of these reasons we should tentatively expect that the presence and frequency of an accredited college or university in a county would be positively correlated with county median household income, all else equal. On the other hand, if colleges and universities in Midwestern rural counties are relatively small in size, the number of high-skilled, high-wage workers they employ (faculty and administrators) may be small relative to the number of low-skilled, low-wage workers employed alongside (clerical staff, maintenance and grounds crews, cafeteria workers, and cleaning and housekeeping employees). If this is the case, then the presence of colleges and universities in rural counties may be associated with lower median household income through a "payroll effect" that dominates the opposing income-boosting effects of colleges and universities. All of the above theoretical possibilities, of course, hinge on the assumption that college or university employees take equally proportional residence in the county of their employment. However, if one of these two groups of university employees is more heavily represented within the county residential population than the other, it will serve to reinforce or suppress the "payroll effect" that universities may have on household income. If most of the high-skilled and high-wage university employees take residence in the county where they are employed, any "payroll effect" depressing county household incomes would be negligible. But, if most of the high-skilled and high-wage university employees commute from outside their county of employment (perhaps from a neighboring MSA), while the relatively lower-skilled university workers reside inside the county, the "payroll effect" universities may have on household income would be much stronger.

Finally, a number of additional control variables are included in the analysis to measure potential economic, demographic, and racial/ethnic diversity effects on household income at the county level: county poverty rate, percentages of African Americans, Hispanic or Latinos, Asians or Orientals, and females in the county population, and the median age of the county population. Racial and ethnic minorities may influence county household income levels in at least two different ways. If minorities are relatively poorer as a group, we would expect counties with higher percentages of minorities to exhibit lower median household income. On the other hand, minorities may offer greater diversity and higher levels of entrepreneurship to county economies, and may also be located in exurbs just beyond the boundaries of large metropolitan areas with higher incomes. If so, when controlling for poverty rates, counties with higher percentages of minorities could be expected to display higher median household income.

Median age of the county population may influence county income levels. If this is a demographic push or pull factor for business development, how might it impact local household income? Counties with a younger population and labor force may be more attractive to potential employers and businesses looking to relocate, possibly increasing income levels as a result of business development. This effect may be independent of the higher levels of education (and thus income) that younger demographic groups are expected to exhibit. On the other hand, an older county population with potentially greater job experience and seniority could have an opposing effect and lead to higher incomes as a result of greater levels of experiential human capital. These theories are tested by including median age as a control variable, alongside the measures for educational attainment and labor force attachment.

Findings and Observations

Tables 8.2 and 8.3 summarize the statistical findings from the eight independent regression models including unstandardized and standardized coefficients (in parentheses), significance levels, and, in the bottom row, each model's r^2 and adjusted r^2. The unstandardized coefficient is the partial slope of the regression plane or, in other words, the dollar impact on the dependent variable resulting from a one-unit change in value on the independent variable, all else constant.[29] The r^2 in each model reveals roughly the percentage of variation in the dependent variable that can be explained by the variance in the independent variables included in each model.[30]

Rural Connectivity to Urban Economies

The consistency in the direction and significance of the geography and commuting variable coefficients across all eight models in tables 8.2 and 8.3 supports one of the main theses of this research: rural areas in close proximity to larger urban/metropolitan areas exhibit higher median household income, all else equal. Simply sharing a border with a metropolitan area (MSA) boosts rural county median household income by between $700 and $1,900 annually according to these findings. And, independent of the effects of geographic location, rural counties with a higher proportion of the labor force commuting outside the county of residence for employment (presumably, but not always, to metropolitan regions with better employment and income opportunities) also exhibit higher median household income.[31] While neither of these effects is overly strong, the consistency in the direction and significance of the relationship reinforces the hypothesis

Table 8.2. Models 1-4

Variable	Model 1	Model 2	Model 3	Model 4
County shares one or more borders with another county that is part of an MSA	783.940***	819.774***	819.734***	1612.169***
	(.063)	(.066)	(.066)	(.130)
Land area in square kilometers	.236*	.236*	.236*	.236*
	(.030)	(.030)	(.030)	(.033)
Water area in square kilometers	.096	.032	.032	.183
	(.014)	(.005)	(.005)	(.027)
Population density: persons per square kilometer of land	71.769***	61.687***	61.700***	107.915***
	(.172)	(.148)	(.148)	(.259)
Interstate highway runs through or crosses county	141.982	130.917	131.034	243.474
	(.011)	(.010)	(.010)	(.019)
Total number of accredited colleges or universities in county	-103.405	-125.343	-124.867	-118.347
	(-.012)	(-.014)	(-.014)	(-.014)
Median age of county population (2006)	-170.646***	-300.385***	-300.279***	353.247***
	(-.092)	(-.161)	(-.161)	(.190)
Percentage of all households unmarried partner same sex	1071.079**	1209.655***	1209.864***	-185.640
	(.032)	(.036)	(.036)	(-.006)
Percentage of population foreign born	132.862*	180.283**	180.230**	141.802
	(.026)	(.035)	(.035)	(.028)
Percentage of workers 16+ working outside county	48.227***	49.347***	49.353***	51.721***
	(.113)	(.116)	(.116)	(.122)
Percentage of population 25+ with bachelors degree or more	106.239***	145.776***	145.765***	131.164***
	(.076)	(.104)	(.104)	(.094)
Percentage of population 25+ with less than a HS diploma				
Percentage of households below poverty line	-662.886***	-824.184***	-823.820***	
	(-.678)	(-.843)	(-.843)	

(continued)

Table 8.2. (continued)

Variable	Model 1	Model 2	Model 3	Model 4
Labor force participation rate	179.146*** (.203)			667.703*** (.755)
Unemployment rate			-1.302 (-.001)	
Employment-to-population ratio				
Female labor force participation rate				
Percentage of population black or African American	-1.463 (-.001)	-22.049 (-.012)	-22.044 (-.012)	4.093 (.002)
Percentage of population Hispanic/ Latino				
Percentage of population Asian/ oriental				
Percentage of population female -1081.852***	-248.546*** (-.062)	-4.438 (-.001)	-4.630 (-.001)	(-.269)
R Square	.901	.893	.893	.810
Adjusted R Square	.899	.890	.890	.806

Significance Measures:
* p < .10 (90% confidence level)
** p < .05 (95% confidence level)
*** p < .01 (99% confidence level)
Standardized partial coefficients are in parentheses

Source: See Methodology section (computations by the author).

Table 8.3. Models 5-8

Variable	Model 5	Model 6	Model 7	Model 8
County shares one or more borders with another county that is part of an MSA	1557.862***	1922.329***	811.372***	704.793***
	(.126)	(.156)	(.066)	(.057)
Land area in square kilometers	.359**	.231	.264**	.248*
	(.045)	(.029)	(.033)	(.031)
Water area in square kilometers	.326***	.208	.015	.126
	(.049)	(.031)	(.002)	(.019)
Population density: persons per square kilometer of land	105.219***	113.612***	60.689***	65.157***
	(.253)	(.273)	(.146)	(.156)
Interstate highway runs through or crosses county	267.908	263.314	131.998	169.220
	(.021)	(.020)	(.010)	(.013)
Total number of accredited colleges or universities in county	3.949	−284.440	−125.995	−31.262
	(.001)	(−.033)	(−.014)	(−.004)
Median age of county population (2006)	303.045***	360.962***	−301.054***	−341.687***
	(.163)	(.194)	(−.162)	(−.184)
Percentage of all households unmarried partner same sex	−4.071	−43.209	1176.869***	1247.484***
	(−.001)	(−.001)	(.035)	(.037)
Percentage of population foreign born	142.236	295.447***	255.933***	255.933***
	(.028)	(.058)		(.050)
Percentage of workers 16+ working outside county	53.812***	68.644***	49.213***	43.616***
	(.126)	(.161)	(.116)	(.103)
Percentage of population 25+ with bachelors degree or more	141.466***	76.612**	170.571***	
	(.101)	(.055)	(.122)	
Percentage of population 25+ with less than a HS diploma				−63.281***
				(−.084)
Percentage of households below poverty line			−816.982***	−788.392***
			(−.836)	(−.807)

(continued)

Table 8.3. *(continued)*

Variable	Model 5	Model 6	Model 7	Model 8
Labor force participation rate				
Unemployment rate			10.055	−25.845
			(.004)	(−.010)
Employment-to-population ratio	614.149***			
	(.749)			
Female labor force participation rate		665.331***		
		(.742)		
Percentage of population black or African American	2.658	−111.624***	−21.935	−23.762
	(.001)	(−.061)	(−.012)	(−.013)
Percentage of population Hispanic/ Latino			200.537***	
			(.056)	
Percentage of population Asian/ oriental			−168.669	
			(−.012)	
Percentage of population female	−999.330***	−293.332***	−2.608	.391
	(−.249)	(−.073)	(−.001)	(.001)
R Square	.813	.790	.894	.889
Adjusted R Square	.809	.786	.892	.886

Significance Measures:
* $p < .10$ (90% confidence level)
** $p < .05$ (95% confidence level)
*** $p < .01$ (99% confidence level)
Standardized partial coefficients are in parentheses

Source: See Methodology section (computations by the author)

that rural counties which are isolated from or lack connectivity with larger urban economies are at a disadvantage in raising incomes and realizing economic development. Conversely, and consistent with Frederic, counties that have both geographic and labor force connections with urban areas seem to do relatively better.[32] Where the division of labor, specialization and labor productivity are enhanced by the larger "extent of the market" offered in cities, the advantages of deeper markets and increased opportunities for trade appear to spill out to the adjoining rural economies and labor force, boosting household income as a result.

A third variable reinforcing the positive effects of "urbanness" on rural economies is population density. Counties with higher population density (persons per square kilometer) exhibit consistently higher median household income as reflected in the positive and significant sign on this coefficient in all eight models. This is likely to be explained by a combination of two primary factors. First, population density may potentially increase the scope for specialization, division of labor and trade, allowing for increased productivity through an extent-of-the-market effect, boosting average incomes as a result of a wider and deeper market in which to participate. In this sense, higher population density may cause household incomes to be higher due to a broader economic base. Second, some endogeneity may be present. Counties with relatively higher household incomes may be an attraction to noncounty residents looking to relocate. If so, then the higher household incomes are a "pull" factor leading to greater in-migration and thus greater population density. In this sense, then, higher county incomes may cause higher population density. It is likely that both of these factors work together, each reinforcing the other, to explain the positive and statistically significant sign on the population density coefficient across all models in tables 8.2 and 8.3.

The presence of an interstate highway does not appear to boost county household incomes when controlling for other factors.[33] As predicted, the sign on the coefficient for this variable is positive, but the relationship is statistically insignificant in all regressions. As theorized above, reduced transportation costs provided by interstate highways to and from external markets likely increases specialization and opportunity for shipping and trade between the diverse economic bases of rural and metropolitan areas, increasing household income as a result. However, the insignificant correlation on this variable across all models forces us to at least tentatively reject this hypothesis. Although the presence of an interstate highway has no independent effect on rural household incomes, it could increase county residents' willingness to access employment opportunities outside their home county which does appear to play a modest role in boosting county household incomes. Confirmation of this connection will have to await future research when better data, such as the number of miles of interstate highway per county, can be employed.

Taken together, the relationships found in the data imply that rural counties and micropolitan economies that exhibit characteristics similar to those of their larger urban siblings have the best chance for economic development. Greater specialization and agglomeration through proximity to metropolitan areas and population density appear to boost productivity and raise household income.

Population Diversity, Educational Institutions and Median Age

The demographic variables in each of the eight models reveal less consistent relationships to county household income when controlling for alternative factors. Nonetheless, there are some tentative conclusions that can be gleaned from the findings, primary among which is that, in general, a more diverse population and workforce are correlated with higher county household income levels. In support of this conclusion, Models 1, 2, 3, 6, and 8 show that a larger proportion of immigrants (foreign-born) is positively correlated with higher household income among the rural counties surveyed. The sign on the coefficient for this variable in all these models is positive and statistically significant at minimum to the 90 percent confidence level. Although the relationship is modest at best, it suggests that immigrants, on balance, boost county income levels, possibly through entrepreneurship in business development, the relative education levels they bring to the county, or both.

Likewise, and consistent with Richard Florida's findings for metropolitan economies, the presence of same-sex partner households is correlated with higher county household income levels, even in the rural and non-MSA counties in this study.[34] Although the relationship is modest, the findings suggest that counties with a higher proportion of same-sex partner households will exhibit slightly higher household income, all else equal. The coefficient on this variable is positive in Models 1, 2, 3, 7, and 8, and statistically significant at minimum to the 95 percent confidence level in each. When controlling for poverty rates, the presence of gay households in the rural counties in this study is associated with a boost in median household income by $1,070 to $1,240 annually.

Why this pattern may emerge, as well as a few caveats, are worth considering. According to Florida, local communities and economies that are more open and tolerant of diversity tend also to encourage higher levels of creativity, artistry, dynamism, and outside-the-box thinking, and thus engender relatively more entrepreneurship than more conservative and traditionalist local economies without the same levels of tolerance.[35] According to Florida, it is not the presence of homosexual households or even immigrants, per se, that boosts local economic development and income. Rather, the relative presence of homosexual and/or immigrant households is itself merely a measure of some underlying characteristic (call it "tolerance" or "dynamism" or "openness") that tends to breed creativity and entrepreneurship in local economies. That same measure is used here as a proxy to detect the presence of those characteristics in rural and nonmetropolitan economies, and is found to support Florida's highly controversial yet ground-breaking thesis: diversity, tolerance, dynamism and openness, as measured by relative levels of immigrants and same-sex partner households in the population, are correlated with higher median household income.

One caveat is in order before placing too much confidence in this interpretation. One among numerous criticisms of Florida's study is that it may fail to isolate the measure on the effects of same-sex partner households from that of the effects of other correlates, such as a local college or university, both of which may have independent effects on local economic development and income levels, and both of which may be highly correlated to each other.[36] That is, the presence of a local university or college may both attract more immigrants and more same-sex partner households, and also lead to higher levels of local economic development and income. Universities would tend to employ higher-skilled and higher-income individuals and, in partnership with local businesses, may spur local business development and entrepreneurship, both of which would have the effect of elevating average measures of local household income. If so, then the positive association that Florida (and we) finds between immigrants, same-sex partner households, and local household income may be spurious unless presence of a university or college is included as a control variable.

In an effort to answer this criticism, this study includes a control variable for the presence and/or frequency of accredited colleges and universities in each Midwestern rural county in all eight regression models. However, and quite surprisingly, as tables 8.2 and 8.3 illustrate, the presence or number of universities and colleges in Midwestern rural counties actually has no impact on median household incomes. In fact, a modest *negative* (but statistically insignificant) association with median household incomes can be observed in seven of the eight models. That is, when controlling for all the other variables that may explain median household income in rural Midwestern counties, the presence of an accredited university or an increasing number of accredited universities or colleges in a county may be correlated with *lower* median household income. This appears to hold true even when controlling for median age, which we would expect to be lower in counties with colleges and universities.[37] Median age is negatively associated with county household income in Models 1–3, suggesting that a younger population is actually correlated with higher median household income in rural counties, independent of the presence of a university or college. In Models 4–6, however, when labor force participation rates or the employment-to-population ratio are included, median age becomes positively correlated with household income, possibly due to an interaction between median age and labor force attachment. Older workers may, in general, have higher rates of labor force participation so that when controlling for this measure, higher median age boosts county household income. In other words, labor force attachment measures likely trump the effect that a younger population has on household income.

How do we interpret these findings? Because the positive correlation between same-sex households and median household income holds even when controlling for the presence of a university or college, we can tentatively dismiss the criticism against Florida's research and accept that the presence of same-sex households (at least in rural Midwestern counties) represents a latent "creative class" factor that boosts income levels independent of the presence or frequency of colleges or universities. Further, the effect that accredited colleges and universities have on median household incomes in rural Midwestern counties is independent of the median age of the population. Younger median age tends to boost household incomes, except when controlling for measures of labor force attachment. This may be a result of younger workers locating in counties with relatively higher incomes, business attraction and development boosting incomes in counties with a younger population and younger workforce, or a combination of both.

Finally, we should cautiously interpret the effects that universities and colleges have on median household incomes in rural counties. Colleges and universities in Midwestern rural counties may be relatively small in size, and the number of high-skilled, high-wage workers they employ (faculty and administrators) may be small relative to the number of low-skilled, low-wage workers employed alongside (clerical staff, maintenance and grounds crews, cafeteria workers, and cleaning and housekeeping employees). If this is the case, then the finding presented here may be explained by a "payroll effect" that dominates any opposing income-boosting factors of colleges and universities, assuming that the college or university employees take residence in the county of their employment. Another way of putting it is that colleges and universities may be generators of high levels of income inequality among their employees (and the counties in which they reside) by splitting their payrolls between extreme high-skilled and extreme low-skilled workers. If the low-skilled jobs and low-skilled workers that form part of a rural university's payroll dominate the high-skilled jobs and high-skilled workers that form the remaining part of that payroll, then the composition of the labor force in that county could be marginally weighted toward lower income households by the presence of that college or university, especially if the rural college or university is a leading employer in that county. Additionally, if the majority of the low-skilled workers employed by the university reside inside the rural county, while a majority of the high-skilled workers commute from outside the county (say, from neighboring metropolitan areas), the presence of the university would further serve to depress median household income within the county where it is located. This is not to suggest, however, that rural Midwestern counties should eschew institutions of higher learning simply because of their potential compositional effects on the local labor force and on household income levels.

The remaining measures of racial/ethnic and gender diversity generally do not provide any further information on the diversity effects of rural county populations on median household income. Proportionate levels of Hispanics (Model 7) in rural county populations are positively and significantly correlated with higher county household income, all else constant, supporting the hypothesis that diversity boosts economic development, perhaps through greater levels of specialization. However, proportionate levels of African Americans and Asians or Orientals seem to have no consistent effect on rural county median household income.[38] This is contrary to the findings for urban areas.[39]

The proportion of females in the county population appears to have an unambiguously negative impact on county median household income, even when controlling for poverty rates or female labor force participation. Models 1, 4, 5, and 6 illustrate a negative and significant correlation between relative female population and household income levels. This finding is likely attributable to the well-known differences between male and female earnings. If females earn less than males, on average, then counties with a higher proportion of females (and thus potentially more female workers and female head-of-household families) could be expected to exhibit modestly lower median household income. Additionally, females are more likely than males to have incomes that fall below the poverty level. And, in Model 1, where county poverty levels are included as a control variable, the negative relationship between the percentage of females in the county and county median household income is smaller, suggesting that females' negative impact on county income levels is attenuated when poverty rates are held constant. Similarly, in Model 6, where female labor force participation rates are included as a control, the negative relationship between the percentage of females in the county and county median household income is also reduced. From this it can be tentatively inferred that counties that can boost female labor force participation and/or reduce overall poverty rates may be able to offset the negative impact of relatively lower female earnings on median household income in the county, even when a relatively larger percentage of females comprise the county population.

Educational Attainment, Labor Force Attachment, and Poverty Rate
A number of expected findings emerge from tables 8.2 and 8.3. These are relationships or correlations that we would expect, and that are predicted by theory and are well established by prior research. They include the results for the educational attainment, labor force attachment, and poverty variables.

Counties with higher levels of educational attainment (Models 1–7) and greater labor force attachment (Models 1, 4, 5, and 6) exhibit higher household incomes, all else constant. These are well-known associations that nonetheless bear emphasis. If county economic development is sought, economic development officials must seek to attract and retain workers with a minimum of a bachelor's degree, and must boost the number of those holding a bachelor's degree or more as a proportion of the county population. Additionally, counties with a larger segment of their population active in the labor force and/or employed in jobs demonstrate higher household incomes. The overall labor force participation rate (Models 1 and 4), employment-to-population ratio (Model 5), and female labor force participation rate (Model 6) exhibit strong positive and statistically significant correlations with median household incomes in rural counties.[40] And, because education levels are positively associated with employability, there is a clear connection: attracting a more educated county population and, as a result, one that is more employable, boosts county household income.[41] Gender in the work force also appears to play a strong and supporting role: counties that create employment opportunities for women and display higher female labor force participation are rewarded with higher household incomes overall. Although this study does not control for the effects of dual-income households, one explanation for this finding may be that counties with higher levels of female labor force participation indicate more dual-income households, which would tend to boost median household income.

Conversely, counties with a higher proportion of high-school dropouts in their population (Model 8) reflect lower household income as we would expect. County residents with less than a high school education are likely to be much less employable and will tend to reduce labor force attachment, lowering household income as a consequence.

Finally, the poverty rate control variable in Models 1–3 and Models 7 and 8 shows a clear negative and strong correlation with household income, as expected, and dominates the models in which it is present. Although poverty rates and income levels are not exactly the same measures, they certainly overlap conceptually so that they are essentially two sides of the same coin; causation likely runs in both directions. Counties with higher (lower) poverty rates exhibit significantly lower (higher) household income levels, all else constant. The variable was nonetheless included as a control variable so that the effects of other predictors of household income could be observed independent of the impact of poverty.

Conclusions: Policy Implications and Recommendations for Future Research

Using standard OLS multiple regression estimation techniques on cross-sectional Census 2000 data from 680 rural (non-MSA) counties across ten Midwestern states, this study finds that counties with relatively higher population density, closer proximity to metropolitan areas, outside-county employment opportunities for their residents, a more educated workforce, and greater labor force attachment exhibit consistently higher levels of median household income. Additionally, and to a lesser degree, counties with relatively more immigrants and a relatively higher proportion of same-sex partner households tend, all else constant, also to exhibit higher median household incomes. These findings tentatively support the theory that rural economies that can capture urban characteristics such as higher population density, greater population diversity, increased human capital, and workforce connections to metropolitan areas exhibit the best chance for economic development. Surprisingly, rural counties with institutions of higher education do not exhibit higher median household income, perhaps owing to a "payroll effect" reinforced by the residential choice and commuting patterns of rural university employees.

This study is meant to be but a preliminary survey investigating factors correlated with household income in non-MSA counties in the Midwest. As such, it is plagued by numerous weaknesses previously highlighted, primary among which are possible endogeneity effects between some of the independent variables and possible omitted variable bias. Nonetheless, the findings in these models are consistent enough with both theory and prior literature that they can offer a preliminary guide to policy making.

Although detailed policy proposals are beyond the scope of this study, the broad policy implications flowing from these preliminary findings seem fairly straightforward. County officials seeking greater economic development and consequently higher incomes for their resident households must seek to attract and retain younger and more educated workers as members of the county population, particularly those holding a bachelor's degree or beyond. Additionally, county officials must create an economic environment and culture where employment and strong ties to jobs and the labor force are encouraged and valued by the largest possible percentage of the population. This would certainly include attracting and retaining businesses by lowering the costs of doing business in the local economy, broadly lowering taxes and regulations, potentially increasing the availability and access to local employment opportunities. The less costly it is for local residents to obtain jobs, either inside or outside their county of residence, the higher the levels of employment and labor force attachment are likely to be.

County officials in rural counties adjacent to larger metropolitan counties should market their counties as a possible destination for home owners who wish to work in urban areas but commute to a residence in a rural neighborhood; so-called bedroom communities. Attracting high-income workers who commute to jobs outside their county of residence would appear to boost local income measures. In pursuit of these goals, it may be possible for local governments in these rural counties to cooperate together to improve infrastructure quantity and quality, especially if this promotes connectivity between the rural county and a larger neighboring metropolitan economy.[42]

Finally, consistent with Florida's thesis, a diverse population and workforce appear important in boosting local incomes in the rural counties surveyed in this study.[43] Counties more open to immigrants, as well as more racially and ethnically diverse, and counties more tolerant of alternative lifestyle choices, would seem to have the dynamic ingredients that spark creativity and entrepreneurship, potentially boosting local incomes as a result. Consistent with this finding, county policy should be fashioned to encourage and invite immigrants of all types to take up residence and start businesses in rural counties. Policies hostile to immigrant or gay populations, including policies that make it difficult for immigrants to easily and quickly become legal citizens and workers, should likewise be repealed. Markusen, Wassall, DeNatale, and Cohen offer policy suggestions for defining and cultivating "creative class" identities for cities that may be applicable to rural communities as well.[44]

Because this study only begins the investigation of factors associated with household income levels in rural Midwestern counties, there is ample room for future research to refine and improve the study. A number of questions remain unanswered. What might be the impact of local measures of educational success in county school systems on county income levels? Could average SAT scores among a county's local school jurisdictions predict local income? Counties with stronger school systems as measured by average SAT scores may attract parents from outside the county who place a high value on their children's education, many of whom are more highly educated themselves. Additionally, counties with successful school systems as measured by average SAT scores may attract business firms relocating from outside the county. If firms hope to have access to a more educated workforce, or to attract workers that place a higher value on education, then they may anticipate relocating to or starting up in counties with more successful school systems. If so, we would expect counties with stronger school systems also to exhibit higher household income levels.

How might the characteristics and variation in local public finance relate to household income levels? Local taxes and business regulations may impact county income levels, and this opens a further avenue for future data gathering and research.[45] Although measures of economic openness or tax and regulatory burden are not available through Census data, it may be possible to construct county-level measures for these variables from alternative sources and estimate their impact on county income.[46] Additionally, public expenditures on schools, parks and recreation areas, and especially local transportation infrastructure could improve income opportunities for local residents. None of these variables were included in the present study and await further investigation.

Finally, what are the occupational effects of the labor force on household income in rural Midwestern counties? One weakness of the present study is that it omits a measure on the composition of occupations at the county level; a measure that may correlate median household income with the employment base of the county's work force. An investigation of this potential relationship is ripe for future research.

In summary, and aside from the limitations of this study, the general conclusions reached are as follows: Successful rural counties will tend to be linked with larger metropolitan and urban economies, not only through interstate highway systems, but through the employment, educational, and human capital opportunities for the workers that reside in the rural counties.

The findings here suggest that rural Midwestern counties that can mimic the characteristics and attributes of the larger urban areas around them will tend to have higher levels of economic development and resulting household income. These characteristics include: population density that deepens and extends opportunities for specialization within the division of labor, a more educated workforce rich in human capital, high levels of labor force attachment, easy access to outside-of-county job and career opportunities (presumably in neighboring metropolitan areas), and a more ethnically and artistically diverse population. It seems that the future economic success of rural counties will depend on how well they link with and support the larger urban economies in their regions.

Appendix A: Model Communities in the Midwest Ranked on Selected Variables[47]

Table 8.4. Top Five Counties on Median Household Income (1999)

1. Union County, OH	$51,743†
2. Rice County, MN	$48,651†
3. Dodge County, MN	$47,437†
4. Leelanau County, MI	$47,062
5. Spencer County, KY	$47,042†

Source: U.S. Census Bureau, Summary File 3 for Census 2000 (www.census.gov)

Table 8.5. Top Five Counties on Median Family Income (1999)

1. Union County, OH	$58,384†
2. Rice County, MN	$56,407†
3. Nicollet County, MN	$55,694
4. Goodhue County, MN	$55,689†
5. Story County, IA	$55,472†

Source: U.S. Census Bureau, Summary File 3 for Census 2000 (www.census.gov)

Table 8.6. Top Five Counties on Per Capita Income (1999)

1. Leelanau County, MI	$24,686
2. Grand Traverse County, MI	$22,111
3. Ottawa County, OH	$21,973†
4. Goodhue County, MN	$21,934†
5. Dickinson County, IA	$21,929

Source: U.S. Census Bureau, Summary File 3 for Census 2000 (www.census.gov)

Table 8.7. Top Five Counties on Aggregate Household Income (1999)

1. La Salle County, IL	$2,091,196,700†
2. LaPorte County, IN	$2,031,608,300†
3. Wayne County, OH	$2,022,327,800†
4. Walworth County, WI	$1,940,368,200†
5. Fond du Lac County: WI	$1,906,750,000†

Source: U.S. Census Bureau, Summary File 3 for Census 2000 (www .census.gov)

Table 8.8. Top Five Most Populous Counties (2000)

1. Wayne County, OH	111,564†
2. La Salle County, IL	111,509†
3. LaPorte County, IN	110,106†
4. Fond du Lac County, WI	97,296†
5. Hardin County, KY	94,174†

Source: U.S. Census Bureau, Summary File 3 for Census 2000 (www .census.gov)

Table 8.9. Top Five Counties on Population Density: Persons Per Square Kilometer (2000)

1. Erie County, OH	120.5†
2. McCracken County, KY	100.8
3. Monongalia County, WV	87.5†
4. Franklin County, KY	87.5†
5. Wayne County, OH	77.6†

Source: U.S. Census Bureau, Summary File 3 for Census 2000 (www .census.gov)

Table 8.10. Top Five Most Educated Counties: Percentage of Adults with Bachelor's Degree or More (2000)

1. Story County, IA	44.5†
2. Monongalia County, WV	32.4†
3. Jackson County, IL	32.0
4. Leelanau County, MI	31.4
5. Jefferson County, IA	31.2

Source: U.S. Census Bureau, Summary File 3 for Census 2000 (www .census.gov)

Table 8.11. Top Five Counties on Labor Force Participation Rate (2000)

1. Iowa County, WI	75.4†
2. Nicolette County, MN	74.9
3. Dodge County, MN	74.2†
4. Steele County, MN	72.9
5. Green County, WI	72.8†

Source: U.S. Census Bureau, Summary File 3 for Census 2000 (www.census.gov)

Table 8.12. Top Five Counties on Employment-to-Population Ratio (2000)

1. Iowa County, WI	72.5†
2. Dodge County, MN	71.7†
3. Nicollet County, MN	71.5
4. Green County, WI	70.5†
5. Steele County, MN	70.4

Source: U.S. Census Bureau, Summary File 3 for Census 2000 (www.census.gov)

Table 8.13. Top Five Counties on Percentage Workers Employed Outside County of Residence (2000)

1. Spencer County, KY	77.9†
2. Trimble County, KY	76.9†
3. Warren County, IN	69.0†
4. Doddridge County, WV	68.9
5. Garrard County, KY	67.4†

Source: U.S. Census Bureau, Summary File 3 for Census 2000 (www.census.gov)

Table 8.14. Top Five Immigrant Counties: Percent Population Foreign Born (2000)

1. Buena Vista County, IA	12.5
2. Nobles County, MN	9.0
3. Watonwan County, MN	8.0
4. Cass County, IL	7.8†
5. Story County, IA	6.9†

Source: U.S. Census Bureau, Summary File 3 for Census 2000 (www.census.gov)

Table 8.15. Top Five Counties on Percentage of All Households Same-Sex Partner (2000)

1. Alexander County, IL	1.18
2. Cook County, MN	1.05
3. Nelson County, KY	1.01†
4. Hart County, KY	.99
5. Shelby County, KY	.95†

Source: U.S. Census Bureau, Summary File 3 for Census 2000 (www.census.gov)

Notes

The author would like to recognize and give special thanks to Kyle Linn, Kate Bedinghaus, and Sarah Forman for their excellent research assistance, and the Grant County Economic Growth Council for its support and review of the initial drafts of this research.

1. Mark B. Lapping, et al., *Rural Planning and Development in the United States* (New York: The Guilford Press, 1989).

2. Lapping, et al., *Rural Planning and Development*; G.J. Lewis, "Rural Communities," in ed. M. Pacione *Progress in Rural Geography* (Totowa, NJ: Barnes and Noble, 1983); Paul B. Frederic, "Review of *Rural Planning and Development in the United States*," *Economic Geography* 66, no. 1 (Jan. 1990): 103–5

3. Amy K. Glasmeier, *The High-Tech Potential: Economic Development in Rural America* (New Brunswick, NJ: Center for Urban Policy Research, Rutgers University, 1991).

4. Timothy J. Fik, "Review of *The High-Tech Potential: Economic Development in Rural America*," *Economic Geography* 68, no. 4 (October 1992): 443–45.

5. Joel Kotkin, *The New Geography: How the Digital Revolution is Reshaping the American Landscape* (New York: Random House, 2000).

6. Christina E. Gringeri, *Getting By: Homeworkers and Rural Economic Development* (Lawrence: University Press of Kansas, 1994).

7. Ann M. Oberhauser, "Review of *Getting By: Women Homeworkers and Rural Economic Development*," *Economic Geography* 73 no. 1 (Jan. 1997): 131–33

8. Richard Florida, *Who's Your City? How the Creative Economy is Making Where to Live the Most Important Decision of Your Life* (New York: Basic Books, 2008).

9. A Metropolitan Statistical Area (MSA) contains one or more central cities of at least 50,000 residents and the surrounding (contiguous) metropolitan counties which may contain smaller towns and suburbs. The Census Bureau defines the geography of an MSA by the percentage of the labor force that is nonagricultural and by the amount of commuting between the surrounding metro counties and the central city or cities contained within the region. See Edwin S. Mills and Bruce W. Hamilton, *Urban Economics*, 5th ed. (Reading, MA: Addison-Wesley Educational

Publishers, 1994). MSAs are comprised of entire counties, not parts or segmented portions of counties.

10. An alternative measure of income or economic output would have been county median family income. However, in bivariate correlations, this measure was found to be nearly perfectly collinear with county median household income so that the two variables are essentially identical in terms of what they measure. The arbitrary decision was made to use median household rather than median family income per county.

11. In order to ensure reliability and validity of findings, an important assumption of multiple regression analysis is that the values in the dependent variable be normally distributed (low positive or negative skewness). Fortunately, the dependent variable, county median household income, exhibited only modest negative skewness with a skewness statistic of -.256, a standard error of skewness of .094, and a skewness z-score of -2.723 which is considered within the acceptable range for multiple regression analysis.

12. E.J. Blakely and T.K. Bradshaw, *Planning Local Economic Development: Theory and Practice*, 3rd ed (Thousand Oaks, CA: Sage Publications, 2002).

13. Adam Smith, *An Inquiry into the Nature and Causes of the Wealth of Nations*, vol. 1 (Chicago: University of Chicago Press, 1976), 21–25.

14. John M. Quigley, "Urban Diversity and Economic Growth," *Journal of Economic Perspective*, 12, no. 2 (Spring 1998): 127–38.

15. The dummy variable was coded as follows. If an interstate highway passed through or ran along the border of a county, that county was assigned a value of "1" for the interstate highway variable. All other counties without an interstate highway were assigned a value of "0". This allows us to test whether the presence of an interstate highway or highways in the county has any impact on household income.

16. Lapping et al., *Rural Planning and Development*.

17. Quigley, "Urban Diversity and Economic Growth."

18. Smith, *An Inquiry the Nature and Causes of the Wealth of Nations*.

19. For an excellent discussion of how both transportation networks and a larger more diverse population offer greater diversity and encourage economic growth for urban areas, see Quigley, "Urban Diversity and Econmic Growth."

20. Florida, *Who's Your City?*

21. The dummy variable for geography was coded as follows. If a rural county shared one or more full or partial borders with another county that was part of a MSA or CMSA in 2000, that county was assigned a value of "1." All other rural counties not adjacent to or sharing a border with an MSA county were assigned a value of "0." This allows us to test whether geographic proximity to urban agglomeration economies has any impact on county median household income.

22. Florida, *Who's Your City?*

23. Paul D. Gottlieb and Michael Fogarty, "Educational Attainment and Metropolitan Growth," *Economic Development Quarterly* 17 no. 4 (2003): 325–36. See also Stephan J. Goetz and Anil Rupasingha, "The Returns on Higher Education:

Estimates for the 48 Contiguous States" *Economic Development Quarterly* 17, no. 4 (2003): 337–51.

24. Gerald A. Carlino, "Do Education and Training Lead to Faster Growth in Cities?," *Business Review of the Federal Reserve Bank of Philadelphia* (January/February 1995): 15–22.

25. Charles S. Colgan and Bruce H. Andrews, "Beyond the Unemployment Rate: Workforce Profiles for Economic Development," *Economic Development Quarterly* 17 no.3 (2003): 240–54. See also John M. McGrath and Ronald Vickroy, "A Research Approach to Tracking Local Economic Conditions in Small-Town America," *Economic Development Quarterly* 17, no. 3 (2003): 255–63.

26. Unemployment rate is calculated as the percentage of the county labor force seeking but not holding a job in 2000; employment-to-population ratio is calculated as the percentage of the county population holding a job in 2000; and, labor force participation rate is calculated as the percentage of the county population in the labor force (i.e., either holding a job or actively seeking employment) in 2000.

27. Richard Florida, *The Rise of the Creative Class: And How it's Transforming Work, Leisure, Community and Everyday Life* (New York: Basic Books, 2002); Laura A. Reese and Gary Sands, "Creative Class and Economic Prosperity: Old Nostrums, Better Packaging?" *Economic Development Quarterly* 22, no. 1 (2008): 3–7.

28. Carlino, *Do Education and Training Lead to Faster Growth?* See also Melanie et al., "The Economic Impact of Educational Institutions: Issues and Methodology," *Economic Development Quarterly* 16, no.1 (2002): 88–95.

29. For example, in Model 1, an increase in population density by one person per square kilometer would lead to an estimated increase in annual county median household income of slightly more than $71, all else equal.

30. Model 1 is the strongest model among those tested, but also contains a weakness in the relatively high level of negative multicollinearity between the county poverty rate control variable and county labor force participation rate. The bivariate correlation between these variables is -.773, and the collinearity tolerance within the model is .20 for both. Because there was not perfect multicollinearity between these two variables and because standard OLS multiple regression techniques are considered robust, Model 1 is retained in table 8.2, and the separate effects of poverty rates and labor force participation rates can be observed in isolation in Models 2 and 4.

31. Theoretically, this could be the result of a commuting compensation differential where higher wages or salaries are paid to workers commuting longer distances outside their county of residence. However, in multiple regression results not shown here, there was not found to be any significant relationship between median household income and rural commuters traveling longer time distances to their places of employment. Thus, we are led to conclude that the higher household income associated with out-of-county commuting is much more a function of the destiny of that commute than the time or distance of the commute.

32. Frederic, review of *Rural Planning and Development in the United States*.

33. As mentioned above, there may be a stronger association between county income and interstate highway networks than what is able to be estimated using the dummy variable in this study. An improved measure of the concept underlying this variable, and one we hope to investigate in future research, is the actual number of interstate highway miles per county.

34. Florida, *Rise of the Creative Class*.

35. Florida, *Rise of the Creative Class*.

36. Gary Sands and Laura A. Reese, "Cultivating the Creative Class: And What About Nanaimo?" *Economic Development Quarterly* 22, no.1 (2008): 8–23.

37. Bivariate correlations in the data indeed bear out this negative association. The bivariate and statistically significant Pearson correlation coefficient between median county age and presence of an accredited university was −.266, suggesting that counties with colleges and universities exhibit lower median age in their populations.

38. Only in Model 6, when controlling for the effects of female labor force participation, does the proportion of African Americans in the county population become significantly correlated with median household income, exhibiting a negative sign on the coefficient. A speculative conjecture is that this is a result of an interaction effect or endogeneity between the presence of female African Americans with low rates of labor force participation, a theory that awaits further exploration in future research.

39. William H. Frey, *Melting Pot Suburbs: A Census 2000 Study of Suburban Diversity* (Washington, D.C.: The Brookings Institution, 2001).

40. Surprisingly, when included in Models 3, 7, and 8, county unemployment rates are not found to correlate with median household income levels in the rural counties in this study. This measure of labor force attachment is highly collinear with the labor force participation rate and the employment-to-population ratio, as expected, and these latter measures appear to be much stronger predictors of household income in rural economies.

41. The data reveal strong and statistically significant bivariate correlations between the educational attainment variable (percentage of adult population with a bachelors degree or more) and labor force participation rate (+.482), employment-to-population ratio (+.456) and female labor force participation rate (+.553).

42. Steven B. Lackey et al., "Factors Influencing Local Government Cooperation in Rural Areas: Evidence from the Tennessee Valley," *Economic Development Quarterly* 16, no. 2 (2002): 138–54.

43. Florida, *Rise of the Creative Class*.

44. Ann Markusen et al., "Defining the Creative Economy: Industry and Occupational Approaches," *Economic Development Quarterly* 22, no.1 (2008): 24–45.

45. County level aggregate and median real estate taxes were obtained from the census data in this study, and numerous variations of these measures were found to be consistently positively related to median household income: counties with relatively higher aggregate or median property taxes, higher aggregate or median property taxes per capita, or higher aggregate-property-tax-to-aggregate-income ratio exhibit higher median household income, all else constant. However, because the causal direction

of this relationship certainly runs from household income to property taxes and not vice versa (i.e., higher property taxes do not "cause" higher incomes), measures of property taxes are not included as predictors of county household income levels.

46. If some measure of economic openness similar to the Index of Economic Freedom found in James Gwartney et al., *Economic Freedom of the World 2007 Annual Report* (Vancouver: The Fraser Institute, 2007) could be computed for U.S. counties, such an index may prove a useful tool in evaluating the effects of economic openness on median household income in the Midwest and elsewhere.

47. County values marked with "†" indicate a rural county that shares a border with an MSA.

CHAPTER NINE

∽

Small, Green, and Good
The Role of Smaller Industrial Cities in a Sustainable Future

CATHERINE TUMBER

Growing up in a small town, I regularly took bus trips with my mom and little sister into "the city": Syracuse. Like most middle-class families in the early 1960s, we had only one car, which my dad drove to work. So we would buy our tickets at the village pharmacy, board the Big Dog, and barrel though miles of farms and sparsely developed land until we reached the highway. Nearing the final stretch, we had to endure the stench of the Solvay chemical works to our right, and the creepy mint green of polluted Onondaga Lake on our left. But we would disembark in Syracuse's vibrant downtown, all glittering lights and vertical planes, filled with department stores, jewelry and candy shops, theaters and movie palaces, "ethnic" food, and people who were interestingly not like us.

Smaller American cities, places like Syracuse—and Decatur, New Bedford, Kalamazoo, Buffalo, Trenton, Erie, and Youngstown—were once bustling centers of industry and downtown commerce, with wealthy local patrons committed to civic improvements and the arts. In the 1970s they began a decline from which they have not recovered. Today, most are scanted as doleful sites of low-paying service jobs, with shrinking tax bases and little appeal to young professionals or to what urban theorist Richard Florida calls the "creative class." In Syracuse itself the center of gravity has shifted northward, toward Carousel Mall, leaving a ghostly downtown where Rite-Aid, now the largest store, presides over parking lots and abandoned commercial buildings.

Historians and economic demographers generally attribute the decline of small-to-mid-size industrial cities in the Midwest and Northeast—once 50,000 to 500,000 people strong—to outsourcing and globalization, and of course that's true. But the history of smaller-city decline is more complex than that. Smaller industrial cities were also victims of post-war development policies better suited to large cities—or rather, that were painful, but less disastrous, for large metropolitan areas.

Extraordinary mid-twentieth century changes in transportation, zoning, housing construction, mortgage financing, and domestic taste facilitated the creation of wide swathes of "bourgeois utopias" that now ring our cities far out into the exurbs. They are the products of a radical transformation of land-use policy that favored vast highway systems, further separating people from their workplaces, energy producers from consumers, and farmers from their markets. Large cities survived these changes and the resulting onslaught of suburban shopping malls in the late 1970s. In smaller cities, however, malls decimated what was left of downtown retail districts already damaged by proportionately massive downtown highway systems that choked off commercial centers from surrounding urban neighborhoods.

Neglect of the smaller city, as both place and idea, continued through the rest of the century. As large-metropolitan real estate values skyrocketed in the 1990s, big cities attracted millions of dollars in capital improvements and large-scale development. New Urbanist designers and architects, often criticized for focusing on planned suburban communities, attracted funding for pedestrian-friendly thoroughfares, mixed-use building, open spaces, and the preservation of historic architecture that enhanced the metropolitan boom. Now, with today's call for reducing our urban carbon footprint, cosmopolitan living is going green. Two recent books proposing models for a low-carbon economy—Thomas Friedman's *Hot, Flat, and Crowded,* and Jay Inslee and Bracken Hendricks's *Apollo's Fire*—speak throughout of "villages" and "large cities." Not a word for the distinctive role smaller industrial cities might play in a low-carbon world.

That is too bad. Smaller industrial cities have idiosyncratic charms of their own, and are worthy of sustained attention and renewal. And, fortuitously, they have a distinctive and vital role to play in the work of the new century. Indeed, they will be critical in the move to local agriculture and the development of renewable energy industries. These tasks will require a dramatic rethinking of land-use policy, and here smaller industrial cities have assets that large cities lack. Their underused or vacant industrial space and surrounding tracts of farmland make them ideal sites for sustainable land-use policies and the productive green economy.

Yet current urban planning models offer little guidance on how we might begin to make those changes. Nor, until recently, has there been a national forum that matches smaller-city renewal initiatives to national needs. The Revitalizing Older Cities Congressional Task Force, which took industrial cities of smaller scale into account, held its first national summit (organized by the Northeast-Midwest Institute) in 2008. Smaller municipal governments must build on this conversation, for they have critical contributions to make to a low-carbon the future.

The Portland, Oregon-based Post Carbon Cities project offers one bold way to start thinking about national policy, with its call for the "relocalization" of cities, a form of decentralization grounded in local food systems and energy resources. An alternative to the traditional idea of "balancing" economic and environmental needs, relocalization aims to maximize both by dramatically reducing reliance on costly and environmentally damaging supply chains—long transportation routes geared to truck or air transportation—while increasing sustainable agriculture and energy security and creating local jobs that cannot be outsourced.

Taking energy security first, smaller industrial cities, with their large parcels of vacant, relatively low-value property and proximate surrounding land, could serve the alternative energy industry well. Smaller cities are not only more likely to be located near sources of clean energy—such as waterways, forests, and fields—but they can also generate more energy proportionate to their size.

One large obstacle for the clean-energy industry and its advocates is that the current energy infrastructure disadvantages them in competition with coal, natural gas, and oil, which together provide about 70 percent of electrical power in the United States. Achieving "grid parity"—the point at which renewable energy is as cheap as or cheaper than power from prevailing sources—is extremely difficult. The grid, built decades ago for local utility monopolies and now used by a deregulated national energy industry, is in a terrible state of disrepair. More immediately, it is oriented toward large "base loads" traveling over long distances to major population centers, a strain that threatens the fragile system. The United States' "third-world grid," as many now call it, is particularly unsuited to storing or transferring small, supplementary loads of electricity—the kind of loads produced by solar and wind energy in their current form. Moreover, keeping energy more local has the advantage of limiting grid transmission loss, which can run as high as 10 percent.

If smaller cities are to reap the benefits of renewable energy development, the transmission and distribution network must be both modernized and decentralized—changes that electrical energy experts agree are necessary anyway. Local contributions to a first-world energy grid would then vary, depending on terrain and natural resources. Hydrokinetic power harvested from underwater ocean currents shows promise in coastal areas. Hydropower from rivers would generate the most electricity in the West and Midwest, where the drop is higher and the water rush more forceful than in other parts of the country. Solar power on a large scale works best in sunny climates, and wind power on the coasts and in the Great Plains. And, according to a *Washington Post* report, geothermal energy tapped from the thirteen Western states that sit within the trans-Pacific "Ring of Fire" could provide up to half of the nation's current level of electricity output.

But smaller contributions from alternative energy sources should not be overlooked. Small hydropower, defined as producing up to ten megawatts of electricity (enough to support 10,000 homes), is underdeveloped in the United States, lagging far behind Canada, Australia, New Zealand, parts of Asia, and the European Union, where it is found mostly in its fast-developing smaller cities. In New England, a number of projects are under way that will generate three megawatts or less, enough to power a hospital, large shopping center, or small factory. As ideal sites for new energy industries, smaller cities would in turn gain from job creation.

Alternative energy technologies are in various stages of development, but one thing is already clear: if they work, they will require space that dense metropolitan areas cannot provide. Solar power, which among alternative energies has come closest to achieving grid parity, can make use of rooftops and awnings in big cities, but offers far greater potential when staged on ground mounts on polluted brownfields, suburban greyfields, or open land. One of the world's largest solar farms, sitting on more than one thousand acres in Kramer Junction in California's Mojave Desert, consists of row upon row of solar panels, which power generating stations at the facility. According to the company that operates it, at capacity, it produces enough power (150 megawatts) to support 150,000 homes. A good rule of thumb, at this point, is that one megawatt of solar-generated power requires about eight acres of land.

Wind power, unless sited offshore, also requires large tracts of land. And, by definition, biomass and biogas technologies require farm and forest land to generate the raw resources required, as well as space for the physical plant that conducts the conversion. This year BioEnergy Solutions announced a partnership with Vintage Dairy, of Riverdale, California (just outside Fresno) to convert manure from its 5,000 cows into methane by flushing animal waste into an anaerobic-digester, a covered lagoon "equal in size to the area of nearly five football fields and over three stories deep."

As ideal sites for new energy industries, smaller cities would in turn gain from job creation. A 2007 American Solar Energy Society report claimed that renewable energy and energy-efficient industries had already created nearly 8.5 million jobs in the United States, a little more than half in indirectly related fields such as accounting, information technology, and trucking. Many are blue-collar jobs in maintenance and manufacturing. A September 2008 proposal from the Apollo Alliance estimates that its New Apollo Program—a renewable energy proposal on a scale akin to that of the Kennedy administration's space program—could create five million "high-quality" green-collar jobs over the next decade. Indeed, many have pointed out that bold low-carbon policy initiatives could launch the next Industrial Revolution. The Obama administration has signaled its support for Apollo's broad aims for energy policy, though the extent of its commitment was murky as of 2010.

The proximity of abundant, relatively cheap land also gives smaller cities a structural advantage in meeting the growing demand for local, sustainable agriculture. As Michael Pollan demonstrates in his best-selling *The Omnivore's Dilemma*, agribusiness puts down an enormous carbon footprint. Sustainable agriculture and animal husbandry not only produce more nutritious food and less cruelty to animals, they are also far less dependent on petroleum for long-distance transportation, fertilizer, and neurotoxic pesticides (not to mention antibiotics). Building on the work of organic farmers and environmental activists since the 1970s, Pollan's call for relocalizing agriculture coincides with rising alarm about the perils of climate change and dependence on foreign oil. Even the United Nations, which has long embraced agribusiness as the key to famine prevention, is beginning to recognize the role of sustainable, localized practices in food security. The change in public perceptions has created a critical mass of "locavores," most living in big cities far from the heart of agribusiness, who are driving a growing market for organic products.

Farmers' markets, community-supported agriculture, community gardens, and green roofs have become increasingly popular, forcing big supermarket chains to offer local, organic produce. New York City alone went from two farmers' markets in 1979 to more than forty-five in 2008. Meanwhile, the appeal of farming, on a smaller, more diversified, independent model, is growing among young adults and mid-life professionals. The number of organic farms in New York State almost doubled between 2003 and 2007, from 404 farms to 735. And the number of people aged forty-five to fifty-four operating farms of under fifty acres shot up by 70 percent. Increasingly, urban professionals are investing in farmland and taking on agricultural work as a second vocation.

If urban farming—growing food within city limits or on nearby small-scale market farms—and sustainable agriculture in general are to succeed, however, they must be integrated with the larger workforce and with urban and regional planning. Detroit, home to one of the country's first urban farms, pioneered this work. As of 2008, eighty acres throughout the city had been appropriated for agriculture and were under cultivation through the Detroit Garden Resource Program Collaborative. Its member organizations provide training in soil management and crop cultivation, bee-keeping, orchard building, composting, and the like through various faith communities and the local schools, and provide on-the-job training and summer employment to teens and adults. The yield for 2007 was 120 tons of food and promises to grow much higher. The county treasurer's office allowed the nonprofit Urban Farming to grow produce on twenty tax-foreclosed vacant properties in 2008.

To some extent, the urban agriculture movement is primarily a big-city phenomenon, not least because large cities have received disproportionate publicity and funding. The W. K. Kellogg Foundation sponsors one of the larger and more daring philanthropic initiatives. Its Food and Fitness program provided planning grants to nine community-based projects that emphasize access to local food and physical exercise among disadvantaged families. Six of them are located in big cities (including Detroit), two in rural areas, and only one in a smaller city—Holyoke, Massachusetts.

Funding and advocacy organizations have nothing against smaller city initiatives. Far from it. Kellogg's Ricardo Salvador notes that "the metaphor of sustainability itself is lots of small communities, whether they are city neighborhoods in densely populated areas or small rural communities." As Daniel Lerch, of Post Carbon Cities puts it: "This is not just an issue of scale. Very soon we'll see cities of any size going down the path of sustainability with regard to food and watershed."

By minimizing the importance of scale, however, sustainability advocates could be missing the large, strategic regional and economic advantages smaller cities can offer a national policy over the long term. Martin Bailkey, coauthor of a 2000 Lincoln Institute of Land Policy working paper on the history and viability of entrepreneurial "farming inside cities" says "it shouldn't matter whether farms are fifty or sixty miles from, say, New York City, or ten miles from a smaller city like Madison, Wisconsin." But he notes that postindustrial cities with declining populations, particularly in the Midwest, are better positioned to shift urban land-use policy toward farming.

Even more intriguing, he says, is the notion that the "mosaic" of smaller cities located in the heartland could one day anchor a regional agricultural shift from industrial monoculture to more localized biodiversity. Large farms now used for federally subsidized commodity crops—mainly corn and soy—could over time be made available in smaller parcels for market farming on a scale that cannot be undertaken within city limits.

The Land Connection, based in Evanston, Illinois, is working to do just that. One program helps heirs to farmland put agricultural easements on their property, and its training and transition programs assist farmers who want to replace monoculture with sustainable, organic practices. Founder Terra Brockman says that some of the newer farmers, who may be first-timers or returning to the family business, "are making the decision to sell in smaller cities . . . where the demand didn't exist fifteen years ago." What they need, says Brockman, "is really quite simple: land, trained farmers, local processing facilities (which disappeared in the sixties), and logistical transportation."

Developing an effective transportation infrastructure is critical to making smaller cities hubs in a relocalized, agricultural economy. As Kellogg's Gail Imig suggests, it might be easier for smaller cities "to work out local distribution systems for transporting food" than for big cities. Still, federal leadership will be crucial. Gayle Peterson of The Headwaters Group Philanthropic Services—consultants for foundations ranging from Kellogg, Mott, and Weyerhouser to community foundations—says: "There is a huge movement among foundations supporting regional food systems uniting networks of cities and towns in a large agricultural food basket . . . but there are as yet no group initiatives that cut across the issues." Her colleague, John Sherman, adds: "If anything significant is to take place, the thrust will have to come from economic development agencies" that can provide government funding and coordinated policy leadership.

One nonprofit, the Michigan Land Use Institute (MLUI), is emerging as a model of state and regional planning. One of the projects it supports, The Grand Vision, aims to integrate economic opportunities into a working rural landscape and provide land-use experts to help grassroots groups organize and manage their campaigns.

Located in the area around Traverse City, a large town of 14,532 that anchors a "micropolitan statistical area"—a term established in 2003 denoting a new federal census standard—with a population of 131,342, The Grand Vision emerged in 2006 when plans for a highway bypass and bridge around

Traverse City met with community protest. With the cooperation of Senators Debbie Stabinow and Carl Levin and U.S. Representative Dave Camp, federal highway funding was diverted to a two-year community-planning process. The process was coordinated by consultants with the full involvement of local citizens, municipal bodies, businesses, environmental groups, and social services agencies, all organized into "charrettes."

One of MLUI's highly successful programs is Farm to School, which is part of a growing nationwide movement that connects local farm products with school cafeterias. MLUI links the program to a larger state initiative based on a study showing that helping farmers sell to local supermarkets and farmers' markets could increase net farm income in Michigan by nearly 16 percent and generate up to 1,889 new jobs.

Smaller cities might also be better able than large ones to recover for market-farming purposes land lost to suburban sprawl. Filmmaker Nancy Rosin—who produced a documentary on the history of Rochester, New York's farmers' market—explains that before the rise of grocery store chains after World War I, small-market farming appealed to working people, particularly immigrants from Italy and Eastern Europe, who brought their horticultural skills with them. They grew food on city lots where they lived and, over time, grew much larger quantities in the adjacent suburbs—or what we would now call suburbs—in particular, Irondequoit, less than ten miles from Rochester's downtown market. A sizeable number, she says, held full-time jobs with companies such as Kodak and became known as "Kodak farmers." By mid-century Irondequoit "had the largest square footage of greenhouse glass in the world to support the demand for food in a climate with long, cold winters." A fifty-something Irondequoit native who blogs for the *Rochester Democrat and Chronicle* brings that world to life:

> I grew up in the Flats, on St. Joseph Street. My dad was born there in the old homestead, his parents farmers. My siblings and I were raised there. Although it had changed from when my dad was growing up, I still remember all the farming that went on down there. The greenhouses, the tractors, listening to the frogs on a hot summer night . . . it was like living in the country. A drive through the Flats today shows quite a different story. The farms are gone. There are no tractors going up and down the street with trailers bobbing behind them. The greenhouses are gone. Most of the "old timers" have passed. There are houses where there were fields and wetlands. There has been a lot of change.

By the early 1960s Irondequoit was fast being paved over, making way for homes, highways, and strip malls. In 1963, the once-powerful Irondequoit

Grange closed and later became the House of Guitars. The gigantic Irondequoit Mall opened in 1990, and, today, after only eighteen years in business, it is considered officially "dead," with less than 50 percent retail occupancy and an uncertain future. What should become of such worn-out retail outlets, which were multiplying by the thousands across the country even before the 2008 economic downturn?

A happier future for a smaller city like Rochester, where Kodak alone shed some 45,000 jobs over the past twenty-five years, may involve the restoration and growth of sustainable food systems. One of Kellogg's earliest Food and Fitness pilot programs tried to do just that on several acres where a small vineyard tended by an Italian family years ago still grows. (The program is currently languishing due to conflicts among the community organizations that originally established it.) A series of community "Vision Plans" similar to those in Traverse City called for continuing an existing program of riverfront development, as well as more affordable housing, mixed-use buildings, and pedestrian-friendly streets—all familiar New Urbanism strategies. One recent charrette also called for tearing down part of the Inner Loop freeway, built in 1965, that circles the downtown business district. Here is another idea: why not turn the roof and vast parking lot of Irondequoit Mall into a solar "brightfield," and the indoor space into hydroponic market farms? Why not rebuild those greenhouses? And why not introduce green job-training programs in Rochester, a city that has one of the highest high-school dropout rates in the nation?

There is no question that the infrastructure of large metropolitan areas can and must be redesigned and retrofitted for energy efficiency. And not surprisingly, that is where green urban planners have been focusing their efforts: after all, big cities contribute the largest share of the world's carbon output. But focusing on big cities may also reflect what urban historian James J. Connolly calls "metropolitan bias." Even those who have written about smaller urban areas, he argues, have "made little effort to distinguish large and smaller cities from each other," treating them as "essentially interchangeable case studies of developments that unfolded on a national and even an international scale." That model, established by sociologist Louis Wirth's influential 1938 essay "Urbanism as a Way of Life," assumes continued modernization, growth, and centralization of political and economic power in big cities. The idea of the "metropolis as the quintessential urban form" was further reinforced by the postmodern cultural turn, which saw global cities as "sites" for the formation of "transnational" identities; by implication, smaller places are repositories of more provincial, outmoded, and "destructive nationalisms."

If we temper the metropolitan bias that pervades the sustainable cities movement, green advantages and opportunities distinctive to smaller cities come into focus. But we first must abandon the perpetual-growth paradigm and, when appropriate, embrace shrinkage, not as decline but as a framework for creative reinvention. Several American cities are taking a cue from Europe's Shrinking Cities project, spurred by radical population decline particularly in the former East German Republic. Youngstown, Ohio, whose population dropped from 170,000 to 82,000 with the decline of the steel industry, was the first American city to make downsizing a matter of formal policy. The Youngstown 2010 initiative had spent upward of $3 million as of 2008 to demolish vacant houses and buildings; open access to the Mahoning River; cut back sewage, plowing, and other costly services; further concentrate the population; and open green space for parks and agriculture.

Other so-called weak-market cities have launched similar efforts, with greater emphasis on environmental sustainability. In 2008 nearby Cleveland's Neighborhood Progress, Inc. announced a major project, supported by a grant from the Surdna Foundation, exploring the possibility of turning vacant city lots into agricultural and renewable energy sites. Similar plans are under way in Flint, Michigan, which now owns 10 percent of the city's vacant property through the Genesee County Land Bank.

Meanwhile, we need to revisit the cultural mythology about smaller places. Sociologist Kenneth Johnson's 2006 study, which tracked demographic changes in rural America, found that since 2001 rural population gains have swung modestly upward in an "uneven" pattern. "Gains have been greatest," he writes, "in the fringes of metropolitan areas and in rural areas that are proximate to metropolitan areas that include smaller cities and that contain natural and recreational amenities." Johnson's study also contradicts two seemingly intractable stereotypes. Immigrants, particularly Latinos, "are dispersing more widely" and account for much of this small metro growth, thus belying the notion that large urban areas are the exclusive preserve of "transnational" pluralism. And rural does not necessarily equal farming. Johnson shows that "the proportion of the rural workforce employed in manufacturing is nearly double that in agriculture," while "many rural areas have also now become thriving centers of recreation and retirement."

A new literature is taking shape that recognizes the distinctive characteristics and potential of smaller cities. From the *Journal of Urbanism*, launched in March 2008, to recent studies by the Brookings Institution's Jennifer S. Vey, to PolicyLink's reports *To Be Strong Again: Renewing the Promise in Smaller Industrial Cities* (2008) and *Voices from Forgotten Cities: Innovative Coalitions in America's Older Small Cities* (2007), to the work of Ball State

University's Center for Middletown Studies, small cities are gradually being taken seriously again. That quiet shift reflects changes in the rest of the world. A 2008 UN population study predicted that, by the end of that year and for the first time in history, half the world would live in urban centers and that the trend toward cities would continue, with most of the growth taking place in cities of less than half a million. China alone has talked of building 400 small cities by 2020, to accommodate its migrant rural population. All of this is attracting attention from urban planners and architects. But the growing interest in smaller cities also reflects an imaginative resizing, a spiritually overdue compression of the gigantic, "unsustainable" ambitions of economic-bubble culture.

Considering the longstanding but growing urban-rural divide, small-to-intermediate-size cities may offer the best of both worlds. For all the rural romanticism of the 1970s-era homesteading movement—or, for that matter, the vaunted folksiness of "small-town values"—urban life has its allure. Smaller industrial cities are large enough to offer the diversity, anonymity, and vibrancy of urban culture, as well as levels of density that offer efficiencies of scale. They are also small enough to maintain proximity to their natural riches, from fertile land for sustainable food production to renewable energy resources.

An inversion is at work here: placing smaller cities at the center of analysis leads to an imaginative template that is *decentralized, deconcentrated, relocalized.* One of the Obama presidential campaign's strokes of genius involved bypassing big-city power centers, where self-appointed national leaders claimed to speak for all minorities, and talking directly with the decentralized grid of smaller-city community organizations across the land. As policymakers rethink the American agricultural and energy economies, they too should be looking at smaller cities. Small-municipal leaders, for their part, have much to gain in the twenty-first century low-carbon world if they have the eyes to see it.

Index

~

About the Contributors

Janet R. Daly Bednarek is professor of history at the University of Dayton, where she has taught since 1992. She has written extensively on both urban planning and aviation history, particularly in relation to the place where those two fields come together—the history of American airports. Her major publications include *The Changing Image of the City: Planning for Downtown Omaha, 1945–1973* (1992) and *America's Airports: Airfield Development 1918–1947* (2001). Her article, "The Flying Machine in the Garden: Parks and Airports, 1918–1938," first published in *Technology and Culture* (Summer 2005), was selected for inclusion in ed. Jacqueline Jones, *Best American History Essays 2007* (2007). She is currently working on a manuscript on the history of American airports since 1945.

James J. Connolly is professor of history and director of the Center for Middletown Studies at Ball State University. His publications include *An Elusive Unity: Urban Democracy and Machine Politics in Industrializing America* (2010), *Decentering Urban History: Peripheral Cities in the Modern World*, a special issue of the *Journal of Urban History* (editor, 2008), and the *Triumph of Ethnic Progressivism: Urban Political Culture in Boston, 1900–1925* (1998). He has published numerous essays and articles on U.S. urban, ethnic, and political history.

Allen Dieterich-Ward is assistant professor of history at Shippensburg University. He is a specialist in environmental, economic, and urban history with a research focus on the development of metropolitan Pittsburgh during the twentieth century. Recent publications include "Beyond the Metropolis: Metropolitan Growth and Regional Transformation in Postwar America," coauthored with Andrew Needham, *Journal of Urban History* 36:1 (November 2009) and "From Mill Towns to "Burbs of the 'Burgh": Suburban Strategies in the Post-Industrial Metropolis," in eds. Mark Clapson and Ray Hutchison, *Suburbanisation in Global Perspective*, vol. 10 of *Research in Urban Sociology* (2010). He is currently completing a book entitled *From Mills to Malls: Politics, Economy and Environment in Metropolitan Pittsburgh*.

Alison D. Goebel is a PhD candidate in the department of anthropology at the University of Illinois, Urbana–Champaign. Her dissertation investigates how middle-class white identities and structures of privilege are reconfigured through economic restructuring, and the role of small-city spaces in these changes. Her fieldwork research was supported by grants from the National Science Foundation and the Wenner-Gren Foundation. She has presented her findings at the American Anthropological Association, the Association of American Geographers, and the Labor and Working Class Histories Association. She will defend her dissertation in fall 2010.

Michael J. Hicks is associate professor of economics and director of the Center for Business and Economic Research at Ball State University. He holds economics degrees from Virginia Military Institute and the University of Tennessee and has been on the faculty at Tennessee, Marshall University, and the Air Force Institute of Technology. He is coauthor of *Local Government Consolidation* (forthcoming 2010) and author *The Local Economic Impact of Wal-Mart* (2007). He has published more than 40 refereed papers, over 100 technical reports, and writes a syndicated weekly economics column.

Thomas E. Lehman is professor of economics at Indiana Wesleyan University. He holds a Ph.D. in Urban Economics and Public Affairs from the University of Louisville. He has written and published widely on the payday lending industry and local economic development issues in Indiana. He has coauthored studies on the determinants of rental prices in urban housing markets. Most recently, his research has been focused on using Census data to investigate the predictors of local economic development and growth in Midwestern towns and counties that lie outside of metropolitan regions. Recent publications include "Why Rents Rise," in ed. John Gilderbloom, *Invisible City: Power, Place and Poverty*, (2007), with others, and "Payday

Lending and Public Policy: What Elected Officials Should Know," *Indiana Policy Review* (Winter 2007): 18–28.

S. Paul O'Hara is assistant professor of history at Xavier University. His specializes in U.S. urban, social, and cultural history and is the author of numerous essays and articles on industrial cities, particularly Gary, Indiana. His forthcoming work, *Gary, The Most American of All American Cities*, will be published in 2011. He is also the author of "Envisioning the Steel City: The Legend and Legacy of Gary, Indiana" in eds. J. Cowie and J. Heathcott, *Beyond the Ruins: The Meanings of Deindustrialization* (2003) and "Working-Class Utopia: Work, Masculinity, and Vice in Post-war Gary, Indiana," a paper presented to the 2009 Newberry Seminar in Labor History.

Catherine Tumber is writing a book on the promise of America's small-to-midsize older industrial cities in a low-carbon future. She is currently a research affiliate with the MIT Department of Urban Studies and Planning's Community Innovators Lab. Catherine is the author of *American Feminism and the Birth of New Age Spirituality* (2002) and coeditor with Walter Earl Fluker of *A Strange Freedom: The Best of Howard Thurman on Religion and Public Life* (1998). She has a doctorate in U.S. history from the University of Rochester, and has worked as an editor for the *Boston Phoenix* and the *Boston Review*. Her essays and reviews have appeared in both publications as well as in *Book Forum*, the *Wilson Quarterly*, the *Washington Post*, *In These Times*, and *Commonweal*, among others.

LaDale Winling is visiting assistant professor at Temple University and has a Ph.D. in Architectural History and Theory from the University of Michigan, along with Master's degrees in public history and urban planning. His dissertation is titled "Building the Ivory Tower: University Development and the Politics of Urban Space." In it, he uses campus planning as a lens to examine the role of American universities in urban development and the tensions between administrators, politicians, students, and communities. His publications have appeared in the *Journal of Planning History*, the *Journal of Urban History*, *Technology and Culture*, the *Journal of the Society of Architectural Historians*, and the *Journal of Social History*.